Cook... Celebrate!

Christine Ramos

Copyright ©, Christine Ramos, 2024

All rights reserved. No parts of this book may be reproduced without the written permission of the publisher.

First Edition

Other books written by Christine Ramos...

"Encountering God... Personally!"

"Seeking God... Intentionally!"

"Accompanying Jesus... Imperfectly!"

"Trusting God... Patiently!"

Table of Contents

January...4

February..36

March..61

April..80

May..102

June...125

July..148

August..168

September....................................189

October..204

November....................................228

Advent..251

December....................................257

Christmas Season........................271

Lent..291

Holy Week...................................304

Easter Season..............................312

Post Pentecost Feast Days............321

Sacramental Celebrations............323

Recipe Index................................330

About the Author.........................333

Acknowledgements.....................334

January

*Let us begin this prayer, this book, this sacred New Year,
with the Sign of the Cross:
In the name of the Father, and of the Son, and of the Holy Spirit.
Amen!*

Prayer for the New Year

*Holy Trinity, what is it we need, more than anything, in this New Year?
Your Holy Presence.
I intentionally place You within this New Year.
I place You within our marriage, within our family, within our home.
I place You in the homes of our friends and neighbors.
I place You in our parishes, in our communities, in our cities, and states.
I place You in our country. I place You in all countries.
I place You in our world. I place You in our universe.
I place you in all that you have so abundantly created.
May Your Holy Presence saturate our very being.
May You bring Your Divine Love,
Peace, Hope and Joy in every place You are.
May we see Your Light and be Your Light to all.
Grant this prayer in the name of Jesus Christ, our Lord.
Amen.*

New Year's Day/Mary, Mother of God/Day of Peace

Happy New Year! Today we see before us, a fresh start. A new beginning. A time to wipe the slate clean. Another year has come and gone. We thank the Holy Trinity for gifting us another year! We ask Them to bless us, protect us, heal us, save us. As we trust in Them, we look forward to all the blessings They will bring to our lives. We also honor Our Lady, the Queen of Peace, the Mother of the Most High. Let us take time to ask our Blessed Mother to graciously intercede for us so we may walk more closely in the Divine Peace of her Son, our Lord, Jesus Christ.

Blessed Mother, Queen of Peace, we thank you for your intercession to the Holy Trinity on behalf of our prayers. We celebrate this new day, this new year,
in the hope of permeating God's peace within ourselves, within our homes, within our communities, within our country, within our world.

Mary, Mother of God, graciously intercede for us.
Holy Trinity, we adore You! Hear and answer our prayers.

+++

"Do not look forward in fear to the changes in life; rather, look to them with full hope, that as they arise, God, Whose very own you are, will lead you safely through all things, and when you cannot stand it, God will carry you in His arms.

Do not fear what may happen tomorrow; the same understanding Father Who cares for you today will take care of you then and every day. He will shield you from suffering, or will give you unfailing strength to bear it.
Be at peace, and put aside all anxious thoughts and imaginations."
-- St. Francis de Sales, Doctor of the Church

"The world offers you comfort, but you were not made for comfort. You were made for greatness."
-- Pope Benedict XVI
Food for the Soul: Trust in the Lord. Place your life in His Hands.
St. Francis de Sales, pray for us.
Blessed Mother, graciously intercede for us.
Holy Trinity, we adore You! Hear and answer our prayers.

Challah Bread

Challah is a Jewish bread eaten on Jewish Sabbaths and major holidays. Sounds like the perfect bread to celebrate our New Year!

Ingredients:
- 1 cup water
- 1/4 cup canola oil
- 2 Tbsps sugar
- 1 large egg
- 1 tsp vanilla
- 1/2 tsp salt
- 3 1/4 cups flour
- 1 package of instant yeast

Directions: Using a bread machine, add water, oil, sugar, egg, vanilla, salt, and flour (in that order) to the pan. Make a small well in the center of the flour and add yeast to that well. Set on the "dough" cycle. Once the cycle is complete, remove dough from the bread machine pan. Punch down dough. Shape loaf to desired shape and place on a parchment paper lined baking sheet. Cover dough lightly with a kitchen towel or plastic wrap. Allow to rise for 1 hour. Uncover dough. Bake at 350 degrees for 30-35 minutes. Remove from oven. Rub a knob of unsalted butter over the crust of the bread as soon as it is removed from the oven.

Try this recipe another way...
+++By making a **Holiday Fruit Nut Challah!** Add 1 cup of chopped red and green glazed/candied cherries into the dough. Feeling a little nutty after the holidays? Add in 1/2 cup of chopped walnuts along with the cherries! Now that's festive! Just make sure to add these extra ingredients only when the bread machine beeps *during* the dough cycle. The beep is the signal that lets you know it's time to add in any extra ingredients.

Rose Bowl Parade (January 1)
Confetti Veggie Wreath

My Dad loved to watch the Rose Bowl Parade on New Year's Day and I always have, too! The pomp, the circumstance, the fresh, floral beauty, all so appropriate for celebrating this very first day of the new year. So, while we are watching the parade and the bowl games of the day, how about munching on a fresh veggie dip, beautifully presented on a buttery crescent roll dough? It's a great pull-apart appetizer to share with all those loved ones who may drop by to wish a blessed "Happy New Year"!

Ingredients:
- Two 8 oz cans of crescent roll dough, your choice of regular, buttery, or Hawaiian flavor

Cream Cheese Mixture Ingredients:
- 8 oz cream cheese, softened
- 1/2 cup mayonnaise
- 1 tsp half and half
- 1 tsp seasoning salt

Topping Ingredients:
- 1 freshly shredded cheese of your choice
- 2 cups of finely chopped frozen mixed vegetables, thawed and pulsed in the food processor
- 1/4 cup green onion, thinly sliced

Directions: Preheat oven to 375 degrees. Prepare an ungreased 14 inch round pizza pan. Open the crescent roll cans. Do not unroll dough, keep the roll together. Cut the roll into 8 pieces. Do the same for the second can, as well. Place the 16 pieces, cut side up, in an 11 inch circle. Bake for 15 - 20 minutes, until golden brown. Cool for 5 minutes on the pan, then move to a platter. Cool completely. Prepare the cream cheese mixture: In a small bowl, add cream cheese, mayo, half and half, and seasoning salt. Mix until well blended. Set aside. Finely shred cheese of your choice. Set aside. Pulse thawed mixed (formerly frozen) vegetables in the food processor so they are finely chopped, like confetti. Set aside. With kitchen shears, thinly slice green onions. Set aside. Spread cream cheese mixture evenly on top of baked crescent roll wreath. Top cream cheese mixture with confetti veggies evenly. Top veggies with green onions. Top with finely shredded cheese. Rolls will pull apart into individual servings. Store leftovers in refrigerator.

Try this recipe another way...
+++By making a ***Confetti Veggie Pizza!*** Unroll the crescent dough and place in a single layer in a 9 x 13 inch pan. Continue with the recipe as directed.

January Birthday Cake

<u>Chocolate Pound Cake</u>

Celebrating a Birthday this month? We are!
I made this cake for my sister's birthday many years ago, and she loved it!
Hope you will, too!

Ingredients:
- 7 oz semisweet chocolate, chopped
- 3 oz unsweetened chocolate, chopped
- 2 sticks unsalted butter, softened
- 2 cups sugar
- 4 large eggs
- 2 tsps vanilla
- 3 Tbsps brewed coffee, cooled
- 2 1/4 cups flour
- 1/2 tsp salt
- 1 tsp baking soda
- 1 1/4 cups buttermilk

Directions: Preheat oven to 350 degrees. Well oil a 12 cup Bundt pan using a pastry brush. Set aside. In a small bowl, combine the semisweet and unsweetened chocolate. Melt chocolate in microwave until smooth. Set aside. In a large mixing bowl, cream butter and sugar together until light and fluffy. Add in eggs, one at a time, beating after each egg. Mix in chocolate, vanilla, and coffee. In a small bowl, with a fork, mix together the flour, salt, and baking soda. Add flour mixture, alternately, with the buttermilk, into the chocolate batter, and mix. Do not overmix. Pour cake batter into the oiled Bundt pan. Bake for 1 hour, or until a toothpick inserted comes out clean. Cool cake in the pan for 10 minutes. Cover the cake with a plate and invert to remove cake from the pan. Once the cake has completely cooled, dust with powdered sugar.

Serving Suggestion:
Top with ice cream, whipped cream, ground pecans, and a maraschino cherry!

Feast of St. Basil (January 2)
Patron saint of hospital administrators.
"A good deed is never lost; he who sows courtesy reaps friendship, and he who plants kindness gathers love."
Food for the Soul: How can you be the Love of God to those around you today?
St. Basil, pray for us.
Blessed Mother, graciously intercede for us.
Holy Trinity, we adore You! Hear and answer our prayers.

Cream Puff Day (January 2)

Whipped Cream Puffs
A perfectly light dessert to satisfy any sweet tooth!

Pastry Shell Ingredients:
- 1 cup water
- 1 stick unsalted butter
- 1 cup flour
- 4 large eggs

Whipped Cream Filling:
- 1 cup heavy cream
- 3 Tbsps powdered sugar
- 1 Tbsp vanilla pudding mix (to stabilize whipped cream)
- 1/2 tsp vanilla

Directions: Preheat oven to 400 degrees. Prepare a large baking sheet by lining it with parchment paper. Set aside. Prepare the pastry shells: In a medium saucepan, heat water and butter until boiling. Remove saucepan from heat. Add flour and mix. Beat in eggs, one at a time. Drop shell batter, by tablespoonfuls, onto the baking sheet, leaving an inch between the pastry shells. You can also make a longer eclair shell, if you choose, by connecting two or three tablespoonfuls together. Bake shells for 20 minutes. Remove them from the oven and prick each shell several times with a toothpick. (This will make them a bit hollow in the center.) Return shells to the oven to bake for 5 more minutes. Remove shells from oven and cool completely. Prepare the whipped cream topping. In a small cold metal bowl, beat heavy cream, powdered sugar, vanilla pudding, and vanilla until thick. Do not overmix. Place a large dollop of whipped cream filling onto the bottom half of the pastry shell. Top with the pastry "cap". Sprinkle tops with powdered sugar. Store filling and filled cream puffs in the refrigerator.

Try this recipe another way...
+++By making ***Strawberries and Cream Puffs!*** Slice up some strawberries into thin slices and add them on top of the whipped cream filling. Dreamy!

The Holy Name of Jesus (January 3)

"Wherefore, God also has highly exalted Him, and given Him a name which is above every name: That at the name of Jesus every knee should bow, in heaven and on earth, and under the earth, and every tongue declare that Jesus Christ is Lord, to the glory of God the Father."
(Philippians 2: 9-11)
Food for the Soul: Rejoice in the Precious Name of Jesus!
Sweet Jesus, we honor Your glorious Name! Have mercy on us.
Blessed Mother, graciously intercede for us.
Holy Trinity, we adore You! Hear and answer our prayers.

Feast of St. Elizabeth Seton (January 4)
Patron saint of Catholic schools, widows, and seafarers.
"The heart preparing to receive the Holy Eucharist should be like a crystal vase."
Food for the Soul: Let us examine our hearts and make them ready for Jesus.
St. Elizabeth Seton, pray for us.
Blessed Mother, graciously intercede for us.
Holy Trinity, we adore You! Hear and answer our prayers.

Spaghetti Day (January 4)

Alfredo Sauce
We often think of serving spaghetti with a red sauce, but it can also be wonderful topped with a rich, creamy, cheesy, Alfredo sauce. Three ingredients are all you need!

Ingredients:
- 2 cups heavy cream
- 1 stick unsalted butter
- 1 cup Parmesan cheese, freshly grated
- Salt and pepper, to taste.

Directions: Combined cream and butter in a medium saucepan. Stirring constantly, cook on medium heat until slightly thickened. Add Parmesan cheese to sauce. Stir constantly until cheese is melted and sauce is creamy. Serve over cooked spaghetti, fettuccine, or egg noodles. Add some shredded cooked chicken or cooked shrimp, if desired. Top with extra grated Parmesan cheese.
Try this recipe another way...
+++By making some ***Roasted Garlic Alfredo Sauce!*** You can start by roasting a head of garlic in the air fryer...Take a head of garlic and cut about 1/4 inch off the top so you can see the inside of the garlic cloves. Place the head of garlic in a piece of foil. Surround the head of garlic with the foil, like a cup. Pour a tablespoon of canola or olive oil, or more, over

the head. Lightly salt and pepper. Wrap the head and seal in the foil. Place in the air fryer for 15 - 20 minutes at 370 degrees. Remove from the air fryer. Open the foil carefully, being careful of any steam. Cool the garlic for 5 - 10 minutes. Squeeze the cloves of the garlic head into a small bowl and mash the garlic. Add the amazing, fragrant, roasted garlic to the cream and butter in the recipe for the Alfredo Sauce. Mangia, mangia!

Feast of the Epiphany

"The Magi are filled with awe by what they see – heaven on earth and earth in heaven; man in God and God in man; they see enclosed in a tiny body, the One Whom the entire world cannot contain."
-- St. Peter Chrysologus

Food for the Soul: Let us place ourselves with the Christ Child and behold His Majesty!

St. Peter Chrysologus, pray for us.
Blessed Mother, graciously intercede for us.
Holy Trinity, we adore You! Hear and answer our prayers.

<u>Buttery Starlight Cookies</u>

I often make these cookies for Christmas, but they would be wonderful to celebrate the Epiphany. I'm sure you will enjoy these delicate, melt-in-your-mouth bites!

Cookie Ingredients:
2 sticks of unsalted butter, softened
1/3 cup of heavy cream
2 cups flour
Cookie Bottom and Top Ingredients:
1/4 cup of sugar (plain or colored sugar)
Decoration Ingredients:
1 bag of Candy Melts/Candy Wafers (any color)

Directions: Preheat the oven to 375 degrees. Prepare the cookie sheets, parchment paper lined. Combine the butter, heavy cream, and flour in a medium bowl. Scoop a large teaspoonful of dough and roll it into a ball. Flatten the ball into a disc. Press both sides of the disc lightly into some sugar. Place sugared cookie discs on prepared cookie sheet, about an inch apart. With a fork, poke holes into the cookie discs so they do not get too puffy while baking. Bake for 7 - 9 minutes, until slightly puffy, but not golden brown. (They will look pale.). Remove cookies from sheets and cool completely. Melt the candy wafers and drizzle over the tops of the cookies. Allow the candy topping to cool and set. Store at room temperature in a cookie tin. Use wax paper in between layers.

Feast of St. John Neumann (January 5)
St. John encouraged the formation of communities among Catholic students attending secular universities.

"To holy people, the very name of Jesus is a name to feed upon, a name to transport. His name can raise the dead and transfigure and beautify the living."

Food for the Soul: The name of Jesus is like no other. Show reverence to His Holy Name.

St. John Neumann, pray for us.
Blessed Mother, graciously intercede for us.
Holy Trinity, we adore You! Hear and answer our prayers.

Fried Chicken Caesar Tenders

So many young people love to eat chicken tenders. This is a chicken tender that adults will love as well! Juicy and flavorful with a light crunch. Serve with your favorite dipping sauces: ranch, sweet and sour, honey mustard, barbecue, lemon garlic mayo, buffalo, hot honey, honey soy mayo... oh dear, so many choices...which one to choose?

Ingredients:
- Chicken tenderloins, about 1 1/2 - 2 lbs

Marinade Ingredients:
- 1/3 cup canola oil
- 1/3 cup + 2 Tbsps creamy Caesar dressing
- 2 Tbsps Worcestershire sauce
- 1 tsp apple cider vinegar
- 1 tsp lime juice
- 1 tsp garlic powder

- 1 tsp onion powder
- 1/2 tsp black pepper
- Your choice of bread crumbs, panko bread crumbs, flour, or your favorite breading mix

Directions: Mix together all of the marinade ingredients (canola oil, creamy Caesar dressing, Worcestershire sauce, apple cider vinegar, lime juice, garlic powder, onion powder, black pepper) in a medium sized bowl. Using a fork, poke holes into the chicken tenderloins, 3-4 times with each tenderloin. Turn them over and do the same on the other side.Place the tenderloins in the marinade and mix until they are completely covered in the marinade. Pour the marinade and chicken into a gallon freezer bag. Remove as much air as possible from the bag, then seal. Refrigerate for two hours. (You can marinate up to 12 hours.). Preheat deep fryer to 370 degrees. Prepare a paper towel lined baking sheet.Prepare a medium bowl with your choice of breading. Take a tenderloin out of the marinade and bread it with crumbs or flour. Place tenderloin in the fryer. Fry until golden brown. Remove and place on paper towel line baking sheet. Continue with the rest of the tenders. Serve tenders with a variety of dipping sauces.

Try this recipe another way...
+++By making ***Chicken Caesar Tenderloins!*** Instead of breading and frying them, cook them in a large skillet with 3 Tbsps canola oil. Cook on each side of about 3 minutes. Serve on top of mashed potatoes, with stuffing, or by themselves with some veggies.

Whipped Cream Day (January 5)

Whipped Cream Vanilla Biscuits
I was always intimidated to make biscuits, but this recipe is so easy! They may not be made in the traditional way, but, boy are they good!

Ingredients:
- 2 cups self-rising flour
- 1 Tbsp sugar

- 2 cups heavy cream
- 1 tsp vanilla

Topping Ingredients:
- Sugar for topping (optional)
- 2 Tbsps unsalted butter, melted, for topping

Directions: Preheat oven to 500 degrees. Prepare a baking sheet, parchment paper lined.In a medium bowl, mix the self-rising flour with the sugar. Add in the heavy cream and the vanilla. Mix until combined. Do not overmix. Drop biscuits by large tablespoonfuls onto a parchment paper lined pan. Sprinkle sugar on tops, if desired. Bake for 10 minutes. Remove biscuits from the oven. Brush tops with melted butter. Serve warm, slathered with unsalted butter.

Try this recipe another way...
+++By making some savory **Garlic Cheese Cream Biscuits!** Omit the vanilla and don't top the biscuits with sugar. Mix in a cup of freshly shredded cheese to the dough (cheddar, colby) and brush some melted garlic butter on the tops before they go in, and after the biscuits come out of the oven. Sounds like some pure savory biscuit delight!

Feast of St. André Bessette (January 6)
Patron saint of the rejected.
St. André encourages devotion to St. Joseph.

"It is surprising that I am frequently asked for cures, but rarely for humility and the spirit of faith. Yet, they are so important."

Food for the Soul: Don't we do the same? Let us pray for an increase in our faith and humility.

St. André Bessette, pray for us.
St. Joseph, pray for us.
Blessed Mother, graciously intercede for us.
Holy Trinity, we adore You! Hear and answer our prayers.

Feast of St. Raymond of Peñafort (January 7)
Patron saint of canon lawyers and all lawyers.

"May the God of love and peace, set your hearts at rest and speed you on your journey, may He, meanwhile, shelter you from disturbance by others in the hidden recesses of His love, until He brings you, at last, into that place of complete plentitude, where you will repose forever, in the vision of peace, in the security of trust, and in the restful enjoyment of His riches."

Food for the Soul: Let us pray for peace in our hearts, for a restful dwelling in God's heart.

St. Raymond of Peñafort, pray for us.
Blessed Mother, graciously intercede for us.
Holy Trinity, we adore You! Hear and answer our prayers.

God's Word of the Day (January 8)

"The Lord bless you and keep you; the Lord make His face shine upon you and be gracious to you; the Lord turn His face toward you and give you peace."
(Numbers 6:24-26)

Food for the Soul: Pray this blessing upon all those you meet today.

Blessed Mother, graciously intercede for us.
Holy Trinity, we adore You! Hear and answer our prayers.

English Toffee Day (January 8)

Chippy Toffee Cookies

Whenever I make my brittle, I always have some crushed brittle bits after I break it into pieces.. This is a wonderful way of putting those crunchy bits to a delicious use!

Ingredients:
- 4 sticks of unsalted butter, softened
- 1 cup sugar
- 2 tsp vanilla
- 1 cup crushed potato chips (choose a light, crisp brand of chips, not kettle chips)
- 3 cups flour
- 2/3 cup toffee bits (or some crushed English toffee or brittle)

Directions: Preheat oven to 350 degrees. Prepare a parchment paper lined cookies sheet. In a large bowl, cream together butter, sugar, and vanilla. Add potato chips to butter mixture. Combine. Add flour. Combine. Do not overmix. Stir in toffee bits. On the prepared pan, drop by teaspoonfuls, about an inch apart. Bake for 10 - 15 minutes, until golden brown. Remove from cookie sheet and cool completely. Dust with powdered sugar.

Try this recipe another way...
+++By making ***Chippy Choco-Chip Cookies!*** Substitute the toffee bits for chocolate chips.
+++By making ***Chippy PB Chip Cookies!*** Substitute the toffee bits for peanut butter chips.
+++By making ***Chippy Toffee Nut Cookies!*** Instead of 2/3 cup toffee chips, add 1/3 cup of toffee bits and 1/3 cup chopped walnuts.

Toffee Crunch Oatmeal Cookies

The flavors of the toffee, the oats, the coconut, and the almonds work so well together!

Ingredients:
- 2 sticks unsalted butter, softened
- 1 cup light brown sugar
- 1 cup sugar
- 2 large eggs
- 1 tsp vanilla
- 2 cups flour
- 1/4 tsp baking soda
- 1/4 tsp salt
- 1 cup oatmeal (rolled oats)
- 10 oz toffee bits
- 1 cup sweetened coconut flakes
- 1 cup sliced almonds, broken into pieces
-

Directions: Preheat oven to 350 degrees. Prepare cookie sheet, parchment paper lined. In a large bowl, cream together butter and sugars. Beat in eggs and vanilla. Add flour, baking soda, and salt. Mix well. Do not overmix. Stir in oatmeal. Stir in toffee bits. Stir in coconut flakes. Stir in almonds. Drop cookie batter by teaspoonfuls onto the prepared cookie sheet, 1 inch apart. Bake for 15 minutes until golden brown. Remove from oven and cool slightly on pan. Carefully remove cookies from pan. Cool completely. Store in cookie tins.

God's Word of the Day (January 9)

"When Jesus spoke again to the people, He said, 'I am the Light of the World. Whoever follows me will never walk in darkness, but will have the light of life.'"

(John 8:12)

Food for the Soul: Seek the Light and turn away from darkness in all you do today.

Blessed Mother, graciously intercede for us.
Holy Trinity, we adore You! Hear and answer our prayers.

God's Word of the Day (January 10)
"The people living in darkness have seen a great light; on those living in the land of the shadow of death, a light has dawned."
(Matthew 4:16)
***Food for the Soul: Jesus shines His Light upon you today.
Bask in His Light!***
*Blessed Mother, graciously intercede for us.
Holy Trinity, we adore You! Hear and answer our prayers.*

God's Word of the Day (January 11)
"Do not gloat over me, my enemy! Though I have fallen, I will rise. Though I sit in darkness, the Lord will be my light."
(Micah 7:8)
Food for the Soul: Sometimes, we fall. Sometimes we are in the darkness. But Jesus offers His Hand to help us up, to light our path and show us the way!
*Blessed Mother, graciously intercede for us.
Holy Trinity, we adore You! Hear and answer our prayers.*

God's Word of the Day (January 12)
"Your Word is a lamp unto my feet and a light to my path."
(Psalm 119:105)
***Food for the Soul: The Word of God has the answers for your life.
Seek His Wisdom.***
*Blessed Mother, graciously intercede for us.
Holy Trinity, we adore You! Hear and answer our prayers.*

Feast of the Baptism of Our Lord (2nd Sunday of January)
"The Lord was Baptized, not to be cleansed Himself, but to cleanse the waters, so that those waters, cleansed by the flesh of Christ which knew no sin, might have the power of Baptism."
-- St. Ambrose of Milan

Food for the Soul: Jesus brings His Holiness to all, so our souls may be saved!

St. John the Baptist, pray for us.
St. Ambrose of Milan, pray for us.
Blessed Mother, graciously intercede for us.
Holy Trinity, present at this Baptism, hear and answer our prayers.

Feast of St. Hilary (January 13)
"God the Word became flesh, that through His Incarnation, our flesh might attain to union with God the Word."

Food for the Soul: Pray in union with the Holy Trinity today. Place Them in your midst.

St. Hilary, pray for us.
Blessed Mother, graciously intercede for us.
Holy Trinity, we adore You! Hear and answer our prayers.

God's Word of the Day (January 14)
"Blessed are the peacemakers, for they shall be called sons of God."
(Matthew 5:9)

Food for the Soul: May we bring God's peace into our relationships today.

All the Holy Saint, Souls, and Angels of God, pray for us.
Blessed Mother, graciously intercede for us.
Holy Trinity, we adore You! Hear and answer our prayers.

God's Word of the Day (January 15)
"If possible, so far as it depend on you, live peaceably with all."
(Romans 12:18)

Food for the Soul: May we bring God's peace within our homes today.

Blessed Mother, graciously intercede for us.
Holy Trinity, we adore You! Hear and answer our prayers.

God's Word of the Day (January 16)
*"And let the peace of Christ rule in your hearts,
to which, indeed, you were called in one body."*
(Colossians 3:15)
Food for the Soul: May the peace of God quiet our mind today.
*Blessed Mother, graciously intercede for us.
Holy Trinity, we adore You! Hear and answer our prayers.*

Feast of St. Anthony (January 17)
Abbot. Patron saint of animals, cattle, and butchers.
"Whoever you may be, always have God before your eyes."
Food for the Soul: Live today with God's Will in mind.
*St. Anthony, pray for us.
Blessed Mother, graciously intercede for us.
Holy Trinity, we adore You! Hear and answer our prayers.*

God's Word of the Day (January 18)
"Let not your hearts be troubled, neither let them be afraid."
(John 14:27)
Food for the Soul: Trust in the Lord without worry or fear.
*Blessed Mother, graciously intercede for us.
Holy Trinity, we adore You! Hear and answer our prayers.*

God's Word of the Day (January 19)
*"In peace I will both lie down and sleep; for You alone,
O Lord, make me dwell in safety."*
(Psalm 4:8)
**Food for the Soul: Hand over all worries to God;
rest peacefully in His Strength and Might.**
*Blessed Mother, graciously intercede for us.
Holy Trinity, we adore You! Hear and answer our prayers.*

Popcorn Day (January 19)

Chrissy's Kettle Corn

Crunchy, tender, sweet, salty, buttery! It's a favorite of our family and friends. Why buy some at the theater or county fair when you can have that heavenly kettle corn aroma coming right from your kitchen?!

Ingredients:
- 1/3 cup of popcorn kernels (I use Orville's)
- 3 1/2 Tbsps sugar
- 1/2 tsp salt
- 5 Tbsps canola oil

Directions: Prepare a large parchment paper lined cookie sheet for the popped popcorn. Set aside. In a stovetop hand-crank popcorn popper, add oil and heat until hot over medium high heat. In a small bowl, combine popcorn kernels, sugar, and salt. Stir together. When the oil is very hot, pour in the kernels, sugar, and salt. Cover the pot and stir the kernels constantly. As soon as the kernels begin to pop, lower heat to medium. Continue to stir constantly. When the kernels stop popping, remove the pot from the heat. Pour the kettle corn onto a parchment paper lined baking sheet. Lightly salt. Remove any kernels that did not pop. Store in a gallon freezer bag. Will stay fresh for a few days.

Try this recipe in another way...
+++By making **Cinnamon Sugar Popcorn!** Just add 1 tsp of cinnamon to the recipe.

God's Word of the Day (January 20)
"But you are a chosen race, a royal priesthood, a holy nation, a people for His own possession, that you may proclaim the excellencies of Him Who called you our of darkness into His marvelous light."
(1 Peter 2:9)
***Food for the Soul: Meditate on who God says you are:
a blessed Child of God.***
*Blessed Mother, graciously intercede for us.
Holy Trinity, we adore You! Hear and answer our prayers.*

Martin Luther King Day (third Monday of January)
*"If we have no peace, it is because we have forgotten
that we belong to each other."
-- St. Teresa of Calcutta*
***Food for the Soul: See the eyes of Jesus in everyone
you meet today, even those who are difficult.***
*St. Teresa of Calcutta, pray for us.
Mother Mary, Queen of Peace, graciously intercede for us.
Blessed Mother, graciously intercede for us. Holy Trinity, we adore You!
Hear and answer our prayers.*

<u>*Sous Vide Pork Chops*</u>
Since we have a chance to be together on this national holiday, let's gather for a great dinner! Once you try sous vide pork chops, you won't want to make them any other way! They are so tender and juicy! Plus, you can pretty much prepare them and then forget about them while they are cooking, so you can prepare the rest of the meal.

Ingredients:
- Center cut pork chops, bone-in
- Meat tenderizer
- Onion powder
- Garlic powder

Directions: Prepare the sous vide at 142 degrees. Season pork chops with the meat tenderizer, onion powder, and garlic powder on both sides. (Season lightly with the meat tenderizer so they will not be too salty.). Place 2 pork chops within a vacuum sealed bag. Place in the sous vide container. Continue to do the same with as many pork chops as you may have, placing no more than 2 pork chops in a bag. Sous vide for 2 hours. Remove chops from bags. Serve with *Creamy Onion Gravy* and *Cornbread Cranberry Apple Stuffing*.

Try this recipe another way...
+++By making *Fried Sous Vide Pork Chops!* After removing the sous vide cooked chops from the bag, bread them in your favorite seasoned breading. Place them on a baking sheet and allow them to rest for 15 minutes so the breading will stay on the chops during the frying process. Preheat the deep fryer to 370 degrees. Then, fry them in the deep fryer until golden brown. (Remember, the chops will already be cooked, so all you will need to do is crunch up that breading!). Place on a paper towel lined baking sheet to absorb any extra oil. Serve.

Cornbread Cranberry Apple Stuffing

Make it easy on yourself and use your favorite stovetop stuffing mix as a base for this recipe. It is enhanced by adding the tart and sweet flavors of apple and cranberry.

- **Ingredients:**
- Cornbread stuffing box mix
- 1 large apple, peeled, cored, shredded
- 1/2 cup dried cranberries

Directions: Prepare the stuffing mix according to the package on the stovetop or in the microwave, except, when you heat the water, add the dried cranberries so they begin to rehydrate and plump up. After the bread crumbs are added to the butter and water, add the shredded apple. Continue with the package directions. Serve with pork chops and top with creamy onion gravy.

Creamy Onion Gravy

Buttered, sautéed onions. Great for a steak or on a burger. Add some heavy cream to them and you have an out-of-this-world gravy to serve at a special celebration dinner!

Ingredients:
- 3 Tbsps unsalted butter
- 2 medium sweet onions, thinly sliced
- 1 1/2 cup heavy cream
- Salt to taste

Directions: Melt butter on medium heat in a large skillet. Add thinly sliced onions to the butter. Cover pan and cook for 4 minutes. Uncover pan and stir the onions. Add a tablespoon of water. Cover and cook for 4 minutes. Repeat this process every 4 minutes over the next 20 minutes. You don't need to add water each time, since that may water down the onion flavor too much. Occasionally, you may need to add a bit more butter. You just don't want the onions to get too browned. When the onions are finished cooking, they should be very soft, lightly golden, and buttery. Add in the heavy cream. Simmer for 5 minutes, stirring frequently. The sauce will thicken. Salt to taste. (If you want to add some pepper to taste, use white pepper.). Serve over Sous Vide Pork Chops...or Instant Pot Pork Tenderloin Medallions...or slices of Air Fryer Chicken...or mashed potatoes...or Cornbread Cranberry Apple Stuffing...or egg noodles...

Feast of St. Agnes of Rome (January 21)
Patron saint of girls and virgins.
"Christ has made my soul beautiful with the jewels of grace and virtue. I belong to Him Whom the Angels serve."
Food for the Soul: What do you need to do to make your soul beautiful in the eyes of the Lord?
*St. Agnes of Rome, pray for us.
Blessed Mother, graciously intercede for us.
Holy Trinity, we adore You! Hear and answer our prayers.*

Day of Prayer for Unborn Children (January 22)
"You are called to stand up for life! To respect and defend the mystery of life always and everywhere, including the lives of unborn babies, giving help and encouragement to mothers in difficult situations. You are called to work and pray against abortion."
-- St. John Paul II
Food for the Soul: Pray for all the mothers who are contemplating abortion. Pray that they may understand there is a great purpose for their child's life...
Our Lady of Guadalupe, pray for us.
St. John Paul II, pray for us.
Blessed Mother, graciously intercede for us.
Holy Trinity, we adore You! Hear and answer our prayers.

God's Word of the Day (January 23)
"In the same way, let your light shine before others, so that they may see your good works and give glory to your Father Who is in heaven."
(Matthew 5:16)
Food for the Soul: Do good today for the greater glory of God!
Blessed Mother, graciously intercede for us.
Holy Trinity, we adore You! Hear and answer our prayers.

Pie Day (January 23)
Creamy Comfort Chicken Pot Pie
I chose a savory pie for a cold day in January. This recipe is for an open face pie, but you can always double the crust recipe if you would like to place a crust on top. Just remember to make a few slits in that top crust before baking, so the steam can escape.

Pie Crust Ingredients:
- 1 1/2 cups flour
- 1/4 tsp salt
- 1 stick unsalted butter, melted
- 2 vanilla creamers

Chicken Filling Ingredients:
- 1/2 stick unsalted butter
- 3 Tbsps flour
- 1/2 tsp salt
- 1/8 tsp pepper
- 1/2 tsp onion powder
- 1/2 tsp garlic powder
- 1/4 tsp chicken powder
- 1 cup chicken broth, low sodium
- 1 cup half and half
- 2 cups shredded cooked chicken
- 3/4 cups cooked vegetables (peas, corn, carrots, etc)

Directions: In a large nonstick skillet, melt butter. Stir in flour and cook for a minute or two. Slowly stir in broth on low heat. Stir in salt, pepper, onion powder, garlic powder, and chicken powder. Stir in half and half. Cook, stirring constantly, until sauce begins to thicken. Then cook 2 additional minutes. Add cooked chicken and cooked vegetables. Combine. Prepare the pie crust. Combine the melted butter, salt, creamers, and flour. Do not overmix. Press the dough into an 8 x 8 inch square pan or 8 or 9 inch pie pan. Add chicken filling to pie crust. Bake at 385 degrees for 30 minutes, until crust is golden brown. Remove from oven. Allow pie to set for 5 minutes before cutting and serving.

Try this recipe another way...
+++By making ***Chicken ala King ala Biscuits!*** Instead of making the chicken filling in a pie crust, serve it over some fresh, hot, homemade biscuits. You can use the recipe for Whipped Cream Vanilla Biscuits (January 5) by changing it into a savory biscuit recipe. Omit the vanilla and omit sugaring the biscuit tops before baking. You can even add 1/2 cup of freshly shredded cheese (cheddar or colby jack) to the dough. Then, just break open those fresh baked biscuits and top with the warm, rich, comforting, creamy, chicken goodness!

Feast of St. Francis de Sales (January 24)
Patron saint of DeSales University.

"We all have a vocation. We believe that God has placed us in this life to fill a special need that no one else can accomplish."

Food for the Soul: Pray that God may gives you the wisdom and strength to be what He desires you to be and to do what He desires you to do.

St. Francis de Sales, pray for us.
Blessed Mother, graciously intercede for us.
Holy Trinity, we adore You! Hear and answer our prayers.

Peanut Butter Day (January 24)

Peanut Butter Chip Cookies

I remember making these cookies on an extremely cold, snowy day in January, so many, many years ago. How comforting it was to have the aroma of peanut butter cookies surrounding me as they were baking in the oven, as I sipped some hot cocoa, snuggled up in a warm blanket, watching an old movie...

Ingredients:
- 3/4 cup of unsalted butter, softened
- 1 cup sugar
- 1/2 cup brown sugar
- 1 tsp vanilla
- 2 large eggs
- 2 cups flour
- 1 tsp baking soda
- 12 oz peanut butter chips

Directions: Preheat oven to 350 degrees. Prepare the cookie sheet, parchment paper lined. In a large mixing bowl, cream butter and sugar. Add eggs and beat in. Add flour and baking soda. Mix until combined. Do not overmix. Stir in peanut butter chips. On a parchment paper lined baking sheet, drop by large teaspoonfuls onto the pan, leaving an inch in between cookies. Bake for 10 - 12 minutes. Remove from oven and allow cookies to cool. Store in a cookie tin. Makes about 5 dozen cookies.

Try this recipe another way...
+++By making *Nutty Peanut Butter Chip Cookies!* Add in 1/2 cup of chopped peanuts for an added crunch!
+++By making *Chocolate Peanut Butter Chip Cookies!* Try with 6 oz of peanut butter chips and 6 oz of chocolate chips.
+++By topping the cookies with a *Peanut Butter Drizzle!* Melt 2 Tbsps of creamy peanut butter with a 1/2 Tbsp of unsalted butter. Add a 1/2 - 3/4 cup of powdered sugar and mix together. Then drizzle over the cooled cookies. Talk about a peanut butter extravaganza!

Peanut Butter and Jelly Bars
Bring back the flavorful duo of your youth...in cookie bar form!

Ingredients:
- 1 1/2 cups of flour
- 1/2 cup sugar
- 3/4 tsp baking powder
- 1/2 cup unsalted butter
- 1 large egg
- 3/4 cup grape jelly or raspberry preserves
- 10 oz peanut butter chips, divided
-

Directions: Preheat oven to 375 degrees. Oil a 9 inch square glass pan. In a large bowl, stir together flour, sugar, and baking powder. Cut in butter. (Or place these ingredients in a food processor and pulse until coarse crumbs.). Add the egg and blend well. Reserve half of this mixture. Set aside. Press remaining half of the mixture into the bottom of the prepared pan. Place jelly/preserves in a small bowl. Heat in microwave for about 20 - 30 seconds, until spreadable. Spread the jelly/preserves evenly over the crust in the pan. Sprinkle 1 cup of the peanut butter chips over the jelly/preserves. Place the rest of the peanut butter chips (2/3 cup) in the remaining flour mixture. Combine. Sprinkle this mixture over the top. Bake for 25 - 30 minutes or until lightly browned. Cool completely in the pan. Cut into 16 bars. Serve.

The Conversion of St. Paul the Apostle (January 25)
Patron saint of writers, publishers, musicians, and evangelists.
*"I did not receive it from any man, nor was I taught it;
rather, I received it by revelation from Jesus Christ."*
(Galatians 1:11 - 16)
Food for the Soul: Seek the Wisdom of God today.
St. Paul, pray for us.
Blessed Mother, graciously intercede for us.
Holy Trinity, we adore You! Hear and answer our prayers.

God's Word of the Day (January 26)
*"May the Lord give strength to His people!
May the Lord bless His people with peace!"*
(Psalm 29:11)
**Food for the Soul: Receive all the blessings
God has in store for you today.**
Blessed Mother, graciously intercede for us.
Holy Trinity, we adore You! Hear and answer our prayers.

Feast of St. Angela Merici (January 27)
**Patron saint of the sick, disabled, physically challenged people,
and those grieving the loss of their parents.**
"The last word that I address to you and one I urge upon you with all the ardor of my soul, is that you live in harmony, united together in one heart and one will. Be bound to one another by the bonds of charity, treating each other with respect, helping one another, bearing with each other in Christ Jesus: if you really try to live like this, there is no doubt that the Lord, our God, will be in your midst."
**Food for the Soul: Work together with the people of God.
We are all brothers and sisters in Christ.**
St. Angela Merici, pray for us.
Blessed Mother, graciously intercede for us.
Holy Trinity, we adore You! Hear and answer our prayers.

Feast of St. Henry de Osssó y Cervelló (January 27)
Priest, founder of the Society of St. Teresa of Jesus.
"I will live, sleep, speak, listen work, suffer – I will do everything, I will suffer everything in union with Jesus, with the same divine intention and sentiments that Jesus had and with which He suffered, which is what Jesus wants of me."
Food for the Soul: Seek union with Jesus in whatever you do today.
*St. Henry, pray for us.
Blessed Mother, graciously intercede for us.
Holy Trinity, we adore You! Hear and answer our prayers.*

Chocolate Cake Day (January 27)

Triple Threat Chocolate Cake
Chocolate cake mix, chocolate pudding, and chocolate chips, all in one cake! That's a lot of chocolate!

Ingredients:
- 15.25 oz chocolate cake mix
- 1/2 cup sugar
- 1 small package of instant chocolate pudding mix
- 4 large eggs, beaten
- 1 cup sour cream
- 3/4 cup water
- 3/4 cup canola oil
- 1/2 cup mini semisweet chocolate chips (or milk or white chocolate chips)

Directions: Preheat oven to 325 degrees. Oil a 9 x 13 inch glass pan. In a large bowl, stir together cake mix, sugar, and pudding mix. Mix in beaten eggs, sour cream, water, and oil until well blended. Fold in chocolate chips. Pour into the prepared pan. Bake for 45 - 55 minutes, or until toothpick inserted into the center comes out clean. Remove cake from oven. Cool completely. Dust with some powdered sugar.

Feast of St. Isaac of Nineveh (January 28)
Syrian bishop, theologian, and monk.
"If God is slow in answering your request, or if you ask and do not promptly receive anything, do not be upset, for you are not wiser than God."
Food for the Soul: We don't know everything, especially when we think we do.
St. Isaac of Nineveh, pray for us.
Blessed Mother, graciously intercede for us.
Holy Trinity, we adore You! Hear and answer our prayers.

Feast of St. Ephrem the Syrian (January 29)
Patron saint of spiritual leaders.
"Scripture brought me to the Gate of Paradise, and the mind stood in wonder as it entered."
Food for the Soul: The Word of God is like a love letter to you. Have you taken time to read it? To wrap your heart around it? To rejoice in it?
St. Ephrem, pray for us.
Blessed Mother, graciously intercede for us.
Holy Trinity, we adore You! Hear and answer our prayers.

Chinese New Year (2nd new moon after Winter Solstice)

Honey Walnut Shrimp
This is one of my favorite dishes to order at our local Chinese restaurant. Now, I'm so happy I can make it for us at home

Ingredients for Glazed Walnuts:
- 1/2 cup walnuts (or more if you like glazed walnuts)
- 1 Tbsp butter
- 1 Tbsp brown sugar

Ingredients for Sauce:
- 1/2 cup mayonnaise
- 2 Tbsps honey
- 1 Tbsp lemon or lime juice
- 2 - 3 Tbsps sweetened condensed milk

Ingredients for Shrimp:
- 12 oz large raw shrimp, peeled and deveined
- 1/2 cup rice flour

Directions: Prepare the glazed walnuts. In a medium skillet, melt butter and brown sugar. Add in the walnuts. Heat on medium heat until walnuts are glazed and toasted. Set aside. Prepare the sauce. In a small bowl, mix together the mayonnaise, honey, lemon juice, and sweetened condensed milk. Taste and add a little more lemon juice, or a little more sweetened condensed milk to your taste. Set aside. Preheat fryer to 375 degrees. When the fryer is up to temperature, toss the shrimp in the rice flour until coated, in a large bowl. Immediately fry shrimp until golden. Place shrimp on paper towel lined baking sheet. Warm sauce until warm in the microwave, about 30 seconds. Toss shrimp with sauce. Top with glazed walnuts. If you would like, serve honey walnut shrimp over some fluffy rice cooked in lemon juice flavored water and finished with some salted butter.

Try this recipe another way...
+++By making ***Honey Walnut Chicken!*** Substitute the shrimp for some chicken tenderloins and cut them into nuggets. Coat them in the rice flour, then fry the nuggets.

Apricot Cream Cheese Wontons
Out of fortune cookies for your homemade Chinese dinner?
Then making some of these tasty treats!

Ingredients:
- Wonton wrappers (often found by the produce section of the grocery store)
- Equal parts cream cheese (softened) and apricot preserves

Small bowl of water

Directions: Preheat fryer to 370 degrees. Prepare a paper towel lined baking sheet. On some wax paper, lay out your wonton wrappers. (Have a small bowl of water and a pastry brush nearby.) Brush the edges of the wrappers with a little water, so they will stick together when folded. In another small bowl, stir together equal parts of cream cheese and apricot preserves until well blended. In the center of each wonton wrapper, place a teaspoonful of the cream cheese mixture. (Do not overfill.) Fold the wrappers over so they form a triangle. Press the edges together to seal. After you have filled and sealed as many wontons as you want, fry the wontons in the deep fryer until golden brown. Place wontons on paper towel lined baking sheet. Allow to cool for 2 minutes. Dust with powdered sugar and serve. (Be careful! The filling will be hot!)

Try this recipe another way...
+++By making **Fried Cream Cheese Wontons with Brandied Apricot Sauce!** Instead of combining the cream cheese with the apricot preserves, just fill the wontons with a tsp of cream cheese, fry them, and dust them with powdered sugar. Prepare an **Apricot Brandy Sauce** by mixing together some apricot preserves with a bit of brandy. Warm this mixture slightly in the microwave, then dip the fried cream cheese wontons into the sauce.

+++By making **Fried Wonton Cinnamon Crisps with Apricot Brandy Sauce!** Forget about filling the wontons at all! Just cut the wonton wrappers in half and fry them up until golden brown. Right out of the fryer, sprinkle the hot wonton strips with cinnamon sugar. Serve with the warm **Apricot Brandy Sauce** (recipe above) to dip in and devour! So incredibly easy and delicious!

God's Word of the Day (January 30)
"And the peace of God, which surpasses all understanding, will guard your hearts and your minds in Christ Jesus."
(Philippians 4:7)
Food for the Soul: Allow Christ's peace to guard your heart from fear and worry.
Blessed Mother, graciously intercede for us.
Holy Trinity, we adore You! Hear and answer our prayers.

Feast of St. John Bosco (January 31)
Patron saint of editors, publishers, youth, apprentices, and magicians.

"Enjoy yourself as much as you like – if only you keep from sin."
***Food for the Soul: God wants you to enjoy your life. He loves you!
But, welcome God's pure joy without the pains of sin.***
*St. John Bosco, pray for us.
Blessed Mother, graciously intercede for us.
Holy Trinity, we adore You! Hear and answer our prayers.*

February

February Birthday Cake

Creamy Ricotta Cheesecake

Celebrating a Birthday this month? We are!
This is one of my personal favorites! For my February birthday, I would often ask my Mom to make this cheesecake for me. It was always so rich and creamy! Definitely a special cheesecake to celebrate a joyous day.

Ingredients:
- 1 lb ricotta cheese, as dry as possible (can also use instead, small curd cottage cheese)
- 16 oz cream cheese, softened (two 8 oz packages)
- 1 1/2 cups sugar
- 4 large eggs, slightly beaten
- 1/3 cup corn starch
- 2 Tbsps lemon or lime juice
- 1 tsp vanilla
- 1 stick of unsalted butter, melted
- 16 oz sour cream
- Butter cookie crumbs, ground finely (or graham cracker crumbs)

Directions: Preheat oven to 325 degrees. Oil a 9 inch spring form pan. Lightly dust bottom of pan with cookie crumbs. In a large bowl, add ricotta cheese and cream cheese. Beat on high until smooth and creamy. Blend in sugar at high speed. Blend in eggs, continuing at high speed. On low speed, mix in corn starch, lemon juice and vanilla. Continuing on low speed, mix in melted butter (slightly cooled) and sour cream. Pour cheesecake batter into prepared pan. Bake for 1 hour and 10 minutes, or until firm around the edges. Turn off oven and leave cheesecake in the oven for 2 hours. After two hours, remove from oven and cool completely. Chill in refrigerator. Remove sides of pan. Cut and serve.

Serving Suggestion:
Top slices with chocolate syrup, caramel sauce, warmed raspberry preserves, fresh fruit, lemon curd, or fresh whipped cream. But, be sure to try a slice plain, too. It is amazing all on its own!

God's Word of the Day (February 1)

"Great peace have those who love Your Law; nothing can make them stumble."
(Psalm 119:165)
Food for the Soul: Choose to walk in God's ways today, in everything you do.
Blessed Mother, graciously intercede for us.
Holy Trinity, we adore You! Hear and answer our prayers.

Ice Cream for Breakfast Day (February 1)

Oatmeal Topped with Apple Cinnamon Ice Cream

Hot/cold...breakfast/dessert...where two worlds happily collide! The ice cream will act as a melty, creamy, sweet topping to a humble, ordinary bowl of oatmeal!

Ingredients:
- A bowl of oatmeal, however you like to make it
- 1-2 tsps of raisins or dried cranberries (optional)
- 1-2 tsps of salted butter ^
- 1 tsp brown sugar
- A sprinkle of cinnamon

Apple Cinnamon Ice Cream Ingredients:
- 1 apple, peeled, cored, shredded
- 1 cup heavy cream
- 2 Tbsp cool whip
- 1/4 cup Splenda sugar blend
- 2 vanilla creamers
- 1 tsp cinnamon

Topping Ingredients:
- Chopped nuts of your choice

Directions: The night before, prepare the ice cream. Combine ingredients to make the ice cream. Add to your ice cream maker. Freeze. The following morning, prepare the oatmeal. (This is when I would add the raisins/dried cranberries to the oatmeal, in the milk or water, so they will be plump and not so chewy.). Add the butter, sugar, and cinnamon. Be sure the oatmeal is piping hot so it will melt the ice cream as soon as the scoop is placed on top. Place a scoop of the ice cream on top of the oatmeal. Top with chopped nuts.

Feast of the Presentation of Our Lord (February 2)
"Simeon gave back Jesus to His Mother, He was only suffered to keep Him for one moment. But, we are far happier than Simeon. We may keep Him always, if we will. In Communion He comes, not only into our arms, but into our hearts."
-- St. John Vianney
Food for the Soul: Visit with Jesus today. He impatiently waits for you.
Sweet Christ Child, hear our prayers.
St. John Vianney, pray for us.
Blessed Mother, graciously intercede for us.
Holy Trinity, we adore You! Hear and answer our prayers.

Groundhog Day (February 2)

Apple Pie Dumplings with Cinnamon Apple Ice Cream
The question this morning is, will the groundhog see his shadow or not? Will there be 6 more weeks of winter, or will there be 6 more weeks until spring? Wait a minute...don't they both mean the same thing?! Either way, it sounds like a great time to make some warm, comforting, apple dumplings as we wait until spring has sprung...

Apples for the Dumplings
- 2 apples: peeled, cored, and sliced into 8
- 1 Tbsp of lime or lemon juice
- 1 Tbsp of Splenda brown sugar blend

Pie Dough for the Dumplings
- 1 1/2 cups flour
- 1 stick unsalted butter, melted
- 1/4 tsp salt
- 2 vanilla creamers

Caramel Sauce
- 3/4 stick unsalted butter
- 1/4 cup Splenda brown sugar blend
- 2 vanilla creamers + Heavy cream, a few Tbsp (optional)
- 1/2 cup diet ginger ale

Homemade Cinnamon Apple Ice Cream
- 1 apple, peeled, cored, shredded
- 1 cup heavy cream
- 2 Tbsp cool whip
- 1/4 cup Splenda sugar blend
- 2 vanilla creamers
- 1 tsp cinnamon

Directions: Ice Cream: Combine ingredients to make the ice cream. Add to your ice cream maker. Freeze. Preheat oven to 350°. Grease an 8 x 8 inch glass baking pan with oil. **Apples:** Peel and core two apples, then cut each apple into eighths. Place the slices in a bowl. Sprinkle lime (or lemon) juice and a little brown sugar over the apple slices. (For more tender apples, cook the coated apples in a little butter over medium heat in a frying pan for about three minutes or so. Cool apples before moving on to Step 4.). **Pie Dough:** Mix pie dough ingredients together. Divide the dough into 12 balls, about the size of a large walnut. Flatten the ball in the palm of your hand and shape the dough around each apple slice. (You will have 4 slices of apples left over. Eat them up and enjoy! You deserve a nutritious snack!) Place the dumplings into the greased 8 x 8 glass pan, leaving a little room in between each dumpling. **Caramel Sauce:** In a small saucepan over medium heat, melt butter, the brown sugar blend, vanilla creamers, and salt together. Heat until sugar melts.

Then add some heavy cream, if you have some. Pour this mixture over the dumplings in the pan. Pour the ginger ale around the edges of the pan. Try avoid pouring it directly on top of the dumplings. Bake the dumplings until their crust is lightly golden, about 35 minutes. Serve the dumplings warm with ice cream. Spoon the extra caramel sauce from the baking pan over the ice cream and dumplings. **Makes 1 dozen Apple Pie Dumplings.**

Feast of St. Blaise (February 3)
Patron saint of throat illnesses, animals, and candlemakers.
"Through the intercession of St. Blaise, bishop and martyr, may God deliver you from every disease of the throat and from every other illness."
Food for the Soul: Hand over all that ails you, to Jesus, our Healer.
St. Blaise, pray for us.
Blessed Mother, graciously intercede for us.
Holy Trinity, we adore You! Hear and answer our prayers.

God's Word of the Day (February 4)
"Let all that you do be done in love."
(1 Corinthians 16:14)
Food for the Soul: May all that you do today be done mindfully and lovingly, in God's name.
Blessed Mother, graciously intercede for us.
Holy Trinity, we adore You! Hear and answer our prayers.

Feast of St. Agatha (February 5)
Patron saint of breast cancer patients.
"Lord, my creator, you have protected me since I was in the cradle. You have taken me from the love of the world and given me patience to suffer."
Food for the Soul: Offer your cross to Jesus today. Carry it bravely, in love for Him.
St. Agatha, pray for us.
Blessed Mother, graciously intercede for us.
Holy Trinity, we adore You! Hear and answer our prayers.

Feast of St. Paul Miki (February 6)
Patron saint of Japan.

"Like my Master, I shall die upon the cross. Like Him, a lance will pierce my heart so that my blood and my love can flow out upon the land and sanctify it to His Name."

Food for the Soul: Praise Jesus for all the martyrs! May you be so brave in your love for Him!

St. Paul Miki, pray for us.
Blessed Mother, graciously intercede for us.
Holy Trinity, we adore You! Hear and answer our prayers.

God's Word of the Day (February 7)

"If you love Me, you will keep My commandments."
(John 14:15)

Food for the Soul: Be mindful in your choices today, that everything you do, gives honor to Jesus.

Blessed Mother, graciously intercede for us.
Holy Trinity, we adore You! Hear and answer our prayers.

Feast of St. Josephine Bakhita (February 8)
Patron saint of the Sudan and victims of human trafficking.

"Be good, love the Lord, pray for those who do not know Him. What a great grace it is to know God!"

Food for the Soul: Say a prayer today for those who do not know God, that their eyes and hearts may be opened to Him.

St. Josephine Bakhita, pray for us.
Blessed Mother, graciously intercede for us.
Holy Trinity, we adore You! Hear and answer our prayers.

God's Word of the Day (February 9)

"We love because He first loved us."
(1 John 4:19)

Food for the Soul: Show God's love to someone you know today.

Blessed Mother, graciously intercede for us.
Holy Trinity, we adore You! Hear and answer our prayers.

Pizza Day (February 9)

Southwest Side of Chicago Deep Dish Pizza

One thing you can be sure of, we Chicagoans do enjoy our pizza! Especially deep dish. It's great when you can make it at home to share, fresh out of the oven, with those you love!

Dough Ingredients:
- 1 1/2 teaspoon granulated sugar
- 1 1/3 cups of water
- 1 teaspoon salt
- 1/8 teaspoon cream of tartar
- 1/2 cup plus 3 tablespoons canola oil
- 3 1/2 cups flour
- 1 packet instant yeast

Filling Ingredients:
- 1 lb deli sliced part skim mozzarella, more if you like it extra cheesy
- 1 pound bulk Italian sausage, shaped into tiny meatballs, cooked
- 1 medium onion, diced and cooked until tender
- 4 sweet peppers, cored, sliced thinly, cooked until tender (I cook mine in the air fryer for 15 minutes, stirring and spraying a little oil on them every 5 minutes)

Pizza Sauce Ingredients:
- 2 cans of tomato sauce, 8 oz each
- 1/2 tsp garlic powder
- 1/2 tsp onion powder
- Oregano powder, quick sprinkle
- 2 tsp brown sugar, heaping
- Salt sauce to taste
- Grated Parmesan, for topping and garnish

Pan Preparation:
Two 9 inch cake pans coated with:
3 tablespoons unsalted butter, melted (if you would like a garlic butter crust, add some garlic powder to the melted butter). Reserve 1 tbsp of the melted butter to brush on crust edges before baking. Makes two 9 inch pizzas.

Directions: Place dough ingredients in bread machine in order, with instant yeast last. Run on dough setting. Leave dough in machine for one extra hour after end of cycle. Remove dough and place in an oiled bowl. Punch down and let dough settle for 15 more minutes. While dough is in the bread machine, prepare fillings. Cook sausage. Cook onion. Cook peppers. Prepare sauce to taste. Allow fillings and sauce to cool. Set aside. Position an oven rack in the middle of the oven and preheat to 450 degrees. Coat bottom and sides of two 9 inch cake pans with 1 Tbsp melted butter for each pan. Place pans in fridge for 5 minutes. Remove pans from fridge. Divide the dough in half and spread across the bottom and up the sides of each of the pans. Cover entire bottom in mozzarella, all the way up to the edge, pushing dough up the sides of the pan as you place the slices. Divide the filling ingredients in half. Cover the cheese layer completely with sausage meatballs. Layer with onions, peppers. Top with sauce. Sprinkle top with grated parmesan. Brush 1 Tbsp melted butter on crust edges. Bake until golden around the edges, about 25 minutes. Remove from oven. If you desire, brush some more melted butter onto the edges of the crust. Allow to rest for 5 minutes. Slice and serve. **Each pizza serves 3 - 4 people.** (If you only want to make one pizza, store half of the dough in an oiled, covered bowl in the fridge for up to ten days. When you want to use it, remove it from the fridge and let it rest at room temperature for about two hours before placing it into the pan.)

Super Bowl (second Sunday of February)

Chris' Caramel Corn

Paul and I are big football fans and we do enjoy a great Super Bowl game, even if our hometown team, "da Bears", are not playing. Good food is a part of the game experience, and we can tell you, this treat is a real touchdown! Buttery, salty, sweet. It is one of my friend's favorites (Michelle)! You can even make it ahead of time, too, so it will be ready for the big game. Just know that when you make it, the aroma will make it difficult for you not to eat it right away! I like to mix the caramel corn with some buttered popcorn, for an even more sweet and salty combo. Or you can make some fresh cheesy popcorn and mix it with the caramel corn for the ultimate Chicago style popcorn mix!

Ingredients for freshly popped popcorn:
- 2/3 cup popcorn kernels (I use Orville's)
- 5 Tbsps canola oil
- 1/2 tsp salt

Ingredients for Caramel Corn:
- 3/4 cup brown sugar
- 1 stick unsalted butter
- Salt (use only on unsalted popcorn)
- About 5 - 6 cups freshly popped popcorn, or store bought buttery or cheesy puffcorn (or some of each) to avoid those pesky kernels!

Directions for freshly popped popcorn: Prepare a large parchment paper lined cookie sheet for the popped popcorn. Set aside. In a stovetop hand-crank popcorn popper, add oil and heat until hot over medium high heat. In a small bowl, combine popcorn kernels and salt. Stir together. When the oil is very hot, pour in the kernels and salt. Cover the pot and stir the kernels constantly. As soon as the kernels begin to pop, lower heat to medium. Continue to stir constantly. When the kernels stop popping, remove the pot from the heat. Pour the popcorn onto a parchment paper lined baking sheet. Lightly salt. Remove any kernels that did not pop. Store in a gallon freezer bag. Will stay fresh for a few days.

Directions for Caramel Corn: Divide the freshly popped popcorn (or puffcorn) in half and pour into two large bowls. Melt the unsalted butter in a medium saucepan. Add in the brown sugar. Stir constantly. Cook on medium heat for about 2 - 3 minutes, or until mixture has gotten to a thin, golden syrup. Do not overcook. Pour the syrup over the popcorn/puffcorn. Mix thoroughly and carefully to glaze all of the corn. (Note: Popcorn will not be totally covered in the glaze and that's okay!) Lightly salt unsalted popcorn only. Store in a large gallon plastic freezer bag. Caramel Corn will stay fresh for a few days...if it's still around!

Caramel Apple Cream Cheese Dip
Enjoy the flavors of a caramel apple without all the fuss!

Ingredients:
- 8 oz cream cheese, softened
- 3/4 cup packed brown sugar
- 1 Tbsp vanilla
- 1/2 cup chopped/ground cocktail peanuts
- 4-5 Granny Smith apples, cut into wedges, peeled or unpeeled

Directions: In a small bowl, combine cream cheese, brown sugar, and vanilla until smooth. Top the dip with chopped/ground peanuts. Serve with apple wedges. Dip wedges into the dip and enjoy! Note: To keep apples from turning brown, place apple slices in a gallon bag, add a little lemon juice, close the bag and shake the apples to toss in the lemon juice.

Pinwheel Roll-Ups
My Mom used to make a beef dip for us, oh so long ago. I'm sure she got the original recipe from one of the ladies in the Women's Guild at our parish; they were always exchanging their favorite recipes! Over time, I've altered the recipe a bit. I've added more meat, some seasonings, then placed it on a tortilla to make it into an easy, pop-in-your-mouth appetizer...

Ingredients:
- 8 oz cream cheese, softened
- 4 Tbsps mayonnaise
- 2 Tbsps honey mustard
- 3/4 tsp garlic powder
- 3/4 tsp onion powder
- 1/4 tsp meat tenderizer
- 3 packages of Splenda
- Two 2 oz packages of Buddig beef, snipped into small pieces
- 2 Tbsps green onions, snipped into small slices
- 1/2 cup cheddar cheese (or your favorite), freshly grated
- Flour tortillas

Directions: These pinwheels will need to sit in the refrigerator overnight, so plan ahead. In a medium bowl, add cream cheese, mayo, and honey mustard. Stir until combined. Add garlic powder, onion powder, meat tenderizer, and Splenda into cream cheese mixture. Stir until combined. With some kitchen shears, snip the beef slices into small pieces. Add into the cream cheese mixture. With some kitchen shears, snip the green onions into small slices. Combine with cream cheese/beef mixture. Add cheese to the mixture. Combine. Place a flour tortilla on a plate. Spread the cream cheese/beef filling onto the tortilla. Roll the tortilla tightly, jelly roll style. Wrap the rolled tortilla completely in Saran Wrap. This will help make the tortillas very soft and pliable. Continue the same process until all of the filling is gone. Place the Saran wrapped tortilla rolls in a gallon plastic freezer bag. Place the bag in the refrigerator overnight. The next day before serving, unwrap the tortillas, as needed, and cut 1 1/2 - 2 inch slices. Place pinwheels, face up, on a serving plate. Store any leftovers in the refrigerator.
Try this recipe another way...

+++By making this as a ***Cream Cheese Beef Dip!*** Make the filling, but don't use the tortillas. Serve with a variety of crackers and/or chips.

Pigskins in a Blanket
Slice up some hot dogs, wrap them up in a crescent roll, and bake. Add some mustard football "laces" and serve to your hungry, cheering, or booing, guests! Grandchildren approved!

Ingredients:
- 6 of your favorite brand of hotdogs, uncooked, sliced into thirds
- 1 can of crescent dough, each of the 8 crescent triangles cut in half to make 16 triangles

Directions: Preheat oven to 375 degrees. Prepare baking sheet, lines with parchment paper. Cut up hotdogs into thirds. Set aside. Cut crescent dough crescents in half. Roll the hotdog up in the crescent roll dough, starting at the wider end of the dough. Then place them on the baking sheet, tip of the dough side down. Bake for 12 - 15 minutes, or until golden brown. If you would like, add some mustard football laces to the tops. Serve warm with a variety of dipping sauces; ketchup, mustard, honey mustard, barbecue sauce, ranch dressing, etc.

Try this recipe another way:
+++By making **Cheesy Pigs in a Blanket!** Just place a small, thin slice of your favorite cheese on the crescent roll dough before adding the hotdog. Roll up and bake!
+++By making a **Crescent Dog Wreath!** Double the recipe. When you place the crescents dogs on the pan, place them in the shape of a wreath, one right next to another in a double circle. After it is baked, pull apart the crescent dogs! Place a bowl of dip in the center!

Feast of St. Scholastica (February 10)
St. Benedict's twin sister. Patron saint of education.
"She could do more, because she loved more."
-- written by St. Gregory the Great, comparing
St. Scholastica to her brother, St. Benedict.
Food for the Soul: Speak with love today to all you encounter.
St. Gregory the Great, pray for us.
St. Benedict, pray for us.
St. Scholastica, pray for us.
Blessed Mother, graciously intercede for us.
Holy Trinity, we adore You! Hear and answer our prayers.

God's Word of the Day (February 11)
"And so we know and rely on the love God has for us. God is love. Whoever lives in love, lives in God, and God in them."
(1 John 4:16)
Food for the Soul: Rely on God's love through today's challenges.
Blessed Mother, graciously intercede for us.
Holy Trinity, we adore You! Hear and answer our prayers.

God's Word of the Day (February 12)
"As the Father has loved, Me, so have I loved you. Now remain in My love. If you keep My commands, you will remain in My love, just as I have kept My Father's commands and remain in His love."
(John 15:9-10)
Food for the Soul: Think about what it means to "remain in God's love"...
Blessed Mother, graciously intercede for us.
Holy Trinity, we adore You! Hear and answer our prayers.

God's Word of the Day (February 13)
"But You, O Lord, are a God, merciful and gracious, slow to anger, and abounding in steadfast love and faithfulness."
(Psalms 86:15)
Food for the Soul: Praise God for Who He is, to us, His children!
Blessed Mother, graciously intercede for us.
Holy Trinity, we adore You! Hear and answer our prayers.

Feast of St. Valentine (February 14)
Patron saint of happy marriages.
"Love is the most beautiful sentiment the Lord has put into the souls of men and women."
-- St. Gianna Molla
Food for the Soul: Bring love to those in your life today.
St. Valentine, pray for us.
St. Gianna Molla, pray for us.
Blessed Mother, graciously intercede for us.
Holy Trinity, we adore You! Hear and answer our prayers.

Sweetheart Cherries and Cream Scones

You can be sure to get an extra kiss from your sweetheart when you serve them some of these delicious scones! I discovered this recipe many years ago and it is still a favorite. The dough is amazing! The butter and heavy cream "unite" to create a rich crumb, creating a perfect "marriage" with the cherries. Use a heart shaped cutter to really "embrace" this loving occasion!

Ingredients:
- 2 cups + 2 Tbsps flour
- 1/3 cup + 2 Tbsps sugar
- 1 Tbsp baking powder
- 1/2 tsp salt
- 6 Tbsps unsalted butter, cold
- 2/3 cup glazed or maraschino red cherries, chopped
- 1 cup heavy cream
- Sugar, for topping

Directions: Preheat oven to 400 degrees. Prepare cookie sheet, parchment paper lined. In a food processor, add flour, sugar, baking powder, salt and cold butter. Pulse until coarse crumbs. Place flour/butter crumbs Into a medium bowl. Stir cherries into the crumb mixture. Gently stir in heavy cream. Do not overmix. Let stand for 2 minutes. On a lightly powdered sugared surface, press out dough, 1/2 inch thick. Cut into scones, whatever shape you desire. Place scones on a parchment paper lined baking sheet. Sprinkle scone tops with sugar. Bake for 15 minutes. Remove from oven and serve while warm.

Try this recipe another way...
+++By making **Dark Chocolate Cherry Sweetheart Scones!** Substitute the cherries for 1/3 cup of glazed cherries and 1/3 cup dark chocolate chips (or semisweet, or milk chocolate).
+++By making **Blueberry Raspberry Scones!** Substitute the cherries for 1/3 cup whole blueberries and 1/3 cup whole raspberries.
+++By making **Apricot White Chocolate Scones!** Substitute the cherries for 1/3 chopped dried apricots and 1/3 cup white chocolate chips.

+++By making **Tropical Fruit Nut Scones!** Substitute the cherries for 1/4 cup chopped dried pineapple, 1/4 cup sweetened coconut, and enough chopped walnuts to make 2/3 cup of pineapple, coconut and nuts, total.
+++By making **Maple Walnut Scones!** Only add 1/3 cup of sugar. Substitute the glazed cherries for chopped walnuts, and add 1/4 cup of maple syrup to the heavy cream. Sprinkle tops with cinnamon sugar.
+++By making **Holiday Fruitcake Scones!** Substitute the cherries for 1/4 cup glazed cherries, 1/4 cup dried pineapple, and enough chopped pecans to make 2/3 cups of fruit and nuts, total. You can even add a Tbsp of peach brandy into the heavy cream for more of that fruitcake vibe!
+++By making savory **Garlic Cheddar Scones!** Only add 1/3 cup sugar. Substitute the cherries for 2/3 cup of freshly grated cheddar cheese. Also, skip sprinkling the scones with sugar. Instead, brush the tops of the scones with some melted garlic butter before they go into the oven and then, again, after they come out of the oven.

God's Word of the Day (February 15)
"God shows His love for us, in that while we were still sinners, Christ died for us."
(Romans 5:8)
Food for the Soul: Let us place our unworthiness before King of Kings today, and have it be transformed into His amazing love!
Blessed Mother, graciously intercede for us.
Holy Trinity, we adore You! Hear and answer our prayers.

God's Word of the Day (February 16)
"See what kind of love the Father has given to us, that we should be called children of God; and so we are."
(1 John 3:1)
Food for the Soul: Meditate on the fact that you are Child of God... eradicate the lies that tell you, you are not...
Blessed Mother, graciously intercede for us.
Holy Trinity, we adore You! Hear and answer our prayers.

Almond Day (February 16)
Almond Shortbread Bars

The crunchy almond topping adds a nice contrast to this shortbread recipe!

Ingredients:
- 1 cup sugar
- 2 sticks unsalted butter, softened
- 1 large egg yolk (set aside egg white for topping)
- 1/4 tsp almond or vanilla extract
- 2 cups flour

Almond Topping Ingredients:
- 1 Tbsp water
- 1/2 cup sliced almonds
- 1 large egg white

Directions: Preheat oven to 350 degrees. Oil a 15 x 10 x 1 pan. Set aside. In a large bowl, cream butter and sugar. Add egg yolk and extract. Mix. Press dough into prepared pan. In a small bowl, beat egg white with water. Using a pastry brush, brush on dough. Sprinkle top with almonds. Press almonds lightly into the dough. Bake for 15 - 20 minutes. Remove from oven. Cool and cut into squares.

Almond Butterscotch Bars

I'm usually not much of a fan of butterscotch, but the combination of the butterscotch with the almonds is great! I've often made these bars at Christmas time...

Ingredients:
- 1 cup unsalted butter, softened
- 3/4 cup light brown sugar, firmly packed
- 1 tsp vanilla
- 1/2 tsp almond extract
- 1/2 tsp salt
- 2 cups flour
- 1 cup butterscotch chips
- 1 cup slivered or sliced almonds

Directions: Preheat oven to 350 degrees. Set aside an ungreased 15 x 10 x 1 inch pan. In a large bowl, cream together butter and brown sugar. Beat in vanilla and almond extracts and salt. Mix in flour until blended. Press mixture evenly into the pan. Sprinkle butterscotch chips and almonds over cookie dough. Press them into the dough lightly. Bake for 20 - 25 minutes, until golden brown. Remove from oven. Cool. Cut into squares.

Try this recipe another way...

+++By making ***Chocolate Chip Walnut Bars!*** Substitute the butterscotch chips and almonds for 1 cup chocolate chips 1 cup chopped walnuts. Omit the almond extract.

+++By making ***White Chocolate Cranberry Pecan Bars!*** Substitute the butterscotch chips and almonds for 2/3 cup white chocolate chips, 2/3 cup dried cranberries, and 2/3 cup chopped pecans. Omit the almond extract.

+++By making ***Peanut Supreme Bars!*** Substitute the butterscotch chips and almonds for 1 cup peanut butter chips and 1 cup chopped peanuts. Omit the almond extract.

God's Word of the Day (February 17)

"Surely Your goodness and love will follow me all the days of my life, and I will dwell in the house of the Lord forever."
(Psalm 23:6)
Food for the Soul: Welcome God's blessings today!
Live in His love and goodness!
Blessed Mother, graciously intercede for us.
Holy Trinity, we adore You! Hear and answer our prayers.

Presidents' Day (Third Monday of February)

"The Lord has called us from different nations,
but we must be united with one heart and one soul."
-- St. Maria Elizabeth Hesselblad
Food for the Soul: Live as a Child of God among His other Children...
St. Elizabeth, pray for us.
Jesus, guide our leaders to seek Your path for our nation.
Blessed Mother, graciously intercede for us.

Holy Trinity, we adore You! Hear and answer our prayers.

God's Word of the Day (February 18)
*"My command is this: Love each other as I have loved you.
Greater love has no one than this: to lay down one's life for one's friends."
(John 15:12-13)*
Food for the Soul: Bless a friend today to glorify God!
*Blessed Mother, graciously intercede for us.
Holy Trinity, we adore You! Hear and answer our prayers.*

God's Word of the Day (February 19)
*"This is how God showed His love among us: He sent His one
and only Son into the world that we might live through Him."
(John 4:9)*
**Food for the Soul: Praise and thank the Holy Trinity f
or all They have done, all They are doing, and all They will do,
so you may one day join Them in Paradise!**
*Blessed Mother, graciously intercede for us.
Holy Trinity, we adore You! Hear and answer our prayers.*

God's Word of the Day (February 20)
*"Dear friends, let us love one another, for love comes from God.
Everyone who loves has been born of God and knows God.
Whoever does not love, does not know God, because God is love."
(1 John 4:7-8)*
**Food for the Soul: Be aware of your actions today.
How can you be more loving?**
*Blessed Mother, graciously intercede for us.
Holy Trinity, we adore You! Hear and answer our prayers.*

Muffin Day (February 20)

Pineapple Upside Down Cornbread Muffins

Sometimes you may want to enjoy the flavors of a pineapple upside down cake, but don't want to make a whole cake. This yummy muffin solves that problem in a "jiffy"!

Muffins Ingredients:
- 1 large egg, beaten
- 1/3 cup half and half
- 1 Tbsp of the drained pineapple juice
- 1 Tbsp sour cream
- 8.5 oz package of Jiffy corn muffin mix

Pineapple Upside Down Ingredients:
- 3 Tbsps unsalted butter
- 3 Tbsps brown sugar
- 1 can of pineapple tidbits, drained, 18 - 24 tidbits needed
- Maraschino cherries, cut in half and drained

Directions: Preheat oven to 400 degrees. Prepare to have a muffin tin ready, one for 6 muffins, oiled. Place 1/2 Tbsp of butter in each muffin tin. Melt butter in the oven for a few minutes. Remove pan from oven and place 1/2 Tbsp of brown sugar in each tin with the melted butter. In the center, place 1/2 a cherry. Place 3 - 4 pineapple tidbits in each tin on top of the butter/sugar. Set aside. In a small bowl, add the egg, half and half, pineapple juice, and sour cream. Mix together until well combined. Add the corn muffin mix. Stir until well combined. Pour the muffin mixture into the muffin tins, filling each tin equally, about two-thirds full. Bake for 15 - 20 minutes, or until golden brown. Remove from the oven and, immediately and carefully, invert the muffin tin onto a plate. Allow the muffins to cool for a few minutes. Serve while warm or cool completely.

Feast of St. Peter Damian (February 21)
Holy saint dedicated to the Immaculate Heart of Mary.
"May Christ be heard in our language, may Christ be seen in our life, may He be perceived in our hearts."
Food for the Soul: Be mindful today, of what you say, what you do, and why you do it. Are you putting on Christ, bringing Christ, and being Christ to others for God's glory?
St. Peter Damian, pray for us.
Blessed Mother, graciously intercede for us.
Holy Trinity, we adore You! Hear and answer our prayers.

Feast of the Chair of St. Peter (February 22)
Apostle. First pope of the Church.
"Until we have a passionate love for our Lord in the Most Blessed Sacrament, we shall accomplish nothing."
Food for the Soul: Sometimes the tasks we undertake in life seem to get us nowhere. Have they been rooted in the passionate love of Jesus Christ?
St. Peter, pray for us.
Blessed Mother, graciously intercede for us.
Holy Trinity, we adore You! Hear and answer our prayers.

Feast of St. Polycarp (February 23)
Patron saint of earaches.
"Hear me declare with boldness: I am a Christian."
Food for the Soul: May your life today proclaim you are of Christ!
St. Polycarp, pray for us.
Blessed Mother, graciously intercede for us.
Holy Trinity, we adore You! Hear and answer our prayers.

God's Word of the Day (February 24)

"Love is patient, love is kind. It does not envy, it does not boast, it is not proud. It does not dishonor others, it is not self-seeking, it is not easily angered, it keeps no record of wrongs."
(1 Corinthians 13:4-5)

Food for the Soul: Love requires much of us. It is intentional. May we be mindful in our speech and actions today, that all is spoken and done in love.

Blessed Mother, graciously intercede for us.
Holy Trinity, we adore You! Hear and answer our prayers.

Tortilla Chip Day (February 24)

Tortilla Chips and Salsa

Chips and salsa are very easy to make at home! Prepare the salsa ahead of time so the flavors can "meld" together. You can also add some diced jalapeño pepper to make it a little spicy.

Salsa Ingredients:
- 1 container of cherry tomatoes, diced (I use a vegetable chopper or a food dicer...)
- 1 small onion, diced
- 2 cloves of garlic, minced (or a couple of sprinkles of garlic powder)
- 3 - 4 sprigs of cilantro, chopped (optional)
- Sprinkle of salt, to taste
- 3 - 4 Tbsps lime juice
- Jalapeño pepper, diced, if desired

Tortilla Ingredients:
- 10 corn tortillas, each cut into 8 wedges
- Salt or seasoning mix

Directions: Prepare the salsa ahead of serving time. In a medium bowl, add diced tomatoes, onions, and minced garlic (or garlic powder). Stir. Add cilantro, if desired. Stir. Add lime juice. Stir. Salt to taste. Add diced jalapeño pepper, if desired. Stir. Allow salsa to sit in refrigerator for at least an hour, stirring the mixture occasionally. (The lime juice will "marinate" the veggies...). Preheat the deep fryer to 375 degrees. Prepare a cookie sheet, paper towel lined. In small batches, fry the tortillas wedges until golden brown. Remove chips from fryer and place on cookie sheet. Lightly salt/season both sides of the tortillas immediately after they are fried. Serve warm or cooled tortillas with your freshly made salsa.

Try this recipe another way...
+++By making ***Tropical Salsa!*** Add 2/3 cup of pineapple tidbits and some diced jalapeño pepper for a sweet, spicy salsa.

Cinnamon Sugared Tortilla Crisps

I used to order these at a local Mexican restaurant many, many years ago. When Paul and I got married, I tried making them myself. The traditional recipe calls for flour tortillas, but Paul and I enjoy them made with corn tortillas. Either way, serve this crunchy dessert after dinner today and you'll hear everyone say, "Olé!"

Ingredients:
- 10 flour or corn tortillas, each tortilla cut into 8 wedges
- 1/2 cup sugar
- 1 Tbsp cinnamon (add more or less, to your taste)
- 1/2 tsp salt

Directions: Preheat deep fryer to 375 degrees. In a small bowl, combine sugar, cinnamon, and salt. Stir together until combined. With some kitchen shears, cut each tortilla into 8 wedges. In small batches, fry the tortilla wedges until golden brown. Place on paper towel lined baking sheets and immediately, out of the fryer, sprinkle both sides of the tortilla chips with the cinnamon sugar mixture. Served warm or cooled.

God's Word of the Day (February 25)
"Let the morning bring me word of Your unfailing love, for I have put my trust in You. Show me the way I should go, for to You I entrust my life."
(Psalm 143:8)
Food for the Soul: Pray for God's guidance today.
Blessed Mother, graciously intercede for us.
Holy Trinity, we adore You! Hear and answer our prayers.

God's Word of the Day (February 26)
"If I have the gift of prophecy and can fathom all mysteries and all knowledge, and if I have a faith that can move mountains, but do not have love, I am nothing."
(1 Corinthians 13:2)
Food for the Soul: Meditate on the power of the true love of God.
Blessed Mother, graciously intercede for us.
Holy Trinity, we adore You! Hear and answer our prayers.

Feast of St. Gabriel Possenti (February 27)
Patron saint of Catholic youth, students, and those studying for the priesthood.
"I will attempt, day by day, to break my will into pieces. I want to do God's Holy Will, not my own!"
Food for the Soul: There will be a moment today, when you will want to do your will instead of God's Will. Be truthful with yourself, be prepared, and know that it is coming! Be ready to deny yourself and cheerfully submit to Him.
St. Gabriel Possenti, pray for us.
Blessed Mother, graciously intercede for us.
Holy Trinity, we adore You! Hear and answer our prayers.

Toast Day (February 27)

Toasted Bolillo Sandwiches

When I saw "Toast Day", I thought, how exciting and tasty can that be? But, then I remembered a sandwich favorite I make with a toasted Bolillo, which is a Mexican white bread roll. With a sandwich like this, who needs to order from a sandwich shop? You can put whatever meats, cheeses, condiments, veggies, and pickles you desire on your sandwich, but I'll give you the recipe for how I create mine. Pop the cut roll in the air fryer for a few minutes so it gets nice and toasty, top it with a combination of your favorite deli meats, lots of mayo, honey mustard, some onion and tomato slices, and a homemade pickle relish, and it will take the ordinary sandwich to extraordinary!

Ingredients:
- Bolillo rolls
- Mayonnaise
- Honey mustard dressing, or your favorite kind of mustard or dressing (Caesar, French, Italian, or Thousand Island dressing would be really good, too!)
- Shaved ham
- Shaved chicken or turkey breast
- Shaved roast beef
- Thinly slice salami
- Thin slices of your favorite cheese(es)
- Thinly sliced onions
- Thinly sliced vine tomato, sprinkled with salt and garlic powder

Pickle Relish Topping:
- 1 - 2 Tbsps sweet pickle relish
- 2 dill pickle spears, diced
- 1 - 2 Tbsps diced onion

Directions: Prepare the pickle relish. In a small bowl, add the sweet pickle relish, diced dill pickles, and diced onions. Stir together until combined. Taste. Add a little more of whatever ingredient you want until it tastes great to you. Set aside. (For me, the mixture of the sweet pickles and the dill pickles is what makes this relish so good, which is surprising since I don't ever eat dill pickles on anything! The onions also add a nice crunch and flavor.). Slice the tomato and place on a plate. Season the slices, on both sides, with some salt and garlic powder. Set aside. Place a cut Bolillo roll into the air fryer, but keep the roll closed so only the crust of the roll gets crunchy. (In case you do not know, Bolillo rolls are very large! You may only fit one in the air fryer at a time, depending on the size of your air fryer.) Bake at 350 degrees for 3 - 4 minutes, until you get your desired toasty crunch. Remove roll from air fryer. Open cut roll. Generously slather on some mayo to both sides of the roll. Begin to build your sandwich. If you want some cheese, add it to both sides of the roll. Then start with salami and ham on one side, roast beef and chicken on the other side. Then top each side with honey mustard (or try some creamy Caesar or ranch!). Add onion slices to one side and seasoned tomato slices to the other. Then top with the pickle relish. Sandwich the two sides together. Cut in half, serve, and enjoy!

God's Word of the Day (February 28)

"However, as it is written: 'What no eye has seen, what no ear has heard, and what no human mind has conceived' –
the things God has prepared for those who love Him."
(1 Corinthians 2:9)
Food for the Soul: Praise God for His abundant blessings!
Blessed Mother, graciously intercede for us.
Holy Trinity, we adore You! Hear and answer our prayers.

God's Word of the Day (February 29, for Leap Year)

"For I, the Lord your God, hold your right hand; it is I Who say to you, 'Fear not, I am the One Who helps you.'"
(Isaiah 41:13)
Food for the Soul: Ask God for His help today.
Then watch Him come to your aid.
Blessed Mother, graciously intercede for us.
Holy Trinity, we adore You! Hear and answer our prayers.

March

March Birthday Cake

Green River Cake

Celebrating a Birthday this month? We are! Try making this moist, rich cake. It's similar to a pound cake in it's texture. Also, a great dessert to serve on St. Paddy's Day! Enjoy a slice with a cup of Irish Coffee...

Cake Ingredients:
- 3 sticks unsalted butter, softened
- 3 cups sugar
- 5 large eggs
- 2 Tbsps lemon extract
- 3/4 cup green river soda
- 1 - 2 drops green food coloring, or until desired shade of green (optional)

Green River Glaze Ingredients:
- 1 Tbsp unsalted butter, melted
- 3 Tbsp green river soda
- 1 1/4 - 1 1/2 cups of powdered sugar

Directions: Preheat oven to 325 degrees. Well oil a Bundt pan. Use a pastry brush to get into all of the crevices. In a large mixing bowl, cream together the butter and the sugar for 20 minutes. Add the eggs, one at a time, and beat well after each addition. Add the lemon extract. Combine. Add half of the flour. Combine. Add half of the green river soda. Combine. Add the rest of the flour. Combine. Add the rest of the green river soda. Combine. Pour the batter into the well oiled Bundt pan. Bake between 1 hour and 1 hour and 15 minutes, until toothpick inserted in center of cake is clean. Cool cake completely. Dust cake with powdered sugar, or prepare the green river glaze (add small amounts of soda or powdered sugar to get to the desired consistency) and drizzle over the cooled cake.

Try this recipe in another way...
+++By using a different flavored soda! My Mom used to make it with lemon lime soda, but orange, cherry, or even root beer, would be great.

Just change the extract to match the soda flavor and omit the green food coloring.

God's Word of the Day (March 1)

"For the message of the cross is foolishness to those who are perishing, but to us who are being saved, it is the power of God."
(Corinthians 1:18)
Food for the Soul: Gaze upon the crucifix and see Jesus as your Hope, your Love, your Joy, your Peace.
*Blessed Mother, graciously intercede for us.
Holy Trinity, we adore You! Hear and answer our prayers.*

Citrus Day (March 1)
Citrus Roll Biscuits

The sweet flavors of lemon and orange shine through in a rolled biscuit...

Ingredients:
- 1/4 cup canola oil
- 3/4 cup half and half
- 2 cups flour, sifted
- 1 Tbsp baking powder
- 1 tsp salt
- 1/4 tsp baking soda

Citrus Filling Ingredients:
- 1/3 cup sugar
- Zest from 1 small orange
- Zest from 1 small lemon
- 2 Tbsps of unsalted butter, softened

Citrus Glaze Ingredients:
- 1/2 Tbsp orange juice
- 1/2 Tbsp lemon juice
- 1/2 cup powdered sugar, sifted

Directions: Preheat oven to 400 degrees. Oil a 9 inch cake pan. In a medium bowl, mix together the canola oil and the half and half. In another bowl, sift together the flour, baking powder, baking soda, and salt. Add the dry ingredients to the oil mixture. Combine. Do not overmix. In a small separate bowl, mix together the filling ingredients; stir together sugar, orange zest, and lemon zest until combined. Set aside. Roll out the biscuit dough to a 15 x 8 inch rectangle. Spread the filling ingredients over the dough. Roll the dough, like a jelly roll, rolling up from the longer side of the dough. Cut slices, 1 1/2 inch thick. Place slices in the prepared pan. Bake at 400 degrees for 15 minutes. Mix the glaze ingredients together while the biscuits are baking. Remove biscuits from oven. Top biscuits with glaze immediately. Allow to cool for 5 minutes. Serve warm.

God's Word of the Day (March 2)

"But He was pierced for our transgressions; He was crushed for our iniquities; upon Him was the chastisement that brought us peace, and with His wounds, we are healed."

(Isaiah 53:5)

Food for the Soul: Thank Jesus, for taking upon Himself, the sins of the world. Thank Him for the Healing, Saving Power He brings to you today.

Blessed Mother, graciously intercede for us.
Holy Trinity, we adore You! Hear and answer our prayers.

Feast of St. Katharine Drexel (March 3)
Patron saint of philanthropy.

"Peacefully do, at each moment, what at that moment ought to be done. If we do what each moment requires, we will eventually complete God's plan, whatever it is. We can trust God to take care of the master plan when we take care of the details."

Food for the Soul: Be mindful of the details today, knowing God is in charge of the master plan!

St. Katharine Drexel, pray for us.
Blessed Mother, graciously intercede for us.
Holy Trinity, we adore You! Hear and answer our prayers.

Feast of St. Casimir (March 4)
Patron saint of Poland, Lithuania, and young people.
"St. Casimir embraced a life of celibacy, submitted himself humbly to God's Will in all things, devoted himself with tender love to the Blessed Virgin Mary, and developed a fervent practice of adoring Christ present in the Blessed Sacrament."
–– St. John Paul II

Food for the Soul: Live today with a pure heart. Choose God's Will, pray to the Blessed Mother, and adore Jesus in His Holy Presence.

St. Casimir, pray for us.
St. John Paul II, pray for us.
Blessed Mother, graciously intercede for us.
Holy Trinity, hear and answer our prayers.

Pancake Day (March 4)

Ricotta Pancakes with Blueberry Topping
Want to try a different kind of pancake? Then try these delicious cakes, made with ricotta cheese, for some added calcium and protein!

Pancake Ingredients:
- 2 large eggs, separated
- 2/3 cup ricotta cheese, drained
- 1/4 cup half and half
- 6 Tbsps flour
- 2 tsp sugar
- 1/4 tsp baking powder
-

Ingredients for Blueberry Topping:
- 1 can of Blueberry Pie Filling
- 1 tsp lemon juice

Directions for Blueberry Topping: Combine blueberry pie filling with 1 tsp of lemon juice. Heat in a medium pot until warm. Set aside.

Directions for Ricotta Pancakes: Separate eggs. Place whites in a small bowl. Beat until stiff, but still moist. Set aside. Place yolks in a medium bowl. Add the ricotta cheese and the half and half. Mix together. Add the flour, sugar, and baking powder. Mix. Add the beaten egg whites and fold them gently into the batter. Prepare a large nonstick skillet with 1 Tbsp of canola oil and heat the oil on medium, medium high heat. Transfer batter to a 2 cup measuring cup for easy pouring. Pour batter, about 2-3 Tbsps for each pancake, onto the oiled pan. Wait until bubbles appear on top, then flip each pancake. Cook each side until golden brown. For the next batch, be sure to add another Tbsp of canola oil. Allow oil to heat up once again before adding pancake batter. Top pancakes with a spoonful, or two, of the warm blueberry topping. You can always use apple or cherry pie filling, instead!

God's Word of the Day (March 5)
*"For sin shall no longer be your master,
because you are not under the law, but under grace."*
(Romans 6:14)
***Food for the Soul: Live in the grace of God today.
Turn away from sin. Seek God.***
*Blessed Mother, graciously intercede for us.
Holy Trinity, we adore You! Hear and answer our prayers.*

God's Word of the Day (March 6)
*"This Jesus, delivered up according to the definite plan
and foreknowledge of God, you crucified and killed by the
hands of lawless men. God raised Him up, loosing the pangs of death,
because it was not for Him to be held by it."*
(Acts 2:23-24)
***Food for the Soul: Believe in the Mighty Power of our Lord Jesus Christ!
He is Life. He is Healer. He is Redeemer. There is no lie in Who He is!***
*Blessed Mother, graciously intercede for us.
Holy Trinity, we adore You! Hear and answer our prayers.*

Feast Day of St. Thomas Aquinas (March 7)
Patron saint of universities and scholars.
"Grant me, O Lord my God, a mind to know You, a heart to seek You, wisdom to find You, conduct to please You, faithful perseverance in waiting for You, and a hope of finally embracing You."
Food for the Soul: Embrace Jesus with your life today.
St. Thomas Aquinas, pray for us.
Blessed Mother, graciously intercede for us.
Holy Trinity, we adore You! Hear and answer our prayers.

Feast Day of St. John of God (March 8)
Patron saint of hospitals, the sick, nurses, firefighters, alcoholics, and booksellers.
"With outstretched arms He begs us to turn toward Him, to weep for our sins and to become the servants of love, first for ourselves, then for our neighbors. Just as water extinguishes a fire, so love wipes away sin."
Food for the Soul: Love wipes away sin. How powerful is Love!
St. John of God, pray for us.
Sweet Jesus, have mercy on us.
Blessed Mother, graciously intercede for us.
Holy Trinity, we adore You! Hear and answer our prayers.

Feast of St. Frances of Rome (March 9)
"God's Will is mine."
Food for the Soul: May we all come to realize that this is the way to a peaceful, loving, blessed, anointed life lived in Christ.
St. Frances of Rome, pray for us.
Blessed Mother, graciously intercede for us.
Holy Trinity, we adore You! Hear and answer our prayers.

God's Word of the Day (March 10)
"Indeed, under the law, almost everything is purified with blood, and without the shedding of blood, there is no forgiveness of sins."
(Hebrews 9:22)
Food for the Soul: Think about the power of the Precious Blood of Christ today. It is Healing. Cleansing. Redeeming.

Blessed Mother, graciously intercede for us.
Holy Trinity, we adore You! Hear and answer our prayers.

God's Word of the Day (March 11)
"May I never boast, except in the Cross of our Lord Jesus Christ, through which the world has been crucified to me, and I to the world."
(Galatians 6:14)
Food for the Soul: All glory and honor to the Cross of Jesus Christ!
Blessed Mother, graciously intercede for us.
Holy Trinity, we adore You! Hear and answer our prayers.

God's Word of the Day (March 12)
"And being found in human form, He humbled Himself by becoming obedient to the point of death, even death on a cross."
(Philippians 2:8)
Food for Thought: Meditate on the humanity of Christ. He learns. He teaches. He listens. He speaks. He laughs. He cries. He celebrates. He suffers. He hurts. He heals. He even dies. But, He is also God, so powerful and full of might, that death cannot hold Him... He is so magnificent in glory! That is our God!
Blessed Mother, graciously intercede for us.
Holy Trinity, we adore You! Hear and answer our prayers.

God's Word of the Day (March 13)
"For the wages of sin is death, but the free gift of God is eternal life in Christ Jesus our Lord."
(Romans 6:23)
Food for the Soul: Choose life and love today.
Blessed Mother, graciously intercede for us.
Holy Trinity, we adore You! Hear and answer our prayers.

God's Word of the Day (March 14)
*"He who dwells in the shelter of the Most High
will abide in the shadow of the Almighty."*
(Psalm 91:1)
Food for the Soul: Choose to live in God's presence today.
*Blessed Mother, graciously intercede for us.
Holy Trinity, we adore You! Hear and answer our prayers.*

God's Word of the Day (March 15)
*"For you were straying sheep, but have now returned
to the Shepherd and Overseer of your souls."*
(1 Peter 2:25)
***Food for the Soul: Have you returned to God?
Or are you still a straying sheep?***
*Blessed Mother, graciously intercede for us.
Holy Trinity, we adore You! Hear and answer our prayers.*

God's Word of the Day (March 16)
*"As they went out, they found a man of Cyrene, Simon by name.
They compelled this man to carry His Cross."*
(Matthew 27:32)
***Food for the Soul: God asks us to carry our cross.
Let us be brave and do this for Him, Who loves us so much!***
*Blessed Mother, graciously intercede for us.
Holy Trinity, we adore You! Hear and answer our prayers.*

Feast of St. Patrick (March 17)
Patron saint of Ireland.
*"Christ beside me, Christ before me, Christ behind me.
Christ within me, Christ beneath me, Christ above me."*
***Food for the Soul: Live today in the knowledge
that Christ surrounds you in His love!***
*St. Patrick, pray for us.
Loving Jesus, be with us.
Blessed Mother, graciously intercede for us.
Holy Trinity, we adore You! Hear and answer our prayers.*

Instant Pot Corned Beef

Tender. Juicy. Flavorful. Serve with Instant Pot Buttered Cabbage and Instant Pot Buttered Baby Potatoes. Instant Pot, what did I ever do before you came into my kitchen?

- **Ingredients:**
- 3 lb corned beef brisket, flat cut
- 1 can of beef broth plus enough water to make a total of 2 1/2 cups
- 12 oz beer (nothing too bitter)
- 1 Tbsp apple cider vinegar
- 2 tsps light brown sugar
- 2 tsps onion powder
- 2 tsps garlic powder
- The contents of the included packet of pickling spices

Directions: To a 6 quart instant pot, add the beef broth plus water, beer, apple cider vinegar, brown sugar, onion powder, garlic powder, and the contents of the packet of pickling spices. Stir until combined. Remove the brisket from the packaging and rinse under cold water for about a minute, rinsing off any spices already on the brisket. Place the brisket in the instant pot, fat cap side up. Spoon the beer/broth mixture over the brisket. Cover, lock, and seal the lid of the instant pot. Set on the meat cycle with high pressure for 80 minutes. When the cycle is finished, natural release for 30 minutes. Quick release any remaining pressure. Remove corned beef and place it on a plate or cutting board. Tent with foil to remain warm. Trim off the fat cap and discard. Slice the corned beef against the grain. (If you are able to wait, cool the brisket completely and then refrigerate overnight before slicing. It will be much easier to slice the next day. I recommend using a meat slicer to achieve thin slices.). Be sure to reserve some of the remaining cooking juices from the pot. Place the slices in a gallon freezer bag with some of the cooking juices to keep it moist and juicy. Store the brisket in the refrigerator. Then gently warm up the slices in the microwave before using them for a sandwich, or for serving them as part of a dinner.

Sous Vide Corned Beef

Want to try to make another delicious, juicy, tender corned beef brisket appear? Just wave your magic sous vide wand!
Cook it very slowly overnight with little worry or fuss.

Ingredients:
- 3 lb corned beef brisket, flat cut
- Spice packet

Directions: Prepare the sous vide. Set to 165 degrees. Remove the brisket from the packaging and rinse under cold water for about a minute, rinsing off any spices already on the brisket. Place the brisket on a medium baking sheet, fat cap facing up. Place the spices found in the spice packet on the top of the fat cap. Place brisket in a vacuum seal bag. Vacuum and seal bag. Place bag in the sous vide container. Set for 10 hours. Remove bag from water, then remove corned beef from bag (save the juices). Allow corned beef to cool. Refrigerate, if you are able; it will be easier to slice cold. Slice thinly and place slices in a gallon freezer bag with the corned beef cooking juices from the sous vide bag.

Instant Pot Buttered Cabbage

For a Saint Patrick's Irish feast, serve this melt-in-your-mouth cabbage with thin slices of Instant Pot Corned Beef and
Instant Pot Buttered Baby Potatoes!

Ingredients:
- 1 head of Napa cabbage, thinly chopped
- 1 stick of unsalted butter, cut into 8 pieces
- 3/4 cup low sodium chicken broth
- 1/4 cup of corned beef cooking juices, strained

Directions: In an instant pot, add the chicken broth, corned beef cooking juices, and butter pieces. Add in the chopped cabbage. (It's okay if the cabbage goes a little above the "max" line in the pot. It will cook down and all will be fine.). Close, lock and seal the lid. Set to "pressure cook" on high pressure for 6 minutes. When cycle is finished, do a quick release. Stir the cabbage. Set to "sauté" for 5 minutes, to boiling. Allow the juices with the cabbage to cook down. Stir again. Repeat process, if necessary. Once there is less liquid remaining in the pot, remove cabbage, draining any extra liquid. Butter cabbage with some unsalted butter. Salt and pepper to taste. Serve.

Instant Pot Buttered Baby Potatoes

These potatoes are lip-smacking addictive goodness!

Ingredients:

- 1.5-2 lbs baby new potatoes, washed/cut into quarters
- 3 Tbsps butter/margarine, melted
- 1/2 cup chicken or beef broth
- 2 heaping tsps onion soup mix
- 1/2 tsp Onion powder
- 1/2 tsp Garlic powder
- 1 Tbsp butter/margarine (add after cooking, before serving)

Directions: Add melted butter, broth, onion soup mix, garlic powder, and onion powder to the Instant Pot. Stir sauce until well combined. Add the potatoes. Stir together so the potatoes are covered in the sauce. Seal the Instant Pot, click on manual, select high pressure, and cook for 15 minutes. When the cooking is finished, do a natural release after 15 min. Stir the potatoes. Add an extra tablespoon of butter/margarine while hot. Stir again. Transfer to a bowl, pouring the sauce over the potatoes. Serve.

Feast of St. Cyril of Jerusalem (March 18)
Patron saint of catechists.
*"The wider our contemplation of creation,
the grander is our conception of God."*
**Food for the Soul: God's wonders are all around you.
Take time to see and appreciate them!**
St. Cyril of Jerusalem, pray for us.
Blessed Mother, graciously intercede for us.
Holy Trinity, we adore You! Hear and answer our prayers.

Feast of St. Joseph (March 19)
Patron saint of families, fathers, travelers, house sellers and buyers, craftsmen, and the universal Church.

*"In every difficulty, apply to St. Joseph with confidence
and you will never be disappointed."*
--St. Mary MacKillop

"When you invoke St. Joseph, you don't have to say much. You know your Father in heaven knows what you need; well, so does His friend, St. Joseph. Tell him, 'If you were in my place, St. Joseph, what would you do? Well, pray for this on my behalf.'"
-- St. André Bessette

**Food for the Soul: Turn to St. Joseph today.
Ask him for his help and guidance. Seek his wisdom.**
St. Joseph, pray for us.
St. Mary MacKillop, pray for us.
St. André Bessette, pray for us.
Blessed Mother, graciously intercede for us.
Holy Trinity, we adore You! Hear and answer our prayers.

Chicago Style Italian Beef with Gravy

Are you ready for some delicious, flavorful, tender, homemade beef sandwiches for the big game, similar to a local Chicago favorite? We are!

Beef Ingredients:

- 2.5 - 3 pounds top round or eye of round beef
- 1 tsp meat tenderizer
- 1 tsp onion powder
- 1 tsp garlic powder
-

Beef Directions: Prepare the sous vide to 132 degrees. Mix the seasonings together. Rub the mixture onto the beef. Place into a vacuum sealed bag. Place the bag into the sous vide container. Sous vide the beef for 12 - 24 hours. Remove the bag from the sous vide bath. Leave the beef in the bag. Cool down, and refrigerate overnight. The following day, slice beef thinly, against the grain. I recommend using an electric meat slicer for the best results.

Italian Gravy Ingredients:
- 1/4 cup lard, melted
- 2 cans of beef broth, 14.5 oz each
- 2 tsps browning & seasoning Sauce
- 2 tsps lime juice
- 1 tsp dried oregano
- 1/2 tsp chicken or beef powder
- 1/2 tsp black pepper
- 1/2 tsp garlic powder
- 1/2 tsp onion powder

Gravy Directions: Melt the lard in a medium sized pot. Make the beef gravy by combining all of the ingredients into the medium saucepan over medium heat. When the mixture begins to boil reduce the heat and simmer for 5 minutes, then turn the heat down to low. For each sandwich, drop 1/4 pound of sliced beef (separate the slices) into the gravy for 2 minutes. Make sure the gravy isn't boiling. It should be around 180 degrees F. After the beef has soaked in the gravy, use tongs to arrange the beef on a sandwich roll. Dip the roll into the gravy, or spoon some extra gravy on the sandwich just before serving. Top with your choice of hot/mild giardiniera, sweet peppers, or both. You can also top the beef with some mozzarella cheese or some silky cheddar cheese sauce. Yum! And don't forget the napkins! You will need plenty, for sure! Oh, so messy, but, oh so Chicago good!

Ricotta Meatball Sandwiches with Red Gravy

These light, moist, tender meatballs are great on a sandwich or over pasta!

Meatball Ingredients:
- 19 oz package of mild Italian sausage links, meat removed from casing
- 3/4 cup + 1 Tbsp ricotta cheese
- 1 egg
- 1/3 cup + 1 Tbsp shredded Parmesan cheese, finely grated
- 1/3 cup + 1 Tbsp bread crumbs
- 3/4 tsp garlic powder
- 3/4 tsp onion powder

Red Gravy Ingredients:
- 1 jar of your favorite marinara sauce
- 1/4 cup ginger ale
- 1/2 tsp garlic powder
- 1/2 tsp onion powder
- 2 - 3 packages of Splenda
- Salt, to taste

Sandwich Ingredients:
- Italian rolls, toasted
- Shredded mozzarella cheese
- Cooked sweet peppers
- Sautéed sweet onions

Directions: Prepare the meatballs. In a large bowl, break up the sausage, (removed from its casing). In a small bowl, mix together the ricotta cheese and egg. Add the egg mixture to the sausage and mix lightly together. In the small bowl, mix together the Parmesan cheese, bread crumbs, garlic powder and onion powder. Add into the sausage mixture and stir until combined. Do not overmix. Use a tablespoon scoop to measure out the sausage mixture for the meatballs. Lightly roll the mixture into a ball and place on a parchment lined baking sheet. (Makes about 35.) Set aside. Prepare the gravy. In a large nonstick skillet on medium heat, add in the marinara sauce. Rinse the jar out with the ginger ale and add to the sauce. Stir in the garlic powder and the onion powder. Add in the Splenda and salt, to taste. Heat for 5 minutes until sauce is bubbly, stirring occasionally. Lower the temperature to medium low heat and cover the skillet. Place the meatballs into the hot sauce. Cook the meatballs for 45 minutes, without stirring them. (This way, they will set and not fall apart.) Then, gently stir the meatballs in the gravy. Continue to cook the meatballs, covered, for 2 more hours, stirring every half hour. This will result in a tender meatball and a delicious, flavorful gravy. Serve the meatballs on some crunchy, toasted Italian rolls. Top with cooked sweet peppers, sautéed onions, shredded mozzarella cheese, and gravy.

First Day of Spring
COBALT Sandwiches

This COBALT sandwich, made of Chicken, Onion, Bacon, Avocado, Lettuce, and Tomato, is a favorite for Paul and I! It all came together when I had some leftover chicken from the Easy-Breezy Crispy Air Fryer Chicken and leftover Crispy, Sweet and Smoky Breakfast Bacon. I used my vegetable spiralizer and made some shaved rings of red onion, which gave the sandwich a unique burst of flavor! Add in some shredded lettuce, lightly seasoned tomato and avocado slices, mayo and fresh, toasted brioche bread, and you've got yourself a creamy, crunchy, sweet, salty, savory, smoky sandwich packed full of yummy textures and flavors!

Ingredients:
- Chicken slices (leftover **Crispy Skinned Air Fryer Chicken**)
- Onion (preferably a red onion, very thinly sliced or spiralized)
- Bacon (leftover **Fried Bacon**)
- Avocado, sliced, seasoned with lime juice and salt
- Lettuce, shredded
- Tomato, off the vine or home grown, thinly sliced, seasoned with garlic powder and salt
- Mayonnaise or your favorite creamy salad dressing
- Brioche Bread, lightly toasted

Directions: Lightly toast the brioche bread. On one slice of bread, add mayo/dressing, shredded lettuce, chicken and tomato. On the other slice of bread, add mayo, onions, bacon and avocado. Add a bit more mayo/dressing in between the two sides and then sandwich them together. Time to eat and enjoy!

God's Word of the Day (March 20)
"And Jesus said, 'You lack one thing: go, sell all that you have and give to the poor, and you will have treasure in heaven; and come, follow Me.'"
(Mark 10:21)
Food for the Soul: Give to the poor today.
Give something you don't really want to part with!
Blessed Mother, graciously intercede for us.
Holy Trinity, we adore You! Hear and answer our prayers.

God's Word of the Day (March 21)
"For whoever loses his life for My sake will find it. For what will it profit a man if he gains the whole world and forfeits his soul? Or what shall a man give in return for his soul?"
(Matthew 16:25-26)
Food for the Soul: We get protection for our health, our homes, our cars. What protection do we seek for our precious souls?
Blessed Mother, graciously intercede for us.
Holy Trinity, we adore You! Hear and answer our prayers.

God's Word of the Day (March 22)
"My flesh and my heart may fail, but God is the strength of my heart and my portion forever."
(Psalm 73:26)
Food for the Soul: Our bodies are given to us by God for a certain amount of time. God is eternal. Get to know Him.
Blessed Mother, graciously intercede for us.
Holy Trinity, we adore You! Hear and answer our prayers.

Feast of St. Turibius of Mogrovejo (March 23)
Patron saint of native peoples' rights and Latin American bishops.
"Time is not our own and we must give a strict account of it."
**Food for the Soul: Be mindful of how you spend your time today.
Are you using it wisely?**
St. Turibius of Mogrovejo, pray for us.
Blessed Mother, graciously intercede for us.
Holy Trinity, we adore You! Hear and answer our prayers.

God's Word of the Day (March 24)
*"At once the Spirit sent Him out into the wilderness, and
He was in the wilderness for forty days, being tempted by Satan."*
(Mark 1:12)
**Food for the Soul: You may be tempted today. Put on the
armor of God this morning, which is the Word of God.
Be ready for any spiritual battles that may arise.**
Blessed Mother, graciously intercede for us.
Holy Trinity, we adore You! Hear and answer our prayers.

Feast Day of the Annunciation (March 25)
*"If you ever feel distressed during your day, call upon our Lady, just
say this simple prayer: 'Mary, Mother of Jesus, please be a mother
to me now.' I must admit, this prayer has never failed me."*
-- St. Teresa of Calcutta
**Food for the Soul: Call on the Blessed Mother today.
Just like your own Mom, she is so happy to hear from you!!**
St. Teresa of Calcutta, pray for us.
Mary, Mother of Jesus, intercede for us.
Blessed Mother, graciously intercede for us.
Holy Trinity, we adore You! Hear and answer our prayers.

God's Word of the Day (March 26)
"Humble yourselves, therefore, under the mighty Hand of God, so that, at the proper time, He may exalt you."
(1 Peter 5:6)
Food for the Soul: Remember to allow God to exalt you, and not do that job yourself!
*Blessed Mother, graciously intercede for us.
Holy Trinity, we adore You! Hear and answer our prayers.*

God's Word of the Day (March 27)
"Then I turned my face to the Lord God, seeking Him by prayer and pleas for mercy with fasting, sackcloth, and ashes."
(Daniel 9:3)
Food for the Soul: Seek God and humbly kneel before Him.
*Blessed Mother, graciously intercede for us.
Holy Trinity, we adore You! Hear and answer our prayers.*

God's Word of the Day (March 28)
"My soul thirsts for God, for the living God. When can I go and meet with God?"
(Psalms 42:1-2)
Food for the Soul: Meet with God today. No waiting necessary. He always has time for you.
*Blessed Mother, graciously intercede for us.
Holy Trinity, we adore You! Hear and answer our prayers.*

God's Word of the Day (March 29)
"Return to the Lord your God, for He is gracious and merciful, slow to anger, and abounding in steadfast love."
(Joel 2:13)
Food for the Soul: Even though we sin, God still loves us. Return to His loving, forgiving arms.
*Blessed Mother, graciously intercede for us.
Holy Trinity, we adore You! Hear and answer our prayers.*

God's Word of the Day (March 30)
"But when you fast, anoint your head and wash your face, that your fasting may not be seen by others but by your Father, Who is in secret. And your Father, Who sees in secret, will reward you."
(Matthew 6: 17-18)
Food for the Soul: Fast today. And don't tell anyone.
Blessed Mother, graciously intercede for us.
Holy Trinity, we adore You! Hear and answer our prayers.

God's Word of the Day (March 31)
"In this world, you will have trouble. But take heart! I have overcome the world."
(John 16:33)
Food for the Soul: Plan to see God in action today, overcoming your troubles and struggles!
Blessed Mother, graciously intercede for us.
Holy Trinity, we adore You! Hear and answer our prayers.

Pretzel Sunday (Last Sunday in March)

Sugar Crunch Pretzels
A sweet, salty, crunchy snack.
Make a batch or two ahead of time, break apart, and store in a ziplock bag.

Ingredients:
2 cups crushed pretzel sticks
3/4 cup melted butter
3 Tbsps sugar

Directions: Preheat oven to 325 degrees. Prepare the pan: 9 x 13 inch glass pan, ungreased. In a small bowl, mix together crust ingredients, crushed pretzels, melted butter, and sugar. Press into bottom of the pan. Bake for 8 minutes. Remove from oven and cool completely. Break into pieces and enjoy!

April

April Birthday Cake

Cherry Nut Cake

Celebrating a Birthday this month? We are! This is the month my Dad, Stanley, would have celebrated his. He was born on Easter Sunday in 1917. My Dad loved to eat, but he never gained a pound! He had a great metabolism. He especially loved his sweets. For every meal, he ate some kind of dessert with his coffee. He often would stop at the bakery and pick up one of his (and our) favorites, a cherry nut bread, and have some for breakfast the next morning. In fact, those flavors would be great in a cake! Sounds like a plan, Stan! Love you, Dad!

Ingredients:
- 1 cup unsalted butter, softened
- 1 2/3 cups sugar
- 1 tsp vanilla
- 4 large eggs
- 2 cups flour
- 3/4 tsp baking powder
- Pinch of salt
- 2/3 cup sour cream
- 2/3 cup glazed red cherries, chopped
- 1/3 cup chopped walnuts

Directions: Preheat oven to 350 degrees. Generously oil and flour a Bundt pan. In a large bowl, cream butter and sugar until light and fluffy. Add in vanilla. Mix. Add in one egg at a time, beating well after each addition. In a medium bowl, combine flour, baking powder, and salt. Stir together with a fork to sift dry ingredients. Add flour mixture to butter mixture alternately with the sour cream. Mix well after each addition. Gently stir in glazed cherries and walnuts. Pour batter into prepared pan. Bake for 1 hour or until toothpick inserted in center comes out clean. Remove from oven. Cool for 15 minutes in the pan. Then, place a large plate over the cake and invert cake onto the plate. When completely cooled, dust with powdered sugar.

God's Word of the Day (April 1)
"I am the resurrection and the life. Anyone who believes in Me will live, even after dying. Everyone who lives in Me and believes in Me will never ever die. Do you believe this, Martha?"
(John 11:25-26)
Food for the Soul: Do you believe this? Truly? Pray for steadfast faith!
St, Martha, pray for us.
Blessed Mother, graciously intercede for us.
Holy Trinity, we adore You! Hear and answer our prayers.

Feast of St. Francis Paola (April 2)
Patron saint of mariners and naval officers.
"Fix your minds on the Passion of our Lord Jesus Christ. Inflamed with love for us, He came down from heaven to redeem us. For our sake, He endured every torment of body and soul, and shrank from no bodily pain. He, Himself, gave us an example of perfect patience and love. We, then, are to be patient in adversity."
Food for the Soul: If things don't go your way today, practice patience and pray.
St. Francis Paola, pray for us.
Blessed Mother, graciously intercede for us.
Holy Trinity, we adore You! Hear and answer our prayers.

Cherry Nut Bread
Since I started to think about a cherry nut bread, we might as well make one! Why not? Dad, this one's for you, too!

Bread Ingredients:

- 1/4 cup water
- 1 stick unsalted butter, slightly melted
- 1/2 cup sugar
- 1 tsp salt
- 2 large eggs, lightly beaten
- 1 cup half and half
- 2 tsps vanilla
- 4 1/2 cups bread flour
- 1 (1/4-oz.) envelope instant yeast

Filling Ingredients:

- 2/3 cup glazed cherries, chopped
- 1/3 cup walnuts, finely chopped
- 4 Tbsp of unsalted butter, softened, divided in half, for spreading on each of the two loaves, two tablespoonfuls of butter for each loaf

Glaze Topping Ingredients:

- 1/4 cup butter, melted
- 2 tablespoons honey
- 1 large egg white
- 2/3 cup powdered sugar

Icing Drizzle Ingredients: (optional)

- 1 Tbsp half and half
- 1/2 cup (or more) powdered sugar

Directions: Using the bread machine, add water, melted butter (cooled), sugar, salt, eggs, half and half, vanilla, and bread flour. Make a well in the flour and add the yeast to that well. Set machine to the dough cycle. Prepare the cherry walnut filling. In a small bowl, add glazed cherries and chopped walnuts. Stir together. Divide mixture in half. Set aside. When dough cycle is complete, remove dough from machine. Place dough on medium sized nonstick cookie sheet. Punch dough down. Divide dough in half. Turn half of the dough out onto another medium cookie sheet. Press one dough portion into a rectangle. Spread with 2 Tbsp softened butter, then sprinkle half of the cherry walnut filling over the butter. Press the filling lightly into the dough. Roll up dough like a jelly roll. Place seam side down in an oiled 9 x 5 inch loaf pan. Repeat procedure with remaining half of the dough. Prepare the glaze. Spoon the glaze topping over the loaves and spread it over the dough. Cover the pans loosely with plastic wrap; let rise in a warm place (80° to 85°) for 1 hour or until doubled in size. Preheat oven to 350°. Bake 30 minutes or until golden brown, covering with aluminum foil after 25 minutes to prevent excessive browning, if necessary. Cool in pans for 10 minutes. Remove from pans. Cool for another 15 minutes. Slice bread. Serve warm, slathered with butter!

You can also add an icing on top of the baked bread, mixing together 1 tablespoonful of half and half with about 1/2 cup powdered sugar. Drizzle icing over the tops of the cherry nut loaves.

God's Word of the Day (April 3)
"The hour has come that the Son of Man should be glorified. Most assuredly, I say to you, unless a grain of wheat falls into the ground and dies, it remains alone; but if it dies, it produces much grain."
(John 12:23-24)
Food for the Soul: Is God asking you to die to yourself somewhere in your life?
Blessed Mother, graciously intercede for us.
Holy Trinity, we adore You! Hear and answer our prayers.

Burrito Day (April 3)
Breakfast Burrito
Make these burritos ahead and store in the freezer for a quick morning breakfast, or a late night snack!

Ingredients:
- 12 oz package of Bob Evans pork sausage patties, uncooked
- 6 - 8 large eggs
- 1 Tbsp water.
- 6 slices of American cheese, cubed
- 6 - 8 Tbsps salsa
- 6 flour tortillas

Directions: In a medium nonstick skillet, spray some oil into the pan over medium heat. Into the pan, break apart the sausage patties into sausage crumbles. Cook for a few minutes until sausage is no longer pink. Drain, if needed. Place crumbles in a medium bowl. In another medium bowl, beat the eggs with a tablespoon of water. Pour egg into the pan and cook the scrambled eggs. When cooked, scoop eggs into the sausage mixture. Stir. Then add in the American cheese. Stir. Add in the salsa. Stir. In a cloth tortilla warmer, warm the tortillas so they are pliable. Place a tortilla on a plate. Add 1 - 2 heaping tablespoonfuls of the filling to the tortilla. Fold the tortilla, sides in first, then roll upwards. Place seam side down. Finish filling and rolling the rest of the tortillas. Wrap each burrito in plastic wrap and store in the refrigerator or freezer. When ready to eat, unwrap the burrito from the plastic wrap. Wrap the burrito in a paper towel and warm in a cloth tortilla warmer in the microwave for about 1 minute - 1 1/2 minutes from frozen. (Next time you make the burritos, adjust the amount of each ingredient, depending on your taste.)

Feast of St. Isidore of Seville (April 4)
Patron saint of the internet.
"In confession, there is mercy. Believe it firmly, do not doubt, do not hesitate, never despair of the mercy of God."
Food for the Soul: The Divine Mercy of God is real.
Seek it. Ask Jesus for it. Receive it.
St. Isidore of Seville, pray for us.
Blessed Mother, graciously intercede for us.
Holy Trinity, we adore You! Hear and answer our prayers.

Feast of St. Vincent Ferrer (April 5)
Patron saint of builders.
"Whatever you do, think not of yourself, but of God."
Food for the Soul: Be selfless in your actions today.
May they be for God's greater glory.
St. Vincent Ferrer, pray for us.
Blessed Mother, graciously intercede for us.
Holy Trinity, we adore You! Hear and answer our prayers.

God's Word of the Day (April 6)
"He who loves his life will lose it, and he who hates his life in this world will keep it for eternal life."
(John 12:25)
Food for the Soul: Set your sights on heaven and not on earth.
Blessed Mother, graciously intercede for us.
Holy Trinity, we adore You! Hear and answer our prayers.

Feast of St. John Baptist de la Salle (April 7)
Patron saint of teachers.
"Often remind yourself that you are in the presence of God."
***Food for the Soul: Speak and act carefully today.
Be mindful of being in God's presence.***
St. Francis de la Salle, pray for us.
Blessed Mother, graciously intercede for us.
Holy Trinity, we adore You! Hear and answer our prayers.

Coffeecake Day (April 7)

Almond Raspberry Cream Cheese Coffeecake
This coffeecake features three ingredients that totally compliment each other: cream cheese, raspberry preserves, and almonds. I t also would be great made with cherry preserves!

Coffeecake Ingredients:
- 3/4 cup unsalted butter, softened
- 3/4 cup sour cream
- 1 tsp almond or vanilla extract
- 1 large egg
- 3/4 cup sugar
- 2 1/4 cup flour
- 1/2 tsp baking powder
- 1 tsp baking soda
- 1/4 tsp salt

- **Cheese Mixture Ingredients:**
- 8 oz cream cheese, softened
- 1/4 cup sugar
- 1 egg
- 1 tsp vanilla

Topping:
- 1/2 cup raspberry preserves
- 1/2 cup sliced almonds

Directions: Preheat oven to 350 degrees. Oil a 9 inch cake pan. Set aside. In a large bowl, combine flour and sugar. Cut in butter. (You can use a food processor for this step.). Reserve 1 cup of this mixture and set aside for the streusel topping. With the remaining flour, sugar, butter mixture, add baking powder, baking soda, salt, sour cream, extract, and egg. Blend. Spread batter over the bottom of the pan and up 2 inches on the sides (about 1/4 inch thick on the sides). In a small bowl, mix cream cheese, sugar, vanilla, and egg. Blend. Set aside. Top the coffeecake batter in the pan with the cream cheese mixture. Lightly warm the raspberry preserves so it will be spreadable. Spread preserves over the cheese layer. Combine the 1 cup of the reserved flour/sugar/butter mixture with the sliced almonds. Sprinkle over the raspberry layer. Bake at 350 degrees for 45 - 55 minutes. Remove from oven. Cool 15 minutes. Cut and serve.

Try this recipe another way...
+++By swapping out the raspberry preserves for another flavor of preserves! Apricot, lingonberry, blackberry, and strawberry, are all delicious choices. You can also try using different nuts!

God's Word of the Day (April 8)
"If anyone serves Me, let him follow Me; and where I am, there My servant will be also. If anyone serves Me, him, My Father will honor."
(John 12:26)
Food for the Soul: How can you serve God today?
Blessed Mother, graciously intercede for us.
Holy Trinity, we adore You! Hear and answer our prayers.

God's Word of the Day (April 9)
"But whatever were gains to me, I now consider loss for the sake of Christ. What is more, I consider everything a loss because of the surpassing worth of knowing Christ Jesus, my Lord, for Whose sake I have lost all things."
(Philippians 3:7-8)
Food for the Soul: What can you let go of in this life for Christ today?
Blessed Mother, graciously intercede for us.
Holy Trinity, we adore You! Hear and answer our prayers.

God's Word of the Day (April 10)
"I want to know Christ —yes, to know the power of His resurrection and participation in His sufferings, becoming like Him in His death."
(Philippians 3:10)
Food for the Soul: How well do you know our Lord Jesus Christ? Do you make time to know Him better?
Blessed Mother, graciously intercede for us.
Holy Trinity, we adore You! Hear and answer our prayers.

Feast of St. Stanislaus Kostka of Rostkowo (April 11)
Patron saint of novices, youth, young students, and seminarians.
"I want eternity. I was born for greater things."
Food for the Soul: You were born for the extraordinary, the amazing, the glory of God! Don't settle for less!
St. Stanislaus Kostka of Rostkowo, pray for us.
Blessed Mother, graciously intercede for us.
Holy Trinity, we adore You! Hear and answer our prayers.

Feast of St. Lazarus (April 12)
Patron saint of the poor and the sick.
"What good would it have done Lazarus, when he came out of the tomb, if it had not been said, 'Unbind him and let him go'? He came forth bound; not on his own feet, therefore, but by some power leading him. Let this be in the heart of the penitent: when you hear a man confessing his sins, he has already come to life again; when you hear a man lay his bare conscious in confessing, he has already come forth from the sepulcher; but he is not yet unbound. When is he unbound? By whom is he unbound? 'Whatever you loose on earth,' He said, 'shall be loosed in heaven.' Rightly is the loosing of sins able to be given by the Church, but the dead man cannot be raised to life again except by the Lord's calling him interiorly, for this latter is done by God in a more interior way."
— St. Augustine.
Food for the Soul: Reconciliation with God is so intimate, so personal. Run to Him so He may unbind you from your sins. Then you will be free, like Lazarus, to celebrate in His glory!
St. Lazarus, pray for us.
St. Augustine, pray for us.

St. Mary, sister of Lazarus, pray for us.
St. Martha, sister of Lazarus, pray for us.
Blessed Mother, graciously intercede for us.
Holy Trinity, we adore You! Hear and answer our prayers.

Colby Jack Cheese Bread

We bake this bread, which will rise, in celebration and homage to Jesus, Who rose His close friend, Lazarus, from the grave.

Ingredients:
- 3 Tbsps sugar
- 1 tsp salt
- 1 cup water
- 1/3 cup half and half
- 3 1/2 cups flour
- 1 package of instant yeast
- 1 1/2 cups Colby Jack cheese, freshly grated

Topping:
- Knob of unsalted butter

Directions: Using a bread machine, add the sugar, salt, water, half and half, flour, and yeast (in that order) in the pan. Set on "dough" cycle. When the bread machine beeps in the cycle so you can add special ingredients, pour in the grated cheese. When the whole cycle is completed, remove the dough and place in a greased bowl. Punch down the dough. Allow to rest for 15 minutes. Place dough in a greased 9 x 5 x 3 inch loaf pan. Cover lightly with a kitchen towel or plastic wrap. Allow to rise for 1 hour. Uncover dough. Bake in a 375 degree oven for 40 minutes. Remove from oven. Immediately, rub a knob of unsalted butter over the top crust of the bread. Leave the loaf in the pan for 10 minutes. Then, turn over the pan to remove the loaf. Slice and serve warm with softened unsalted, or whipped, butter.

Feast Day of St. Martin I (April 13)
Patron saint of beggars, tailors, and geese.
*"As for my body, God will take care of it. God is with me.
Why should I worry?"*
Food for the Soul: Place your anxieties in God's Hands. He's got this!
St. Martin I, pray for us.
Blessed Mother, graciously intercede for us.
Holy Trinity, we adore You! Hear and answer our prayers.

God's Word of the Day (April 14)
"Let not your hearts be troubled. Believe in God; believe also in Me. In My Father's house are many rooms. If it were not so, would I have told you that I go to prepare a place for you? And if I go and prepare a place for you, I will come again and will take you to Myself, that where I am, you may also be."
(John 14:1-3)
Food for the Soul: God has a plan. He desires you to be with Him, in all His goodness. He speaks Truth, no lies. Dwell on that today.
Blessed Mother, graciously intercede for us.
Holy Trinity, we adore You! Hear and answer our prayers.

Pecan Day (April 14)

Instant Pot Pork Tenderloin Medallions with Savory Pecan Cream Sauce
These pork medallions are wonderful all on their own, but smothering them in this nutty, creamy sauce makes them even more inviting!

Dry Rub Ingredients:
1 tsp meat tenderizer
1 tsp onion powder
1 tsp garlic powder
1/2 tsp black pepper
1 Tbsp light brown sugar

Ingredients:
1 pound pork tenderloin
1 cup low sodium chicken broth
1 Tbsp unsalted butter, quartered

Ingredients for the Pecan Cream Sauce:
- 1 small onion, chopped and sautéed in unsalted butter
- 1 cup cooking juices from the pork, divided
- 1/3 cup pecans
- 1/2 cup heavy cream
- Salt and pepper, to taste

Directions: Prepare the dry rub: In a small bowl, mix together meat tenderizer, onion powder, garlic powder, black pepper, and brown sugar. On a baking sheet, apply the dry rub to the pork tenderloin. Add the chicken broth to the instant pot. Add the butter cubes into the broth. Place the pork tenderloin in the chicken broth. Close, lock, and seal lid. Set to pressure cook cycle for 3 minutes. (Yes, you read that right! Three minutes. Trust me, the pork will be cooked perfectly!) After cycle is finished, natural release for 15 minutes. During the 15 minutes of natural release, sauté the chopped onion, until soft on a nonstick skillet. Then add the pecans into the skillet and sauté with the onions, for 2 minutes more. Remove from heat and set aside. After the 15 minutes of natural release, do a quick release for any remaining pressure. Remove lid. Remove pork and place on a platter. Tent pork with foil to keep warm. Remove the cooking liquid from the pot. Strain, if needed. Place the sautéed onions and pecans, along with 1/2 cup of the cooking liquid into the food processor and blend until smooth. Return this onion/pecan mixture to the skillet. Add another 1/2 cup cooking liquid into the skillet, as well. Salt and pepper, to taste. Cook for 5 minutes. Stir in the heavy cream. Heat until warmed through. Slice the pork into medallions. Place the slices in the sauce. Warm. Serve.

Pecan Pie

Crunchy, toasted pecans. Buttery crust. Warm, ooey, gooey, brown sugar filling. I'll take a slice!

Pie Crust Ingredients:
- 1 stick unsalted butter, melted
- 1 package Splenda
- 1/4 tsp salt
- 2 vanilla creamers
- 1 1/2 cups flour

Filling Ingredients:
- 3 large eggs
- 1/2 cup light brown sugar, packed
- 1/4 tsp salt
- 1 cup light corn syrup
- 1/3 cup unsalted butter, melted
- 1 tsp vanilla
- 1 cup chopped pecans, or whole, if you prefer (easier to cut pie when chopped)

Directions: Preheat oven to 350 degrees. Prepare an 8 x 8 inch square baking pan, ungreased. In a medium bowl, prepare crust. Melt butter. Add Splenda, creamers, and salt. Stir together. Add flour. Mix together until blended. Pat dough into prepared pan, up the sides and on the bottom, evenly. In the same bowl, prepare filling. Add eggs, brown sugar, and salt. Mix together. Add corn syrup, melted butter, and vanilla. Mix together. Add pecans. Mix together. Pour filling into the prepared crust. Bake for 40 - 45 minutes, until crust is golden brown and the filling in the center is set. Remove from the oven. Allow to cool for 30 minutes. Serve warm or chilled with whipped cream and some cinnamon sprinkled on top. Store in the refrigerator. Makes 16 slices.

Try this recipe another way...

+++By making a **Cranberry Pecan Pie!** Add a 1/2 cup of dried cranberries to the filling.

+++By making a **Walnut Pie!** Substitute the pecans for chopped walnuts.

+++By making an **Almond Pie!** Substitute the pecans for sliced or slivered almonds.

Butter Pecan Butter Cookies

Paul's favorite ice cream flavor is Butter Pecan, so I decided to make him these cookies. Wow! What a great, nutty idea!

Ingredients:
- 1 1/2 sticks unsalted butter
- 3/4 cup powdered sugar
- 1/2 tsp vanilla
- 1 cup flour
- 3/4 cup ground pecans

Directions: Preheat oven to 350 degrees. Prepare a parchment paper lined cookies sheet. In a medium bowl, melt the butter In the microwave. Then, add in powdered sugar and mix together. Stir in vanilla. Add flour and mix until blended. Add ground pecans and stir until incorporated. Take a teaspoonful of the dough and roll it into a ball and place on prepared cookie sheet sugared side up. Flatten ball with your fingers. Leave an inch in between cookies, they will spread. Bake for 12 - 14 minutes. Remove from oven. Cool for a minute or two. Remove cookies from pan and place on wax paper to cool. Store in a cookie tin.

God's Word of the Day (April 15)

"He will swallow up death forever; and the Lord God will wipe away tears from all faces, and the reproach of His people He will take away from all the earth, for the Lord has spoken."
(Isaiah 25:8)
Food for the Soul: Meditate on the awesome power of God today.
Blessed Mother, graciously intercede for us.
Holy Trinity, we adore You! Hear and answer our prayers.

Feast of St. Bernadette Soubirous of Lourdes (April 16)
**Patroness of bodily illness, Lourdes, shepherds,
and those ridiculed for their faith.**
*"O my Mother, it is to your heart that I come to lay down the
anguish of my heart; it is there that I draw strength and courage."*
**Food for the Soul: Seek Mary in any troubles today.
Go to her for comfort and strength.**
St. Bernadette Soubirous of Lourdes, pray for us.
Our Lady of Lourdes, graciously intercede for us.
Holy Trinity, we adore You! Hear and answer our prayers.

Banana Day (April 16)

Ultimate Banana Waffles
This banana waffle is one of my favorites, based on a recipe from my friend, Ellen. By adding a warm, glazed banana topping to an already delicious banana waffle, it becomes the ultimate banana breakfast experience!

Waffle Batter Ingredients:
- 1 large egg, separated
- 1/2 cup half and half
- 2 bananas, mashed
- 4 Tbsps melted unsalted butter, cooled
- 1 tsp vanilla
- 1 cup flour
- 1 tsp baking powder
- 1 Tbsp sugar
- 1/8 tsp salt

Glazed Banana Topping Ingredients:
- 2 Tbsps unsalted butter
- 2 Tbsps light brown sugar
- 1 banana, sliced thin

Directions: Prepare the glazed banana topping: Warm a medium nonstick skillet to medium heat. Melt the butter, add the brown sugar. Stir together. Slice a banana into thin slices, then add the slices to the brown sugar mixture in the pan. Stir the bananas in the sugar mixture for a few minutes until they are thoroughly warm, soft, and glazed. Remove from heat. When waffles are ready, spoon topping onto the waffle. Prepare the waffle batter: Separate the egg. Place egg white in a small bowl. Beat until stiff, but moist. Set aside. Place egg yolk in a medium bowl. Beat egg yolk. Add half and half and mashed bananas. Beat together. In a small bowl, mix together flour, baking powder, sugar, salt. Add dry ingredients into the banana mixture. Mix until combined. Do not overmix. Gently fold egg white into batter. Allow batter to rest. Preheat waffle iron. When the waffle iron is ready, spray the waffle iron well with nonstick cooking spray. Pour batter onto the waffle iron. Cook until golden brown. Place waffle on plate. Butter, if desired. Spoon topping over waffle.

Try this recipe another way...
+++By making **Banana Nut Waffles!** Just add 1/4 cup of finely chopped walnuts to the waffle batter.

God's Word of the Day (April 17)
"Do you understand what I have done for you? You call Me 'Teacher' and 'Lord', and rightly so, for that is what I am. Now that I, your Lord and Teacher, have washed your feet, you also should wash one another's feet. I have set you an example that you should do as I have done for you."
(John 13:13-15)
Food for the Soul: How might we do, today, what Jesus has done for us?
Jesus, have mercy on us.
Blessed Mother, graciously intercede for us.
Holy Trinity, we adore You! Hear and answer our prayers.

God's Word of the Day (April 18)
"And Jesus uttered a loud cry and breathed His last. And the curtain of the temple was torn in two, from top to bottom. And when the centurion, who stood facing Him, saw that in this way He breathed His last, he said, "Truly, this man was the Son of God!"
(Mark 15:37-39)
Food for the Soul: Meditate on the centurion and his words. Experience the moment of this divine revelation; the deep sorrow, then the joy of understanding he received in Christ's presence.
Jesus, have mercy on us.
Blessed Mother, graciously intercede for us.
Holy Trinity, we adore You! Hear and answer our prayers.

God's Word of the Day (April 19)
"Get rid of the old yeast, so that you may be a new unleavened batch, as you really are. For Christ, our Passover Lamb, has been sacrificed."
(1 Corinthians 5:7)
Food for the Soul: What "old yeast" do you have in your life to get rid of, so you may truly celebrate in the resurrection of our Lord?
Jesus, have mercy on us.
Blessed Mother, graciously intercede for us.
Holy Trinity, we adore You! Hear and answer our prayers.

God's Word of the Day (April 20)
"The angel said to the women, 'Do not be afraid, for I know that you are looking for Jesus, Who was crucified. He is not here; He has risen, just as He said. Come and see the place where He lay."
(Matthew 28:5-6)
Food for the Soul: Go with the angel. Experience the awesome power and wonder of the resurrection!
Jesus, our Redeemer, we praise You!
Blessed Mother, graciously intercede for us.
Holy Trinity, we adore You! Hear and answer our prayers.

God's Word of the Day (April 21)
*"For I know that my Redeemer lives, and at the last,
He will stand upon the earth."*
(Job 19:25)
**Food for the Soul: Do you proclaim to those around you
that your Redeemer lives?**
*Jesus, our Redeemer, we praise You!
Blessed Mother, graciously intercede for us.
Holy Trinity, we adore You! Hear and answer our prayers.*

Earth Day (April 22)
*"It is not difficult for one seal to make many impressions
exactly alike, but to vary shapes almost infinitely, which is what God
has done in creation, this is in truth a Divine Work."
-- St. Robert Bellarmine*
**Food for the Soul: Take a nature walk today,
and praise God for all the earthly beauty!**
*St. Robert Bellarmine, pray for us.
Blessed Mother, graciously intercede for us.
Holy Trinity, we adore You! Hear and answer our prayers.*

<u>Creamed Peas</u>
*Did you know that peas are my favorite vegetable? Paul loves them, too.
Add them to a cream sauce and that makes it one of my ultimate side dishes!*

Ingredients:
- 1 bag of frozen peas, cooked in the microwave, drained (You can substitute the peas for any vegetable)

Cream Sauce Ingredients:
- 2 Tbsps unsalted butter
- 2 Tbsps flour
- 1/4 tsp salt
- 1 cup half and half

Directions: Melt butter in a small saucepan. Add flour and salt. Stir. Add half and half. Stir. Cook and continue to stir over medium heat until sauce begins to bubble and thicken. (It is very important to continue to stir! Otherwise, the sauce will catch, or stick, to the bottom of the pan.). Continue to cook and stir for another minute more. Add peas and stir. Serve. (If the sauce is too thick, you may add a little more half and half. For a little more depth in flavor, you can always add a few sprinkles of garlic and/or onion powder.)

Try this recipe another way...
+++By making **Cheesy Creamed Peas!** Just add another 1/4 cup of half and half and 1 cup of cheddar, Swiss, American, Colby jack (or whatever your favorite cheese might be), to the ingredients and follow the recipe as indicated. This cheese sauce with some noodles or rice would also make a great side dish!

Cucumber, Radish, Apple Slaw

Crunchy, tart, a little sweet.
A great, refreshing, cold side dish to celebrate the delicious food the earth provides for us all!

Ingredients:
- 6 mini cucumbers, peeled, shredded, and drained
- 8 large radishes, shredded
- 1 Granny Smith apple, peeled, cored, and shredded

Dressing Ingredients:
- 2 Tbsps honey mustard dressing
- 4 Tbsps mayonnaise
- 4 Tbsps apple cider vinegar
- 3 Tbsps lime juice
- 3 packages Splenda
- 1/4 tsp meat tenderizer
- 1/4 tsp garlic powder
- 1/4 tsp onion powder

Directions: Prepare the dressing: In a small bowl, combine the honey mustard, mayo, apple cider vinegar, lime juice, Splenda, meat tenderizer, garlic powder, and onion powder. Stir until combined. Taste. Adjust to taste. In a medium bowl, combine shredded cucumbers, radishes, and apple. Stir together. Top with dressing. Stir until slaw is dressed. Serve. Refrigerate any leftovers.

Feast of St. George, Martyr (April 23)
Patron saint of knights, soldiers, scouts, fencers, and archers.
*"Doubt not. Believe in God and Jesus Christ,
and be baptized, and I will slay the dragon."*
**Food for the Soul: Do you have any dragons to slay today,
in the Name of Jesus Christ?**
*St. George, pray for us.
Blessed Mother, graciously intercede for us.
Holy Trinity, we adore You! Hear and answer our prayers.*

Feast of St. Fidelis of Sigmaringen (April 24)
Patron saint of lawyers.
*"Woe to me if I should prove myself but a halfhearted soldier
in the service of my thorn-crowned Captain."*
Food for the Soul: Pray wholeheartedly, to our Father in Heaven.
*St. Fidelis of Sigmaringen, pray for us.
Blessed Mother, graciously intercede for us.
Holy Trinity, we adore You! Hear and answer our prayers.*

Feast of St. Mark the Evangelist (April 25)
Gospel writer, apostle, and patron saint of Venice.
*"Do not become a disciple of one who praises himself,
in case you learn pride instead of humility."*
Food for the Soul: Praise God for the gifts He give to each of us!
*St. Mark, pray for us.
Blessed Mother, graciously intercede for us.
Holy Trinity, we adore You! Hear and answer our prayers.*

God's Word of the Day (April 26)
"But when one turns to the Lord, the veil is removed. Now the Lord is the Spirit, and where the Spirit of the Lord is, there is freedom. And we all, with unveiled face, beholding the glory of the Lord, are being transformed into the same image from one degree of glory to another. For this comes from the Lord Who is the Spirit."
(2 Corinthians 3:16-18)
Food for the Soul: Pray to the Holy Spirit to transform you, from glory to glory.
Blessed Mother, graciously intercede for us.
Holy Trinity, we adore You! Hear and answer our prayers.

God's Word of the Day (April 27)
"Blessed be the God and Father of our Lord Jesus Christ! According to His great mercy, He has caused us to be born again to a living hope through the resurrection of Jesus Christ from the dead."
(1 Peter 1:3)
Food for the Soul: Meditate on the resurrection and the Divine Mercy of Jesus...
Blessed Mother, graciously intercede for us.
Holy Trinity, we adore You! Hear and answer our prayers.

Feast of St. Gianna Beretta Molla (April 28)
Patron saint of mothers, physicians, and unborn children.
"If you must choose between me and the baby...save the baby!"
Food for the Soul: Pray for mothers who are contemplating an abortion. Pray for the strength and wisdom of the Holy Spirit to be upon them.
St. Gianna Beretta Molla, pray for us.
Our Lady of Guadalupe, intercede for us and all the unborn children.
Holy Trinity, hear and answer our prayers.

Feast of St. Louis de Montfort (April 28)
Saint who had intense devotion to Our Lady.

"If you put all the love of the mothers into one heart, it still would not equal the love of the Heart of Mary for her children."

Food for the Soul: Pray the Memorare each day this week. Maybe it will become a daily habit.

St. Louis de Montfort, pray for us.
Blessed Mother, graciously intercede for us.
Holy Trinity, we adore You! Hear and answer our prayers.

The Memorare
Remember, O most gracious Virgin Mary, that never was it known, that anyone who fled to thy protection, implored thy help, or sought thy intercession, was left unaided. Inspired by this confidence, I fly unto thee, O Virgin of virgins, my mother. To thee do I come, before thee I stand, sinful and sorrowful. O Mother of the Word Incarnate, despise not my petitions, but in thy mercy, hear and answer me. Amen.

Hamburger Day (April 28)
Build-a-Burger Sauce

One day I decided to mix my three favorite hamburger condiments together, because, when I would spread each one on separately, one flavor usually stood out more than the others. Was I surprised with the end result! Tangy. Salty. Creamy. Makes-your-mouth-want-to-water sauce.

The perfect complement to a juicy burger! Try serving your burgers on pillowy soft potato rolls. Layer with American cheese, lightly seasoned tomatoes, and shredded lettuce. And don't forget to add some raw, sweet onion slices for a bit of crunch!

Sauce Ingredients:
- Ketchup
- Honey Mustard Dressing
- Mayonnaise

- Burgers
- Potato rolls

- American cheese
- Raw sweet onion slices
- Vine tomato, sliced and seasoned with a sprinkle of salt and garlic powder
- Shredded lettuce

Directions: For saucing 4 burgers, mix 2 - 3 Tbsps of each condiment together in a small bowl. Place a generous dollop of the burger sauce on each side of the potato roll. Add your choice of burger toppings. On one side of the bun, place the onion. On the other side of the bun, place the lettuce, then the tomato. Place the cheese and burger on top of the tomato. Sandwich the bun together and enjoy!

Feast of St. Catherine of Siena (April 29)
Patron saint of Europe, Italy, fire prevention, and illness.
"If you are what you should be, you will set the whole world on fire!"
Food for the Soul: Is your life setting the world on fire?
Maybe it's time to ask for God's Will in your life...
St. Catherine of Siena, pray for us.
Blessed Mother, graciously intercede for us.
Holy Trinity, we adore You! Hear and answer our prayers.

God's Word of the Day (April 30)
"I pray that from His glorious, unlimited resources, He will empower you with inner strength through His Spirit. Then Christ will make His home in your hearts as you trust in Him. Your roots will grow down into God's love and keep you strong."
(Ephesians 3:16-17)
Food for the Soul: May we plant our spiritual roots in Jesus.
Jesus, we trust in You.
Blessed Mother, graciously intercede for us.
Holy Trinity, we adore You! Hear and answer our prayers.

May

May Birthday Cake

Lemon Blueberry Cake
Infused with a Buttery Lemon Glaze

Celebrating a Birthday this month? We are! If you are, too, try making this cake. It's tangy, moist, and fruity, celebrating the fresh flavors of the upcoming summer!

Ingredients:
- 1 box of blueberry muffin mix (I use the one that starts with a "K" ends with a "Z" brand)
- 2 Tbsp sour cream
- 1 lemon, zested and juiced (seeds removed from the juice)
- 2 Tbsp unsalted butter, melted
- 1/4 - 1/2 cup confectioner's sugar, to taste

Directions Preheat the oven to 350 degrees. Grease an 8 x 8 inch glass baking pan. Combine the blueberry muffin mix with the ingredients listed on the box, as directed, but also add 2 Tbsp of sour cream and the zest of one lemon. Pour into the 8 x 8 pan. Bake for 30-35 minutes. Prepare the Buttery Lemon Glaze while the cake is baking. Melt 2 Tbsp of unsalted butter in a microwave safe bowl. Once melted, add the juice from one lemon. Then add the confectioner's sugar, to taste. (If using the juice of a small lemon, you may use less confectioner's sugar than if using the juice from a larger lemon.). Once the cake is out of the oven, poke holes into the warm cake with a skewer, or even with the tines of a fork. Using a large spoon, spoon the glaze onto the cake so it seeps into the holes, infusing the cake with its buttery, tart/sweet, lemony goodness! Allow the cake to stand for 1/2 hour. Cut into 16 pieces. Serve warm or cold. Store in the refrigerator. Makes 16 slices.

Try this recipe another way...

+++By making ***Orange Cranberry Cake Infused with a Buttery Orange Glaze!*** Instead of the blueberry muffin mix, use the cranberry orange muffin mix. Substitute the lemon with a small orange. Proceed with the recipe.

May Crowning

"Let us run to Mary, and, as her little children,
cast ourselves into her arms with a perfect confidence."
-- St. Francis de Sales
Food for the Soul: Greet Mary with great joy
when you pray, "Hail Mary!"
St. Francis de Sales, pray for us.
Mary, Queen of Heaven, graciously intercede for us.
Holy Trinity, we adore You! Hear and answer our prayers.

Rosettes

Have you ever eaten a rosette? It's a delicate, thin, crispy, light dessert. Some even call them, "Bite of Nothings"! As I was thinking of a recipe for May Crowning, these came to mind because their shape reminds me of a crown. To make this unique dessert, you will require a rosette iron. I have my Mom's set, but if you don't have a set, you can often find them at antique or thrift stores. Rosettes bring back wonderful memories of my Dad helping my Mom in the kitchen, frying them into airy, crispy delights...

Ingredients:
- 2 large eggs, slightly beaten
- 2 tsps sugar
- 1 cup half and half
- 1 Tbsp brandy
- 1 Tbsp vanilla
- 1 cup flour, sifted
- 1/4 tsp salt

Directions: Preheat fryer to 385 degrees. Prepare baking sheet lined with paper towels. In a blender, add eggs, sugar, half and half, brandy, and vanilla. Blend well. Add flour and salt to the blender. Blend until batter is smooth. Pour some of the batter into a ramekin. (Refill with batter, as needed.). Preheat the iron. Heat the iron in the oil for 2 - 3 minutes. After preheating, dab the iron on some paper towels. Then, dip the iron into the batter, but only up the sides of the iron, not over the top! Plunge the batter coated iron into the oil. Eventually, the batter will come off of the iron and fry in the oil. If not, help it off the iron. With tongs, remove the rosette from the oil when it is golden brown, and place on paper towels, top side up. Dip the iron into the oil once again before starting with another rosette, dab the iron on paper towel, and dip into the batter. Fry. Continue this process until all of the batter is gone. Gently dip rosettes in powdered sugar. Store in a large cookie tin. Note: It's a good idea to sample that first rosette, once it is cooled. If it is not crisp, the batter may be too thick. You can always add a little half and half to thin out the batter a bit.

Feast of St. Joseph, the Worker (May 1)
Foster father of Jesus. Patron saint of the worker.

"St. Joseph was a just man, a tireless worker, the upright guardian of those entrusted in his care. May he always guard, protect, and enlighten families."
-- St. John Paul II

Food for the Soul: Ask St. Joseph today to intercede for those we love. Invite him into your home and workplace.

St. Joseph, pray for us.
St. John Paul II, pray for us.
Blessed Mother, graciously intercede for us.
Holy Trinity, we adore You! Hear and answer our prayers.

National Prayer Day (First Thursday of May)

"Prayer is the oxygen of the soul."
-- St. Padre Pio of Pietrelcino

"For me, prayer is a burst from my heart, it is a simple glance thrown toward Heaven, a cry of thanksgiving and love in times of trial, as well as in times of joy."
-- St. Thérèse of Lisieux

Food for the Soul: Do your prayers burst from your heart? Is it the oxygen of your spiritual life? May your conversations with God be lively. May they be well balanced, in speaking and listening.

St. Padre Pio of Pietrelcino, pray for us.
St. Thérèse of Lisieux, pray for us.
Blessed Mother, graciously intercede for us.
Holy Trinity, we adore You! Hear and answer our prayers.

Feast of St. Athanasius of Alexandria (May 2)
Patron saint of theologians and scholars.
"The Saints, while living in this world, are always joyful, as if they were always celebrating Easter."
Food for the Soul: Let us live today with "Hallelujah" on our lips!
St. Athanasius of Alexandria, pray for us.
Blessed Mother, graciously intercede for us.
Holy Trinity, we adore You! Hear and answer our prayers.

Tuna Day (May 2)
Cranberry Walnut Tuna Salad
Dried cranberries and walnuts are tasty additions to an ordinary tuna salad...making it a bit extraordinary!

Ingredients:
- 1/3 cup sour cream
- 1/3 cup mayonnaise
- 1/2 tsp onion powder
- 1/2 tsp garlic powder
- 1/4 tsp celery salt
- 1 1/2 cups albacore tuna, flaked
- 3/4 cup dried cranberries, plumped in hot water
- 3/4 cup ground walnuts
- 1/4 cup diced sweet onions
- 1/4 cup celery, peeled and diced

Directions: In a large bowl, combine sour cream, mayo, onion powder, garlic powder, and celery salt. To the sour cream mixture, add in shredded chicken, plumped cranberries, walnuts, onions and celery. Mix until combined. Chill and allow flavors to meld. Serve on brioche bread, croissants, or rolls. Or...imagine serving on some slices of **Challah Bread *(January 1)***, or on **Colby Jack Cheese Bread *(April 12)***. Simply amazing!

God's Word of the Day (May 3)
"The Lord is my light and my salvation – whom shall I fear?
The Lord is the stronghold of my life – of whom shall I be afraid?"
(Psalm 27:1)
Food for the Soul: Discuss your fears with God today.
Allow Him to wipe them away.
Blessed Mother, graciously intercede for us.
Holy Trinity, we adore You! Hear and answer our prayers.

God's Word of the Day (May 4)
"For God so loved the world, that He gave His only Son, that whoever believes in Him, should not perish, but have eternal life. For God did not send His Son into the world to condemn the world,
but in order that the world might be saved through Him."
(John 3:16-17)
Food for the Soul: Throughout your day, pray, "Jesus, I love You".
Blessed Mother, graciously intercede for us.
Holy Trinity, we adore You! Hear and answer our prayers.

God's Word of the Day (May 5)
"My grace is all you need, for My power is the greatest when you are weak."
(2 Corinthians 12:9)
Food for the Soul: God, You are my Rock. My Cornerstone.
Blessed Mother, graciously intercede for us.
Holy Trinity, we adore You! Hear and answer our prayers.

Cinco de Mayo (May 5)

Chicken Tamales

In my first book, Paul and I were searching for tamales when I had an encounter with God. A few months later, I tried making my own tamales. They were so good, they were "Paul approved"! The instant pot is the secret to making these perfectly moist tamales.

Chicken Filling Ingredients:
- 6 skinless chicken thighs
- 1 jar of salsa, your choice of heat level (minus a few Tbsps for masa dough)

Tamale Ingredients:
- 2/3 cup of lard
- 1 Tbsp baking powder
- 1/2 tsp salt
- 2 cups masa harina
- 1 can low sodium chicken broth + salsa to make 2 cups
- Corn husks, about 35, cleaned and soaked in water overnight

Directions: Set aside about 3 Tbsps of salsa for the chicken broth you will use for the masa dough. Prepare the chicken filling: Pour half of the jar of salsa in the instant pot. Place the chicken thighs on top of the salsa. Pour the rest of the salsa on top of the chicken. Close, lock, and seal lid. Set to "Poultry" on high for 22 minutes. Natural release for 15 minutes. Remove chicken from pot. Debone the chicken. Shred the chicken meat and mix with the salsa in the pot. Remove the shredded chicken and salsa from the pot and set aside. (Clean the pot so it will be ready for the tamales later.). Prepare the masa dough. In a medium bowl, add lard and baking powder. Whip for 20 minutes, until light and fluffy. (Best to use a stand mixer, if you have one.). Add masa harina, salt, and broth. Whip for 10 minutes. Test dough: Take a 1/2 tsp of dough and place it in a cup of cold water. If it floats, it's ready!

While the dough is whipping, dry corn husks. Apply about 1/4 cup of the masa dough to the wider end of the corn husk with a dough scraper and spread the dough on the wider half only. Add about a tablespoonful, or more, of chicken filling. Fold husk, first left side over, then right side over. Fold end up. (If that was confusing for you, best to refer to a YouTube video on how to create a tamale; it will really help!). Place tamale on a baking sheet, folded side down. Continue with the rest of the tamales until you run out of dough or filling. Use the steamer basket in the instant pot. Then add 2 cups of water to the pot. Line the bottom of the steamer basket with corn husks. Place about 15 of the tamales in the basket. Set on "Steam" for 45 minutes. Natural release for 15 minutes. Open steam vent and then remove lid. Allow tamales to sit in the open pot for 15 minutes. After that, remove tamales and place them on a baking sheet for another 15 minutes. Continue with making the next batch of tamales in the instant pot. You may need to add a little more water to the pot, about 1/4 cup, before starting. When you are ready to eat the tamales, place as many as you are going to eat in a quart size freezer bag with a tablespoon, or two, of water. Partially seal the bag, and microwave for about 1 minute. Remove from bag, unwrap those hot tamales, and serve with salsa and sour cream. (We also buy carnitas and use that for our tamale filling. Just add your favorite salsa to the meat!) Store tamales in the refrigerator. Can also be frozen. Just warm them up in a quart freezer bag with a few tablespoons of water, partially seal, and microwave for about 2 minutes. Add more time, if needed.

Chicken, Cheese, and Bean Flautas

Many authentic Mexican chicken flautas are made with just chicken for the filling, but I like to make them my own "Polish/Mexican" way! So crunchy, creamy, meaty, and cheesy! Easy peasy!

Ingredients:
2 cups shredded cooked chicken
1 cup cheese, freshly grated (cheddar or colby jack)
1 can of authentic refried beans (or your choice of flavor)
Jar of salsa (your choice of brand and heat level)
Corn tortillas

For Serving:
Sour Cream

Directions: Preheat deep fryer to 370 degrees. Warm tortillas in a cloth tortilla warmer in the microwave so they will be pliable enough to roll. Place a tortilla on a plate. Starting toward one end of the tortilla, add a few teaspoons, in layers, of beans, chicken, salsa, and cheese. Do not overfill. Roll tightly and fasten with a toothpick. Fry the flautas in the deep fryer until golden brown. Remove from fryer. Carefully remove the toothpick. Serve with gobs of sour cream on the side!

Feast of St. Dominic Savio (May 6)
Patron saint of the falsely accused and juvenile delinquents.
"I can't do big things. But I want all I do, even the smallest thing, to be for the greater glory of God."
Food for the Soul: *Offer up everything you do today for God's glory. Take none of that glory for yourself.*
St. Dominic Savio, pray for us.
Blessed Mother, graciously intercede for us.
Holy Trinity, we adore You! Hear and answer our prayers.

God's Word of the Day (May 7)
"Be strong and courageous. Do not be afraid or terrified because of them, for the Lord your God goes with you; He will never leave you nor forsake you."
(Deuteronomy 31:6-8)
Food for the Soul: *Where does God need you to be courageous in your life? Don't fear. Go forward. He is right by your side...*
Blessed Mother, graciously intercede for us.
Holy Trinity, we adore You! Hear and answer our prayers.

God's Word of the Day (May 8)
"My flesh and my heart may fail, but God is the strength of my heart and my portion forever."
Psalm 73:26)
Food for the Soul: *When things get rough, just call out to God. He is always listening.*
Blessed Mother, graciously intercede for us.
Holy Trinity, we adore You! Hear and answer our prayers.

Mother's Day (Second Sunday of May)

"Motherhood implies from the beginning, a special openness to the new person: and this is precisely the woman's 'part'. In this openness, in conceiving and giving birth to a child, the woman discovers herself through a sincere gift of self."
— St. John Paul II

"May the Mother of Jesus, and our Mother, always smile on your spirit, obtaining for it, from her Most Holy Son, every heavenly blessing."
— St. Padre Pio

"In trial or difficulty, I have recourse to Mother Mary, whose glance alone is enough to dissipate every fear."
— St. Thérèse of Lisieux

Food for the Soul: Pray the Hail Mary ten times today for your own Mother, living or gone to heaven.

Holy Trinity, we ask You to bless our earthly mothers,
and those in heaven, today and everyday.
Guide them to the promises of eternal life. Amen.

St. John Paul II, pray for us.
St. Padre Pio, pray for us.
St. Thérèse of Lisieux, pray for us.
Blessed Mother, graciously intercede for us.
Holy Trinity, we adore You! Hear and answer our prayers.

Tropical Chicken Salad Pie

*I would make this pie for my Mom, and she always enjoyed it.
She especially liked the addition of the walnuts, coconut, and pineapple.
A unique, savory pie, bursting with flavor, that will impress
your Mom, family, and friends!*

Pie Crust Ingredients:
- 1 stick unsalted butter, melted
- 1 1/2 cups flour
- 1/4 tsp salt
- 2 vanilla creamers
- 1/3 cup Colby Jack cheese, freshly grated

Filling Ingredients:
- 1/3 cup sour cream
- 1/3 cup mayonnaise
- 1/2 tsp onion powder
- 1/2 tsp garlic powder
- 1/4 tsp celery salt
- 1 1/2 cups shredded cooked chicken
- 1 cup pineapple tidbits (small can), drained (reserve 1 Tbsp of pineapple juice)
- 3/4 cup ground walnuts
- 1/2 cup shredded sweetened coconut

Topping:
- 1/2 cup (or more!) Colby Jack cheese, freshly grated

Directions: In a medium bowl, prepare the pie crust. Add the melted butter, flour, salt, creamers, and cheese. Mix together until combined. Do not overmix. Press dough into an 8 x 8 inch square pan, or an 8 or 9 inch pie pan. Poke holes in bottom crust with a fork. Bake at 400 degrees for 10 - 15 minutes until golden brown. Cool crust completely before filling. Prepare filling. In a large bowl, combine sour cream, mayo, onion powder, garlic powder, celery salt, and 1 Tbsp of pineapple juice. To the sour cream mixture, add in shredded chicken, pineapple tidbits, walnuts, and coconut. Mix until combined. Fill cooled pie crust with chicken mixture. Top with shredded cheese. Chill and allow flavors to meld. Cut into slices and serve.

Try this recipe another way!

+++By making a ***Tropical Chicken Salad Sandwich!*** Skip the pie crust and serve it on some brioche bread, croissants, or rolls. Imagine serving it on some slices of **Challah Bread (January 1)**, or on slices of the **Colby Jack Cheese Bread (April 12)! Delish!**

+++By making a ***Ham Salad Pie!*** Substitute the chicken for some diced or shaved ham.

+++By making a ***Turkey Salad Pie!*** Substitute the chicken for turkey.

+++By making a ***Cranberry Walnut Tuna Salad Pie!*** Substitute the chicken for tuna. Instead of using pineapple, add 3/4 cup dried cranberries, plumped. Leave out the coconut and add 1/4 cup chopped sweet onion and 1/4 cup chopped celery for a nice crunch. (Peel the celery before chopping it so it's not stringy.)

God's Word of the Day (May 9)
"But they who wait for the Lord shall renew their strength; they shall mount up with wings like eagles; they shall run and not be weary; they shall walk and not faint."
(Isaiah 40:31)
Food for the Soul: Soar like an eagle today, for the glory of God!
Blessed Mother, graciously intercede for us.
Holy Trinity, we adore You! Hear and answer our prayers.

Feast Day of St. John of Avila (May 10)
Doctor of the Church. Patron saint of the priests in Spain.
"Enlarge your little heart to the immensity of love with which the Father offered us His Son, and with Him, gave us Himself, the Holy Spirit, and all things."
Food for the Soul: Let us adore the Holy Trinity for all the love They bestow upon us!
St. John of Avila, pray for us.
Blessed Mother, graciously intercede for us.
Holy Trinity, we adore You! Hear and answer our prayers.

God's Word of the Day (May 11)
"Fear not, for I am with you; be not dismayed, for I am your God; I will strengthen you, I will help you, I will uphold you with my righteous Hand."
(Isaiah 41:10)
Food for the Soul: Believe in the divine truth of these words: Fear not. God is with you. God will strengthen you. God supports you with His Mighty Hand.
Blessed Mother, graciously intercede for us.
Holy Trinity, we adore You! Hear and answer our prayers.

God's Word of the Day (May 12)
"The Lord is my strength and my song, and He has become my salvation; this is my God, and I will praise Him, my father's God, and I will exalt Him."
(Exodus 15:2)
Food for the Soul: Pray throughout the day:
"God of all Power and Might, I praise You!
Blessed Mother, graciously intercede for us.
Holy Trinity, we adore You! Hear and answer our prayers.

Our Lady of Fatima (May 13)
"According to St. Bonaventure, all the angels in heaven unceasingly call out to her: 'Holy, holy, holy Mary, Virgin Mother of God.' They greet her countless times each day with the angelic greeting, 'Hail Mary', while prostrating themselves before her, begging her as a favor to honor them with one of her requests. According to St. Augustine, even St. Michael, though prince of all the heavenly court, is the most eager of all the angels to honor her and lead others to honor her. At all times, he awaits the privilege of going at her word to the aid of one of her servants."
—St. Louis de Montfort
Food for the Soul: Today in prayer, ask the Blessed Mother to send St. Michael to guard and protect you...
St. Louis de Montfort, pray for us.
Our Lady of Fatima, graciously intercede for us.
Holy Trinity, we adore You! Hear and answer our prayers.

Feast of St. Matthias (May 14)
Patron saint of alcoholics.

"We must combat the flesh and make use of it, without pampering it by unlawful gratifications. As to the soul, we must develop her power by faith and knowledge."

Food for the Soul: Read scripture today to help develop a strong, healthy soul.

St. Matthias, pray for us.
Blessed Mother, graciously intercede for us.
Holy Trinity, we adore You! Hear and answer our prayers.

Feast of St. Isidore (May 15)
Patron saint of farmers and the internet.

"Nothing exists without music, for the universe itself is said to have been framed by a kind of harmony of sounds, and the heaven itself revolves under the tone of that harmony."

Food for the Soul: Take time to listen to some spiritual music today. Meditate on the lyrics. Sing along!

St. Isidore, pray for us.
Blessed Mother, graciously intercede for us.
Holy Trinity, we adore You! Hear and answer our prayers.

God's Word of the Day (May 16)

"Seek the Lord and His strength; seek His presence continually!"
(1 Chronicles 16:11)

Food for the Soul: Be mindful of the Lord's presence throughout the day. Speak to Him. Listen for Him. Adore Him. Praise Him.

Blessed Mother, graciously intercede for us.
Holy Trinity, we adore You! Hear and answer our prayers.

God's Word of the Day (May 17)
*"For the Spirit God gave us does not make us timid,
but gives us power, love and self-discipline."*
(2 Timothy 1:7)
Food for the Soul: Be bold in the Spirit of God within you!
*Blessed Mother, graciously intercede for us.
Holy Trinity, we adore You! Hear and answer our prayers.*

Feast of St. John I (May 18)
Gospel writer. Patron saint of love, loyalty, friendships, and authors.
"Jesus said, 'I am the vine; you are the branches. If you remain in Me and I in you, you will bear much fruit; apart from Me you can do nothing.'"
(John 15:5)
Food for the Soul: Live today as an extension of Jesus.
*St. John I, pray for us.
Blessed Mother, graciously intercede for us.
Holy Trinity, we adore You! Hear and answer our prayers.*

Baking Day (May 18)
Golden Streusel Coffeecake
This coffeecake uses a cake mix for the batter, which is a little bit of a time saver. But even though it isn't completely "from scratch", it sure tastes like it is!

Coffeecake Ingredients:
- 1 cup sour cream
- 3/4 cup canola oil
- 4 large eggs
- 1/2 cup sugar
- 1 box of butter cake mix

Streusel Ingredients:
- 6 Tbsps brown sugar
- 2 tsps cinnamon
- 1 cup ground nuts (walnuts and/or pecans)

Directions: Preheat oven to 325 degrees. Oil a 9 x 13 inch pan. Mix streusel ingredients together in a small bowl. Set aside. In a large bowl, mix together sour cream, oil, eggs, and sugar. Add in butter cake mix. Combine. Pour 1/2 of the cake batter into the oiled pan. Sprinkle 1/2 of the streusel mixture on top of the batter. Then top the streusel mixture with the other half of the cake batter, followed by another layer of the streusel mixture. Bake for 40 minutes. Remove from oven. Cool. Cut into 24 squares. Serve.

Try this recipe another way...
+++By making a *Chocolate Streusel Coffeecake!* Substitute the golden butter with a chocolate cake mix. Add 2/3 cup of mini chocolate chips to the streusel.

Peanut Butter Cup Day (May 18)

Peanut Butter Cup Cheesecake Surprise!
Your guests will get a sweet surprise when they bite into a mini cheesecake with a peanut butter cup hidden in the center! Just be mindful of those who may have a peanut allergy...

Ingredients:
- 24 round peanut butter sandwich cookies
- 24 mini peanut butter cups, unwrapped
- Two 8 oz packages of cream cheese, softened (16 oz total)
- 2 Tbsps sour cream
- 1 cup sugar
- 2 eggs
- 1 tsp vanilla

Peanut Butter Drizzle Ingredients:
- 5 Tbsps creamy peanut butter, warmed
- 3/4 cup powdered sugar, sifted
- 1/2 tsp vanilla
- 3 - 4 Tbsps half and half

Directions: Preheat oven to 350 degrees. Line 24 muffin tins with paper or foil liners. Place one peanut butter sandwich cookie in each of the liners. On top of the cookies, in the center, place one mini peanut butter cup. In a medium bowl, beat cream cheese and sugar until smooth. Beat in the eggs, one at a time. Add the vanilla. Combine. Pour cream cheese mixture into each liner, filling 2/3rds full. Bake for 15 - 20 minutes, or until set. Remove from oven. Cool cheesecakes completely. Prepare the drizzle. In a small bowl, slightly warm the peanut butter in the microwave. Add the powdered sugar and vanilla. Mix until well combined. Add half and half until the desired drizzle consistency. Drizzle over top of cooled cheesecakes. Serve. Store cheesecakes, covered, in the refrigerator.

Try this recipe another way...
+++By making **Caramel Cup Cheesecake Surprise!** Substitute the peanut butter sandwich cookies with vanilla or chocolate sandwich cookies. Substitute the mini peanut butter cups with mini caramel cups.
+++By making **Mint Patty Cheesecake Surprise!** Substitute the peanut butter cookies with mint sandwich cookies. Substitute the mini peanut butter cups with thin mint patties.

God's Word of the Day (May 19)

"But I will sing of Your strength, in the morning I will sing of Your love; for You are my fortress, my refuge in times of trouble."
(Psalms 59:16)
Food for the Soul: Spend time with the Holy Trinity in song.
Blessed Mother, graciously intercede for us.
Holy Trinity, we adore You! Hear and answer our prayers.

Blessed Virgin Mary, Mother of the Church (May 20)

"Mary is the Divine Page on which the Father wrote the Word of God, His Son."
-- St. Albert the Great
Food for the Soul: Call upon the Blessed Mother throughout the day. Seek her guidance. Allow her to lead you to her Son.
St. Albert the Great, pray for us.
Blessed Virgin Mary, Mother of the Church, graciously intercede for us.
Holy Trinity, we adore You! Hear and answer our prayers.

Feast of St. Bernardine of Siena (May 20)
Patron saint of advertising, communications, compulsive gambling, and respiratory problems.

"You must know that when you 'hail' Mary, she immediately greets you! Don't think that she is one of those rude women, of whom there are so many – on the contrary, she is utterly courteous and pleasant. If you greet her, she will answer you right away and converse with you!"

Food for the Soul: Greet Mary, the Mother of Jesus. Share with her your joys, your concerns, your needs.

St. Bernardine of Siena, pray for us.
Mary, Mother of God, graciously intercede for us.
Holy Trinity, we adore You! Hear and answer our prayers.

Feast of St. Christopher of Magallanes (May 21)
Martyr. Patron saint of cancer.

"I am innocent and I die innocent. I forgive with all my heart those responsible for my death. I ask God that the shedding of my blood serve the peace of our divided Mexico."

Food for the Soul: Choose forgiveness today and be generous with it.

St. Christopher of Magallanes, pray for us.
Blessed Mother, graciously intercede for us.
Holy Trinity, we adore You! Hear and answer our prayers.

Feast of St. Rita of Cascia (May 22)
Patroness of impossible causes.

"Let me, my Jesus, share in Thy suffering, at least one of Thy thorns."

Food for the Soul: Are we willing to share in Jesus' suffering?

St. Rita of Cascia, pray for us.
Blessed Mother, graciously intercede for us.
Holy Trinity, we adore You! Hear and answer our prayers.

God's Word of the Day (May 23)
"The Lord will fight for you; you need only to be still."
(Exodus 14:14)
Food for the Soul: Walk through this day in God's presence.
Be still and trust in His strength.
Blessed Mother, graciously intercede for us.
Holy Trinity, we adore You! Hear and answer our prayers.

Turtle Day (May 23)

Turtle Cookies

These cookies are a tribute to my pet turtle, "Paddles", otherwise known as the "run-away turtle", that my sister gave to me when I was a little girl...

Cookie Ingredients:
- 2 sticks unsalted butter, softened
- 1/2 cup sugar
- 1 large egg, separated
- 1 Tbsp water
- 1 tsp vanilla
- 1/4 tsp salt
- 2 cups flour

Turtle Toppings:
- 30 German caramels, unwrapped
- 2 Tbsps half and half
- 1 cup chopped pecans
- 1 cup semisweet chocolate chips

Directions: Preheat oven to 375 degrees. Prepare cookie sheet, lined with parchment paper. In a medium bowl, cream butter and sugar. Add in egg yolk, vanilla, and salt. (Place egg white in a small bowl. Set aside.). Add flour to the sugar/butter mixture and blend. Do not overmix. Add 1 Tbsp water to the egg white. Beat together until frothy. Place the chopped pecans into a small bowl. Take a teaspoonful of dough and roll it into a ball. Roll ball into the egg white and then into the nuts. Place on the cookie sheet. Continue to do this until sheet is filled with cookie balls.

With your thumb, make an indentation in the center of each cookie. In a medium saucepan, add the caramels and half and half. Heat until caramels and cream are melted into a caramel sauce. Fill each cookie indentation with the caramel sauce. Bake for 10 - 12 minutes. Remove from the oven. Remove cookies from pan and allow to cool. Melt chocolate chips and drizzle over tops of cookies. Allow chocolate to set. Store in cookie tins. Place wax paper in between layers.

Try this recipe in another way...
*By making **Chocolate Drizzled Raspberry Cookies!** Instead of the caramel filling, use raspberry preserves. Substitute the pecans with chopped walnuts.

Turtle Cups

Another cookie variation on the "turtle" candy...
who can resist some more caramel goodness?

Crust Ingredients:
- 1 stick unsalted butter, softened
- 3 oz cream cheese, softened
- 1 cup flour

Filling Ingredients:
- 50 German caramels, unwrapped
- 3 Tbsps half and half
- 1 1/2 cups pecans, finely chopped
- 1 cup semisweet or milk chocolate chips

Directions: Preheat oven to 350 degrees. Get mini muffin tins ready for 24 mini tarts. Prepare the crust: In a medium bowl, cream together the butter and 3 oz cream cheese. Stir the flour into the butter mixture. Do not overmix. Divide dough into 24 balls. Mold each ball into each of the 24 mini muffin tins. Bake crusts for 10 - 15 minutes, or until golden brown. Remove from oven. Cool tart crusts completely. In a medium saucepan, melt caramels with half and half on medium heat, stirring constantly. Place a spoonful of caramel in each cup. Top caramel with a small spoonful of finely chopped pecans. Melt chocolate. In each cup, place a small dollop of chocolate on top of the pecans. Allow cups to cool. Store cups in a cookie tin at room temperature. Place wax paper in between layers.

God's Word of the Day (May 24)
"My soul is weary with sorrow; strengthen me according to Your Word."
(Psalms 119:28)
Food for the Soul: Acknowledge your sorrow, then hand it over to Jesus. He will console you and give you His strength.
Blessed Mother, graciously intercede for us.
Holy Trinity, we adore You! Hear and answer our prayers.

Feast of St. Bede the Venerable (May 25)
Patron saint of scholars.
"Unfurl the sails, and let God steer us where He will."
Food for the Soul: Jesus, take the wheel! I trust in You.
St. Bede the Venerable, pray for us.
Blessed Mother, graciously intercede for us.
Holy Trinity, we adore You! Hear and answer our prayers.

Feast of St. Philip Neri (May 26)
Patron saint of joy and humor.
"We must always remember that God does everything well, although we may not see the reason of what He does."
Food for the Soul: Praise the Lord for His wonders throughout the day. Praise His Holy Name!
St. Philip Neri, pray for us.
Blessed Mother, graciously intercede for us.
Holy Trinity, we adore You! Hear and answer our prayers.

Feast of St. Augustine of Canterbury (May 27)
Patron saint of England.
"Order your soul; reduce your wants; live in charity; associate in Christian community; obey the laws; trust in Providence."
Food for the Soul: Live today as a true follower of Christ.
St. Augustine of Canterbury, pray for us.
Blessed Mother, graciously intercede for us.
Holy Trinity, we adore You! Hear and answer our prayers.

God's Word of the Day (May 28)
"Love the Lord Your God with all your heart, with all your soul, with all your mind, and with all your strength."
(Mark 12:30)
Food for the Soul: Show your love for God in all you do.
Blessed Mother, graciously intercede for us.
Holy Trinity, we adore You! Hear and answer our prayers.

Memorial Day

Dreamy Strawberry Jello Pretzel Bars
A buttery, salty, sweet and crunchy crust, followed by a light, cream cheese layer, and topped with a refreshing strawberry jello layer filled with strawberries! Definitely grandchild approved!

Pretzel Crust Ingredients:
2 cups crushed pretzel sticks
3/4 cup melted butter
3 Tbsps sugar
Cream Cheese Filling Ingredients:
8 oz cream cheese, softened
1 cup sugar
8 oz cool whip
Strawberry Jello Layer Ingredients:
6 oz box strawberry jello
2 cups boiling water
10 oz package of frozen strawberries, partially thawed

Directions: Preheat oven to 325 degrees. Prepare the pan. 9 x 13 inch glass pan, ungreased. In a small bowl, mix together crust ingredients, crushed pretzels, melted butter, and sugar. Press into bottom of the pan. Bake for 8 minutes. Remove from oven and cool completely. After crust is cooled, in a medium bowl, beat cream cheese and sugar. Fold in cool whip. Spread cream cheese mixture over cooled pretzel crust. Make sure to spread the cheese mixture to the ends of the pan. (Seal the pan with that cream cheese mixture! You don't want the jello layer leaking into the crust. It will make the crust soggy. You want the crust nice and crunchy!). In a medium bowl, mix boiling water with the strawberry jello mix. Stir until completely dissolved. Add the partially thawed strawberries. Stir until combined. Pour jello mixture over the cheese mixture. Refrigerate for 2 hours, or until jello layer is set. Cut into 24 squares. Store squares in the refrigerator.

Feast of St. Ursula Ledochowska (May 29)
Patron saint of orphans, educators, and Polish girls.
"You must never ask Jesus to wait."
Food for the Soul:: Have you asked Jesus to wait? Maybe it's time to follow His Holy Plan for your life...
St. Ursula Ledochowska, pray for us.
Blessed Mother, graciously intercede for us.
Holy Trinity, we adore You! Hear and answer our prayers.

Feast Day of St. Paul VI (May 29)
Patron saint of social justice, advocate for peace and advancing interfaith dialogue.
"No more war, war never again. It is peace, peace which must guide the destinies of people and of all mankind."
Food for the Soul: Think about the personal wars in your life. Pray for Christ's peace to overcome them.
St. Paul VI, pray for us.
Blessed Mother, graciously intercede for us.
Holy Trinity, we adore You! Hear and answer our prayers.

Feast of St. Joan of Arc (May 30)
**Patron saint of soldiers, youth, prisoners,
those in need of courage, and those ridiculed for their faith.**
"I am not afraid. I was born to do this."
**Food for the Soul: Pray for the courage to be who
you are to be in the Name of Christ Jesus!**
*St. Joan of Arc, pray for us.
Blessed Mother, graciously intercede for us.
Holy Trinity, we adore You! Hear and answer our prayers.*

Feast of the Visitation of the Blessed Virgin Mary (May 31)
*"Let us live as the Blessed Virgin lived: loving God only,
desiring God only, trying to please God only in all that we do."
-- St. John Vianney*
**Food for the Soul: Pray to the Blessed Mother.
Ask her to help you become closer to her Son.**

*Hail, Mary, full of grace, the Lord is with thee.
Blessed art thou among women, and blessed is the fruit of thy womb, Jesus.
Holy Mary, Mother of God, pray for us sinners, now and at the hour of our death. Amen.*

*St. John Vianney, pray for us.
Blessed Virgin Mary, graciously intercede for us.
Holy Trinity, we adore You! Hear and answer our prayers.*

June

June Birthday Cake (Pie)

Amish Fry Pies

Are you celebrating a Birthday this month? We are! And my oldest sister would have been. She enjoyed anything with raspberries, and I think she would have enjoyed some raspberry fry pies instead of a cake! I sampled some fry pies at an antique fair last year, and they were wonderful! So tender and flaky. Since they are hard to find in our area, of course, I had to learn how to make them!

Pie Crust Ingredients:
- 3 1/2 cups flour
- 3/4 tsp baking powder
- 1 tsp salt
- 1 tsp sugar
- 3/4 cup butter or shortening
- 1 large egg, beaten
- 3/4 cup + 1 Tbsp half and half

- Can of raspberry pie filling (or your favorite filling)
- Small bowl of water

Glaze Ingredients:
- 1 cup powdered sugar, sifted
- 2 Tbsps half and half
- 1/2 tsp vanilla

Directions: Preheat deep fryer to 350 degrees. Prepare a paper towel lined baking sheet. In the food processor, pulse together flour, baking powder, salt, sugar, and butter to create coarse crumbs. Mix in half and half and the beaten egg. Do not overmix. Divide dough into 10 equal pieces. Roll each piece into a ball. Place a ball of dough between two sheets of wax paper. Press down on ball with a large shallow bowl to form a flat circle, about a 1/4 inch thick. On half of the dough, add a few

tablespoons of pie filling. Do not overfill. Moisten the edges of the pie dough with water to create a better seal. Fold the remaining half of the dough over the top of the filling. Pinch the edges together with the tines of a fork. Continue with filling and sealing the rest of the dough balls. Fry the pies, a few at a time, without overcrowding, in the oil. Flip pies until each are golden brown. Remove from oil and place on prepared baking sheet. Cool for a few minutes. Prepare the glaze in a small bowl while pies are cooling. Drizzle pies with the glaze while still warm. (Or, you can top with some powdered sugar.) Cool pies completely. Serve. Store in the refrigerator. Can also be stored in the freezer. Just thaw before serving. Makes 10 hand pies.
(If you would rather bake your pies, place them on a parchment lined cookie sheet. Make a slit in the top of each pie. Bake at 425 degrees for about 15 minutes, or until lightly browned.)

Graduation Celebrations

"Do you desire to study to your advantage? Let devotion accompany all your studies, and study less to make yourself learned that to become a saint. Consult God more than your books, and ask Him, with humility, to make you understand what you read."
-- St. Vincent Ferrer

"I have done what is mine to do. May Christ show you what is yours to do."
-- St. Francis of Assisi

Food for the Soul: Seek God in your vocation in life and be open to the changes He may have in store for you.

St. Vincent Ferrer, pray for us.
St. Francis of Assisi, pray for us.
Blessed Mother, graciously intercede for us.
Holy Trinity, we adore You! Hear and answer our prayers.

Fruity Mini Cheesecakes

These mini cheesecakes are the perfect dessert for a graduation, or any other gathering or celebration!

Ingredients:
- 24 golden sandwich cookies
- Three 8 oz packages of cream cheese, softened (24 oz total)
- 3 Tbsps sour cream
- 1 cup sugar
- 3 large eggs
- 1 tsp vanilla
- 1 can of pie filling, (cherry, blueberry, apple, etc., the flavor of your choice)

Directions: Preheat oven to 325 degrees. Line 24 muffin tins with paper or foil liners. Place one golden Oreo in each of the liners. In a large bowl, beat cream cheese and sugar until smooth. Beat in the eggs, one at a time. Add the vanilla. Combine. Pour cream cheese mixture into each liner, filling 2/3rds full. Bake for 20 minutes, or until set. Remove from oven. Cool completely. Top with pie filling. Store cheesecakes, covered, in the refrigerator.

Serving Suggestions:
+++Top half with cherry pie filling and the other half with blueberry pie filling for a patriotic treat!

Try this recipe another way...
+++By making **Caramel Apple Mini Cheesecakes!** Top with apple pie filling, some chopped peanuts, and drizzle on some caramel sauce!
+++By making **Be My Valentine Mini Cherry Cheesecakes!** Substitute the golden sandwich cookies with red velvet sandwich cookies. Top with cherry pie filling.
+++By making **Chocolate Overload Mini Cheesecakes!** Substitute the golden sandwich cookies with chocolate sandwich cookies. Add a package of mini chocolate chips to the cream cheese filling. Top with hot fudge sauce.

Reflection on the Holy Eucharist (June 1)

"The Eucharist is the sacrament of love: it signifies love, it produces love."
-- St. Thomas Aquinas

Food for the Soul: Jesus is Love Incarnate. Each time we receive Jesus, we receive God's purest gift of the most intense Love.

St. Thomas Aquinas, pray for us.
Precious Body and Blood of Jesus, strengthen and protect us.
Blessed Mother, graciously intercede for us.
Holy Trinity, we adore You! Hear and answer our prayers.

Reflection on the Holy Eucharist (June 2)

"To speak of the Blessed Sacrament is to speak of what is most sacred. How often, when we are in a state of distress, those to whom we look for help, leave us; or what is worse, add to our affliction by heaping fresh troubles upon us. He is ever there, waiting to help us."
-- St. Euphrasia

Food for the Soul: Jesus. Friend. Consoler. Healer. Listener. Companion. Shepherd. Our Answer. Always ready to give us a warm embrace.

St. Euphrasia, pray for us.
Precious Body and Blood of Jesus, strengthen and protect us.
Blessed Mother, graciously intercede for us.
Holy Trinity, we adore You! Hear and answer our prayers.

Chicken Day (June 2)

Crispy Skinned Air Fryer Chicken

Be prepared! While it's cooking, the aroma of this juicy, tender chicken is intoxicating!

Ingredients:
- 1 Whole Chicken, about 3 1/2 - 4 lbs
- 2 Tbsp olive oil
- 1/2 Lemon, cut into two quarters
- 1/4 cup of water

Chris' Seasoning Mix
- 1 tsp Baking Powder
- 1 tsp Onion Powder
- 1 tsp Garlic Powder
- 1 tsp Meat Tenderizer
- 1/2 tsp Pepper

Directions: Preheat the air fryer to 350 degrees. Remove whatever may be inside the chicken. (giblets, neck bones, etc.). Pat the skin of the chicken dry. Rub the chicken skin with olive oil. (Using other oils may cause the chicken to smoke and burn, so be sure to use olive oil.). Mix together the ingredients for my seasoning mix. (Yes, you read that right, baking powder is in the seasoning mix! Use it to achieve an extra crispy skin.) Generously season the outside of the chicken. Lightly oil and season the inside, too, then stuff the two lemon quarters inside the bird. Add 1/4 cup of water to the bottom of the air fryer. (This will add moisture to the bird, plus keep the air fryer from emitting any smoke.) Place the chicken, breast side down, into the air fryer. Cook at 350 degrees for 40 minutes. Carefully flip the chicken over and cook at 350 degrees for an additional 35-40 minutes. (When done, the internal temperature of the chicken should reach 165 degrees.) Carefully remove the chicken from the air fryer, place it on a platter, and let it rest for 15 minutes, tented with foil. Pour the flavorful juices that remain in the bottom of the air fryer into a small bowl. Strain, if desired. Remove the crispy skin from the chicken and set it aside to devour! Carve up the bird and spoon the flavorful juices over the tender, moist slices for even more delicious flavor. Serve and enjoy!

NBA and the Stanley Cup Finals

Ham and Pineapple Cream Cheese Dip
Need something to snack on while your watching the NBA or hockey finals? Serve this dip with some crackers or chips. For an added crunch, top with some chopped walnuts!

Ingredients:
- 8 oz cream cheese, softened
- 4 Tbsps mayonnaise
- 2 Tbsps honey mustard
- 3/4 tsp garlic powder
- 3/4 tsp onion powder
- 1/4 tsp meat tenderizer
- 3 packages of Splenda
- Two 2 oz packages of Buddig ham, snipped into small pieces, or a quarter pound of shaved ham from the deli
- 1 small can of crushed pineapple, well drained
- 2 Tbsps green onions, snipped into small slices
- 1/2 cup cheddar cheese (or your favorite), shredded
- 1/2 cup chopped walnuts (optional)

Directions: In a medium bowl, mix together the cream cheese, mayo, honey mustard until well blended. Stir in the garlic powder, onion powder, meat tenderizer, and Splenda. Add in the ham, crushed pineapple, and green onions. Stir until well blended. Add in the shredded cheese. Top with chopped walnuts, if desired. Serve with a variety of crackers or sturdy chips.

Feast of St. Charles Lwanga (June 3)
Ugandan martyr and patron saint of Catholic action in Africa.
"It is as if you are pouring water on me.
Please repent and become a Christian like me."
(St. Charles said this to the Guardian of the Flame as he was being burnt for his faith.)

Food for the Soul:** **Martyrs of Heaven, instill within us your passionate faith and conviction in our Lord, Jesus Christ.
St. Charles Lwanga, pray for us.
Blessed Mother, graciously intercede for us.
Holy Trinity, we adore You! Hear and answer our prayers.

Reflection on the Holy Eucharist (June 4)
"Since Christ Himself has said, 'This is My Body',
who shall dare to doubt that it is His Body?"
-- St. Cyril of Jerusalem
Food for the Soul:** **Each day this week, before the next time you receive Jesus, prepare your heart and mind to truly grasp the truth and awe of the Holy Eucharist.
St. Cyril of Jerusalem, pray for us.
Precious Body and Blood of Jesus, strengthen and protect us.
Blessed Mother, graciously intercede for us.
Holy Trinity, we adore You! Hear and answer our prayers.

Feast of St. Boniface (June 5)
Patron saint of brewers and tailors.
"The Church is like a great ship, being pounded by the waves of life's different stresses. Our duty is not to abandon ship, but to keep her on her course."
Food for the Soul:** **Be a true follower of Christ. Be an active part of making His Church strong, and not one who actively destroys it.
St. Boniface, pray for us.
Blessed Mother, graciously intercede for us.
Holy Trinity, we adore You! Hear and answer our prayers.

St. Mariam Thresia Chiramel Mankidiyan (June 6)
Patron saint of families.
"God will give eternal life to those who convert sinners and bring them to the right path."
Food for the Soul: Gently lead others to Christ.
St. Mariam Thresia Chiramel Mankidiyan, pray for us.
Blessed Mother, graciously intercede for us.
Holy Trinity, we adore You! Hear and answer our prayers.

Donut Day (June 6)

Chris-cent Donuts

Looking for an easy, yummy dessert? All you need is some crescent roll dough, a fryer, and you are on your way! Then, top with my Buttery Lime Glaze!

Ingredients:
- A tube of crescent roll dough (a sheet of the dough is best)

Directions: Preheat deep fryer to 365 degrees. Open crescent roll tube and unroll the dough onto a cookie sheet. If there are perforations, smooth out the dough until the perforations are gone, so you have one sheet of dough. Then, fold the dough in half, so now you have two layers of dough. Lightly pat the layers together. With a 2 inch donut cutter, cut the dough. (In my opinion, the donut holes turn out even better than the donuts, so sometimes I just make the donut holes...). Use the leftover dough scraps to create another sheet of dough. Fold it in half. Cut more donuts and continue to do use the leftover dough scraps until there is no dough left. Place a few donuts into the hot oil. Wait about 30 seconds and then flip the donuts over to fry the other side for about 30 seconds, or until the dough has puffed up and each side is golden brown. Remove the donuts from the oil and place on a paper towel lined cookie sheet. When all are fried, dip the donuts into my *Buttery Lime Glaze* (next recipe!) after they have cooled for a little bit.

Buttery Lime Glaze

The secret to a smooth, glossy glaze that won't make your donuts soggy is to use butter in the glaze!

Ingredients:
- 2 Tbsps unsalted butter, melted
- 2 tsps of vanilla creamer, or half and half
- 3 tsps lime juice
- 1/2 cup powdered sugar, sifted

Directions: In a medium sized bowl, mix together the melted butter, cream and lime juice. Add in the powdered sugar. Check the consistency. If you would like the glaze to be a little thicker, add more powdered sugar, a little at a time. If it should get too thick, add a little cream or lime juice. Dip the donut tops into the glaze. Set the donuts on a plate to set for a bit.

Serving Suggestion: Instead of the glaze, you can also try covering the donuts with powdered sugar or cinnamon sugar, instead. You can even slice and fill the donuts with your favorite jam. The choice is up to you!

Reflection on the Holy Eucharist (June 7)

"If we paused for a moment to consider attentively what takes place in this Sacrament, I am sure that the thought of Christ's love for us would transform the coldness of our hearts into a fire of love and gratitude."
— St. Angela Foligno

Food for the Soul: Since our eyes do not see the bread transform into His Body and the wine transform into His Blood, we often become nonchalant in receiving Jesus. It is important for us to understand that we are receiving One Who is Divine. One Who is Power and Might. One Who is Everlasting. One Who is Redeemer. One Who is Healer. One Who is Teacher. One Who spiritually transforms our very being.

St. Angela Foligno, pray for us.
Precious Body and Blood of Jesus, strengthen and protect us.
Blessed Mother, graciously intercede for us.
Holy Trinity, we adore You! Hear and answer our prayers.

Reflection on the Holy Eucharist (June 8)
"O sublime humility! O humble sublimity! That the Lord of the whole universe, God and the Son of God, should humble Himself like this and hide under the form of a little bread for our salvation."
-- St. Francis of Assisi

Food for the Soul: Jesus humbly came into this world in the form of a little Baby. He humbly comes into union with us in the form of simple bread and wine. How much God, the King of the Universe, must love us to be so very humble!

St. Francis of Assisi, pray for us.
Precious Body and Blood of Jesus, strengthen and protect us.
Blessed Mother, graciously intercede for us.
Holy Trinity, we adore You! Hear and answer our prayers.

Reflection on the Holy Eucharist (June 9)
"The Eucharist is the full realization of the worship which humanity owes God, and it cannot be compared to any other religious experience."
-- St. John Paul II

Food for the Soul: Humbly listen to what Jesus has to say to you when you receive Him in the Holy Eucharist. You will want to take over the conversation, but refrain from doing so.

St. John Paul II, pray for us.
Precious Body and Blood of Jesus, strengthen and protect us.
Blessed Mother, graciously intercede for us.
Holy Trinity, we adore You! Hear and answer our prayers.

Reflection on the Holy Eucharist (June 10)
"There is nothing so great as the Eucharist. If God had something more precious, He would have given it to us."
-- St. John Vianney

Food for the Soul: Praise God today for the gift of His great love, Jesus!

St. John Vianney, pray for us.
Precious Body and Blood of Jesus, strengthen and protect us.
Blessed Mother, graciously intercede for us.
Holy Trinity, we adore You! Hear and answer our prayers.

Feast of St. Paula Frassinetti (June 11)
**The foundress of the Congregation of the Sisters of St. Dorothy.
Patron saint of the sick.**
*"Our Lord wills that you cling to Him alone! If your faith were greater,
how much more peaceful you would be, even when
great trials surround and oppress you."*
***Food for the Soul: If we truly believe in the truth of Who God really is,
we will not worry. He is our only Help. He is our only Answer.
He is our Strength. He is our Firm Foundation.***
*St. Paula Frassinetti, pray for us.
Blessed Mother, graciously intercede for us.
Holy Trinity, we adore You! Hear and answer our prayers.*

Feast of St. Barnabas (June 11)
Apostle and patron saint of Cyprus.
"Without grace there is no hope, but with it, there is no shortage."
***Food for the Soul: Our God is a God of abundance!
He is abundant in Mercy. In Peace. In Joy. In Love. In Hope.***
*St. Barnabas, pray for us.
Blessed Mother, graciously intercede for us.
Holy Trinity, we adore You! Hear and answer our prayers.*

Reflection on the Holy Eucharist (June 12)
*"When we receive Holy Communion, we experience something
extraordinary – a joy, a fragrance, a well-being that
thrills the whole body and causes it to exalt."*
— St. John Vianney
Food for the Soul: Receive Jesus, then, be still and experience Him.
*St. John Vianney, pray for us.
Precious Body and Blood of Jesus, strengthen and protect us.
Blessed Mother, graciously intercede for us.
Holy Trinity, we adore You! Hear and answer our prayers.*

Feast of St. Anthony of Padua (June 13)
Patron saint of lost things.

"Christians must lean on the Cross of Christ, just as travelers lean on a staff when they begin a long journey."

Food for the Soul: Pray, "Jesus, You are my Rock", throughout your day.

St. Anthony of Padua, pray of us.
Blessed Mother, graciously intercede for us.
Holy Trinity, we adore You! Hear and answer our prayers.

Reflection on the Holy Eucharist (June 14)

"If we only knew how God regards this Sacrifice, we would risk our lives to be present at a single Mass."
-- St. Padre Pio

Food for the Soul: Involve yourself in the Holy Mass. Participate. Converse with the Lord and pray for those who pray along with you.

St. Padre Pio, pray for us.
Precious Body and Blood of Jesus, strengthen and protect us.
Blessed Mother, graciously intercede for us.
Holy Trinity, we adore You! Hear and answer our prayers.

Flag Day (June 14)

Old Glory Scones

A variation of my Sweetheart Scones with a fresh fruit twist!

Ingredients:
- 2 cups + 2 Tbsps flour
- 1/3 cup + 2 Tbsps sugar
- 1 Tbsp baking powder
- 1/2 tsp salt
- 6 Tbsps unsalted butter, cold
- 1/3 cup fresh blueberries
- 1/3 cup fresh raspberries
- 1 cup heavy cream

Directions: Preheat oven to 400 degrees. In a food processor, add flour, sugar, baking powder, salt and cold butter. Pulse until coarse crumbs. Place flour/butter crumbs Into a medium bowl. Stir blueberries and raspberries into the crumb mixture. Gently stir in heavy cream. Let stand for 2 minutes. Do not overmix. On a lightly powdered sugared surface, press out dough, 1/2 inch thick. Cut into scones, whatever shape you desire. Place scones on a parchment paper lined baking sheet. Sprinkle scones with sugar. Bake for 15 minutes. Remove from oven and serve while warm.

Cool Whip Jello

A quick, cool, creamy, easy dessert for a patriotic day!

Ingredients:
Small box of jello mix, red or blue
1 1/4 cups of boiling water
8 oz cool whip

Directions: In a medium bowl, pour in jello mix. Add boiling water. Stir until mix is completely dissolved. Add cool whip to the dissolved jello mixture. Stir until thoroughly combined. Refrigerate for an hour or more before serving. Top with more cool whip, if desired.

Reflection on the Holy Eucharist (June 15)

"If you took all of the good works done by all of the humans who have ever lived in all of history and stacked them up and multiplied them by a million, they wouldn't equal the merit, the virtue, and the worth of one Mass. The Eucharistic Sacrifice is Christ's infinite merit, infinite value."
-- St. Teresa of Avila

Food for the Soul: The Holy Mass reinforces our spiritual yearning for Christ to be received in our minds, to be shared in the words we speak, and to burn with love in the depths of our hearts.

St. Teresa of Avila, pray for us.
Precious Body and Blood of Jesus, strengthen and protect us.
Blessed Mother, graciously intercede for us.
Holy Trinity, we adore You! Hear and answer our prayers.

Reflection on the Holy Eucharist (June 16)
"Our lives must be woven around the Eucharist."
-- St. Teresa of Calcutta
Food for the Soul: We are intertwined with God in His Divinity.
St. Teresa of Calcutta, pray for us.
Precious Body and Blood of Jesus, strengthen and protect us.
Blessed Mother, graciously intercede for us.
Holy Trinity, we adore You! Hear and answer our prayers.

Reflection on the Holy Eucharist (June 17)
"The Eucharist is a fire which inflames us."
-- St. John Damascene
**Food for the Soul: Live a day being on fire for Jesus!
Live His Sacred Plan for your life.**
St. John Damascene, pray for us.
Precious Body and Blood of Jesus, strengthen and protect us.
Blessed Mother, graciously intercede for us.
Holy Trinity, we adore You! Hear and answer our prayers.

Reflection on the Holy Eucharist (June 18)
"There is no doubt that a flood of graces will descend upon your family, and the world, if more souls would become docile pupils of adoration."
-- St. Pope John XXIII
**Food for the Soul: Pray throughout your day,
"Holy Trinity, we adore You!"**
St. Pope John XXIII, pray for us.
Precious Body and Blood of Jesus, strengthen and protect us.
Blessed Mother, graciously intercede for us.
Holy Trinity, we adore You! Hear and answer our prayers.

Feast of St. Romuald (June 19)
Founder of the Camaldolese Benedictines (Hermits).
"Better to pray one psalm with devotion and compunction, than a hundred with distraction."
Food for the Soul: Today, pray the "Our Father", one line at a time, meditating on the words of each line.
St. Romuald, pray for us.
Blessed Mother, graciously intercede for us.
Holy Trinity, we adore You! Hear and answer our prayers.

Juneteenth (June 19)
"Oh, God, to know You is life. To serve You is freedom. To praise You is the soul's joy and delight. Guard me with the power of Your grace here and in all places. Now and at all times, forever. Amen."
-- St. Augustine of Hippo
Food for the Soul: Pray throughout the day, "God, You are great indeed!"
St. Augustine of Hippo, pray for us.
Blessed Mother, graciously intercede for us.
Holy Trinity, we adore You! Hear and answer our prayers.

Tender, Butter Bathed Corn on the Cob
The name says it all!

Ingredients:
- 6-8 mini ears of extra sweet corn on the cob
- 1 cup water
- 1 stick of salted butter
- 1 plastic ziplock bag, gallon size

Directions: Add one cup of water to an instant pot. Place a trivet or a steamer basket inside. Add the corn, ears standing up on an end. Pressure cook on high for ten minutes. Natural release for twenty to thirty minutes. Release excess steam through the air vent before removing the lid. Slice one stick of salted butter into eight pieces. Place the butter into a gallon plastic bag. Add the hot ears of corn from the instant pot and seal the bag, letting the air out of the bag before you seal it. Place the bag on the counter and massage the butter onto the ears of corn. Allow the butter slices to melt onto the corn. Turn the bag over and do the same. Then, leave the corn in the bag, the ears lying in a single layer. Allow the corn to bathe in the butter in the bag for about an hour, massaging the butter onto the corn every fifteen minutes or so. When you massage the butter into the corn, always flip the bag over so the melted butter completely covers all the kernels of corn. Right before serving, open the bag about an inch and warm the buttered corn in the bag in the microwave for two minutes. Use tongs to remove the ears of corn from the bag and place in a serving bowl. Carefully pour the butter over the corn and serve!

Father's Day
(Third Sunday in June)

"St. Joseph was an ordinary sort of man on whom God relied to do great things."
--St. Josemaría Escrivá

"If Joseph was so engaged, heart and soul, in protecting and providing for that little family at Nazareth, don't you think that now, in heaven, he is the same loving father and guardian of the whole Church, of all its members, as he was of its Head on earth?"
-- St. Peter Julian Eymard

Food for the Soul: Pray the Hail Mary ten times for your father today, living or gone to heaven.

Holy Trinity, we ask You to bless our earthly fathers, and those in heaven, today and everyday. Guide them to the promises of eternal life. Amen.

St. Joseph, pray for us.
St. Josemaría Escrivá, pray for us.
St Peter Julian Eymard, pray for us.
Blessed Mother, graciously intercede for us.
Holy Trinity, we adore You! Hear and answer our prayers.

Instant Pot Baby Back Ribs

Do you want ribs that are so tender, they fall off of the bone? Try making them in the instant pot!

Ingredients:
- 1 slab of meaty baby back ribs, between 2.25 - 2.75 pounds
- 1 can of beer, 12 oz.
- 2 Tbs liquid smoke

Chris' Dry Rub
- 2 Tbsp Splenda brown sugar
- 1 tsp onion powder
- 1 tsp garlic powder
- 1 tsp meat tenderizer
- 1 tsp paprika
- 1/2 tsp black pepper

Directions: Prepare the instant pot. Add the beer and the liquid smoke into the bottom of the pot. Place a trivet in the pot. Prepare the dry rub. Combine the seasonings and mix well. Set aside. Prepare the ribs. Remove the ribs from the store packaging. Place the ribs on a large cookie sheet. Turn the ribs over and remove the membrane from the ribs. Cut it slightly at the smallest end and pull it away from the ribs with a paper towel in your hand. It will grip the membrane better than your fingers can. This will help your ribs to be nice and tender. Cut the slab in half. Sprinkle and rub the dry rub seasoning all over the ribs, back, front, and on all sides. Place the ribs all around the instant pot, standing on the tips of the bones. Secure the lid. Make sure the vent is closed. Choose the "Meat" setting and cook on high for 75 minutes. Natural release for thirty minutes. Carefully remove ribs from the instant pot, they may fall off the bone! Place on a foil or parchment lined cookie sheet. Coat the ribs, front and back, with your favorite barbecue sauce. I usually use the "baby" sauce for my baby back ribs. I add a little Splenda brown sugar to it, along with a little lime juice for some super yummy results! Preheat the oven to 375 degrees. Bake the ribs in the oven for eight to ten minutes. Cut the ribs into serving sizes. We often eat these baby back ribs with my tender, butter bathed corn on the cob for a double yum, double wow dinner!

Reflection on the Holy Eucharist (June 20)
"A Holy Hour of adoration testifies to the fact that the Jesus who died on the Cross, is present in the Eucharist, and reigns in Heaven, are identical."
-- St. Pope Pius XII
**Food for the Soul: Adore Jesus in the Blessed sacrament as soon as you are able. In the meantime, pray,
"We adore You, O Christ and we bless You!"**
*St. Pope Pius XII, pray for us.
Precious Body and Blood of Jesus, strengthen and protect us.
Blessed Mother, graciously intercede for us.
Holy Trinity, we adore You! Hear and answer our prayers.*

Feast of St. Aloysius Gonzaga (June 21)
Patron saint of youth and students.
"It is better to be a Child of God than king of the whole world."
Food for the Soul: Praise and thank God for creating you as His precious child!
*St. Aloysius, pray for us.
Blessed Mother, graciously intercede for us.
Holy Trinity, we adore You! Hear and answer our prayers.*

First Day of Summer

Taffy Apple Salad
*Cool, refreshing, tangy, crunchy, salty, sweet...
yummy, fruity flavors to enjoy on a hot summer day!*

Ingredients:
1 large can of pineapple tidbits, drained; (save the juice!)
1 1/4 cup cocktail peanuts or walnuts, whole, chopped, or ground (as to your preference)
2 cups miniature marshmallows
2 1/2 cups diced Granny Smith apples (peeled and cored)
1/2 cup sugar

1 Tbsp flour
1 large egg, well beaten
1 1/2 Tbsp apple cider vinegar
8 oz Cool Whip

Directions: In a large bowl, mix together the pineapple tidbits, marshmallows, cool whip, nuts, and apples. Place bowl in refrigerator. In a medium saucepan, mix together the flour, pineapple juice, sugar, cider vinegar, and egg. Cook over medium heat until slightly thickened. Remove from stove. Cool. Pour the cooked mixture over the pineapple mixture and stir until combined. Cover and refrigerate overnight. Before serving, top with some extra chopped/ground peanuts.

Aloha Bread

This was one of my favorite breads that my Mom would make when I was young. The tropical flavors make this bread shine like the Hawaiian sun!

Ingredients:
- 1/4 cup sugar
- 1/2 tsp salt
- 1/4 cup melted unsalted butter, cooled
- 1 large egg
- 1 banana, mashed
- 1 small can of crushed pineapple, well drained (use juice in recipe)
- 3 1/4 cups flour
- 1 package instant yeast
- Knob of unsalted butter

Directions: Drain crushed pineapple. Place pineapple in a small bowl. Save juice in a separate small bowl. Add water to the juice so it makes 1/2 cup liquid. Set pineapple and juice aside. Using a bread machine, add sugar, salt, butter, egg, mashed banana, pineapple juice, and flour into the pan. Make a well in the middle of the flour and put the yeast in the well. Set to the "dough" cycle. When the cycle beeps to add special ingredients, add in the well drained crushed pineapple. When the cycle is completed, punch down the dough. Place the dough into an oiled 2 quart casserole dish. Cover lightly with a towel or plastic wrap. Allow to rise for 45 minutes. Bake at 375 degrees for 30 - 40 minutes until golden brown. Remove from oven. Rub crust immediately with a knob of unsalted butter. Cool in dish for 5 minutes, then remove from dish. Allow to cool for 15 minutes. Slice and enjoy, slathered with unsalted butter.

Feast of St. Paulinas of Nola (June 22)
Patron saint of the poor and pilgrims.
"Let the rich enjoy their riches, let the kings enjoy their kingdoms. You, O Christ, are my treasure and my kingdom."
Food for the Soul: The problem with desiring riches and kingdoms is they never fully satisfy. Only Christ, truly and completely, satisfies every need and desire we may have.
St. Paulinas of Nola, pray for us.
Blessed Mother, graciously intercede for us.
Holy Trinity, we adore You! Hear and answer our prayers.

Reflection on the Holy Eucharist (June 23)
"Our Lord hears our prayers anywhere, but He has revealed to His servants, that those who visit Him in the Eucharist will obtain a more abundant measure of grace."
-- St. Alphonsus Liguori
Food for the Soul: Receive Jesus in the Holy Eucharist. He unites with us in a most intimate way.
St. Alphonsus Liguori, pray for us.
Precious Body and Blood of Jesus, strengthen and protect us.
Blessed Mother, graciously intercede for us.
Holy Trinity, we adore You! Hear and answer our prayers.

Feast of The Nativity of St. John the Baptist (June 24)
Patron saint of baptism, monastics, hermits, converts, tailors, and prisoners.
"He must increase, I must decrease."
Food for the Soul: Push your ego away, today. Then, there will be ample room for the Holy Trinity to dwell.
St. John the Baptist, pray for us.
Blessed Mother, graciously intercede for us.
Holy Trinity, we adore You! Hear and answer our prayers.

Reflection on the Holy Eucharist (June 25)
"Do grant, oh my God, that when my lips approach Yours to kiss You, I may taste the gall that was given to You; when my shoulders lean against Yours, make me feel Your scourging; when my flesh is united with Yours in the Holy Eucharist, make me feel Your Passion; when my head comes near Yours, make me feel Your thorns; when my heart is close to Yours, make me feel Your spear."
-- St. Gemma Galgani
Food for the Soul: May we come to love Jesus so much that we desire to share in His Passion, as much as in His gift of Eternal Life.
St. Gemma Galgani, pray for us.
Precious Body and Blood of Jesus, strengthen and protect us.
Blessed Mother, graciously intercede for us.
Holy Trinity, we adore You! Hear and answer our prayers.

Feast of St. Josemaría Escrivá (June 26)
Patron saint of those who suffer from diabetes.
"Don't let your life be sterile. Be useful. Blaze a trail. Shine forth with the light of your faith...and light up all the ways of the earth with the fire of Christ that you carry in your heart."
Food for the Soul: Shine for Christ today!
St. Josemaría Escrivá, pray for us.
Blessed Mother, graciously intercede for us.
Holy Trinity, we adore You! Hear and answer our prayers.

Feast of St. Cyril of Alexandria (June 27)
Doctor of the Church.
"As two pieces of wax fused together make one, so he who receives Holy Communion is so united with Christ that Christ is in him and he is in Christ."
Food for the Soul: Unite with Jesus in prayer.
Allow yourself to spiritually be one with Him.
St. Cyril, pray for us.
Blessed Mother, graciously intercede for us.
Holy Trinity, we adore You! Hear and answer our prayers.

Feast of St. Irenaeus (June 28)
Bishop, Doctor of the Church, and martyr.
"Just as bread from the earth, when it receives the invocation of God, is no longer common bread but the Eucharist, made up of two elements, one earthly and one heavenly, so also our bodies, in receiving the Eucharist, are no longer corruptible, for they have the hope of resurrection."
Food for the Soul: Thank God for our hope in His gift of Eternal Life!
St. Irenaeus, pray for us.
Blessed Mother, graciously intercede for us.
Holy Trinity, we adore You! Hear and answer our prayers.

Feast of St. Peter and St. Paul (June 29)
This day honors the martyrdom of these two saints in Rome by Nero.
"And when he had opened the fifth seal, I saw under the altar, the souls of them that were slain for the Word of God, and for the testimony which they held."
(Revelation 6:9-10)
Food for the Soul: Glorify God for all the martyrs of our faith!
St. Peter, pray for us.
St. Paul, pray for us.
Blessed Mother, graciously intercede for us.
Holy Trinity, we adore You! Hear and answer our prayers.

Reflection on the Holy Eucharist (June 30)

"It is not to remain in a golden ciborium that He comes down each day from Heaven, but to find another Heaven, the Heaven of our souls in which He takes delight."
-- St. Thérèse of Lisieux

Food for the Soul: Heaven lies within us!
Let us rejoice in knowing we are of God!

St. Thérèse of Lisieux, pray for us.
Precious Body and Blood of Jesus, strengthen and protect us.
Blessed Mother, graciously intercede for us.
Holy Trinity, we adore You! Hear and answer our prayers.

July

July Birthday Cake

Cherry Berry Buckle
Are you celebrating a birthday this month?
If so, enjoy the flavors of summer with this fruity duo!

Cake Ingredients:
2 sticks unsalted butter, softened
1 1/2 cups sugar
4 large eggs
2 Tbsps sour cream
3 cups flour
3 tsps baking powder
1 tsp vanilla
1/2 can cherry pie filling
1/2 can blueberry pie filling

Streusel Ingredients:
1/4 cup unsalted butter, cold
1/2 cup flour
1/2 cup sugar

Directions: Preheat oven to 350 degrees. Oil a 9 x 13 inch glass pan. Set aside. In a large mixing bowl, cream together butter and sugar. Add eggs and beat into butter mixture. Add sour cream and vanilla and beat into mixture again. Add flour and baking powder. Mix until combined. Do not overmix. Put 3/4 of the batter into the prepared pan. On top of the batter, dollop spoonfuls of the cherry and blueberry filling, being careful to stay away from the edges of the pan. (Remember to only use 1/2 can of each!). Take the remaining 1/4 of the batter and dollop spoonfuls over the fruit fillings. In a small bowl, prepare the streusel topping by cutting the butter into the flour and sugar until it resembles coarse crumbs. (Even more convenient is using a food processor for this step.). Sprinkle the streusel over the top of the cake. (It may seem like a lot of streusel, but be sure to use it all. That crunchy, buttery streusel takes the cake over the top!). Bake for 45 - 50 minutes. Remove from oven and allow to cool. Cut into 24 squares

Feast of St. Junípero Serra (July 1)
Patron saint of California.
"Always forward, never turn back."
**Food for the Soul: Live in the moment, in the present.
So many times we dwell in the past, with our focus on what was.
Focus on what is. After all, the God we worship is "I Am"!
Move forward with Him.**
St. Junípero, pray for us.
Blessed Mother, graciously intercede for us.
Holy Trinity, we adore You! Hear and answer our prayers.

Fruit Day (July 1)

Instant Pot Apricot Chicken
This recipe certainly dresses up some ordinary chicken thighs and turns them into a fruity delight!

Ingredients:
- 6 skinless chicken thighs
- 1/2 cup low sodium chicken broth
- 1 tsp garlic powder
- 1 tsp onion powder
- 1/2 tsp black pepper
- 1 packet onion soup mix
- 1 cup Catalina salad dressing
- 2/3 cup apricot jam
- 8 dried apricots, cut in quarters

Directions: In a small bowl, mix together low sodium chicken broth, onion soup mix, garlic powder, onion powder, and black pepper. Add 1/4

of this mixture into the pot. Add the chicken thighs to the pot. Place the apricot quarters on top of the chicken. Pour the Catalina dressing on top of the chicken. Spoon the apricot jam over that. Then pour the broth mixture over and around the chicken. Close, lock, and seal the instant pot. Set on the poultry cycle on high pressure for 20 minutes. When cycle is completed, natural release for 15 minutes. Then do a quick release to remaining pressure. Remove lid. Serve chicken, spooning the sauce over the chicken. If the sauce is not thick enough, thicken it with a cornstarch slurry. In a small bowl, mix together 1 Tbsp of cornstarch with 1 Tbsp of cold water. After the chicken is removed from the pot, put on the sauté setting. When the sauce begins to bubble, stir in the slurry and continue to stir until the sauce thickens. Turn the sauté setting off. Spoon sauce over chicken.

Serving suggestion: *Serve with rice cooked in low sodium chicken broth, 1/2 tsp garlic powder, and 1/2 tsp onion powder. Add some chopped dried apricots and a tablespoon of salted butter to the cooked rice. Warm until apricots are plump. Serve the chicken over the rice, spooning the sauce over the chicken and rice, as well.*

God's Word of the Day (July 2)
"May the God of hope fill you with all joy and peace in believing, so that by the power of the Holy Spirit, you may abound in hope."
(Romans 15:13)
Food for the Soul: Pray to the Holy Spirit today.
Ask Him to bestow upon you His richest blessings.
Blessed Mother, graciously intercede for us.
Holy Trinity, we adore You! Hear and answer our prayers.

Feast of St. Thomas the Apostle (July 3)
Patron saint of judges and architects.
"Humility, which is a virtue, is always fruitful in good works."
Food for the Soul: Be humble in all you do today.
St. Thomas, pray for us.
Blessed Mother, graciously intercede for us.
Holy Trinity, we adore You! Hear and answer our prayers.

Independence Day (July 4)

"The nation...doesn't simply need what we have. It needs who we are."
—St. Teresa Benedicta of the Cross (Edith Stein)

**Food for the Soul: Be active in the world,
in the Name of Jesus Christ our Lord!**

St. Teresa Benedicta of the Cross, pray for us.
Blessed Mother, graciously intercede for us.
Holy Trinity, we adore You! Hear and answer our prayers.

Pickled Mini Cucumber and Onion Salad

Cool. Crunchy. Tangy. A tasty, refreshing accompaniment to any meal!

Ingredients:
- 6 - 8 mini cucumbers, peeled
- 1 small sweet onion or a small red onion, skin removed
- 1 cup apple cider vinegar or white vinegar
- 1/2 cup water
- 3/4 cup sugar
- 1/2 tsp celery salt
- 1/2 tsp garlic powder
- 1/2 tsp onion powder

Directions: Grate (use a large grate) or spiralize cucumbers and onion into thin ringlets. Toss together in a medium heat resistant bowl. (If there is too much onion for your taste, feel free to not add all of it.). Combine the vinegar, water, sugar, celery salt, garlic powder, and onion powder into a medium saucepan on medium heat. Bring vinegar mixture to a boil. Pour the hot mixture over the cucumbers and onions. Stir until well combined. Place in a covered container and allow to marinate in the refrigerator for at least 1 hour. (If you can leave it longer, that would be better for the pickling process.). Serve as a side, or as a topping to some shredded lettuce and halved cherry tomatoes. You can also use it as a topping for a burger, a sandwich, or even a hot dog!

Feast of St. Anthony of Zaccaria (July 5)
Priest, catechist. Patron of physicians and the Barnabite order.
"Prayer is not knowledge and human understanding,
but the Spirit within your heart."
Food for the Soul: Allow the Holy Spirit to guide your prayer.
He will speak on your behalf.
St. Anthony of Zaccaria, pray for us.
Blessed Mother, graciously intercede for us.
Holy Trinity, we adore You! Hear and answer our prayers.

Feast of St. Maria Goretti (July 6)
Patron of chastity, rape victims, purity, girls, and forgiveness.
"Let us love the Cross very much, for it is there that we discover our life,
our true love, and our strength in our greatest difficulties."
Food for the Soul: Look to the Holy Cross for your inspiration today.
St. Maria Goretti, pray for us.
Blessed Mother, graciously intercede for us.
Holy Trinity, we adore You! Hear and answer our prayers.

God's Word of the Day (July 7)
"Rejoice in hope, be patient in tribulation, be constant in prayer."
(Romans 12:12)
Food for the Soul: Let all you do be an unending prayer to God!
Blessed Mother, graciously intercede for us.
Holy Trinity, we adore You! Hear and answer our prayers.

God's Word of the Day (July 8)
"Rejoice in the Lord, always; again, I will say, rejoice."
(Philippians 4:4)
Food for the Soul: Live today in the joy of the Lord!
Blessed Mother, graciously intercede for us.
Holy Trinity, we adore You! Hear and answer our prayers.

St. Augustine Zhao Rong and Companions (July 9)
Chinese Priest, martyred, along with 119 of his companions.
"Blessed are they who are persecuted for righteousness' sake,
for theirs is the kingdom of heaven."
(Matthew 5:10)
Food for the Soul: Honor the martyrs who gave their lives in their love forGod.
St. Augustine Zhao Rong and Companions, pray for us.
Blessed Mother, graciously intercede for us.
Holy Trinity, we adore You! Hear and answer our prayers.

God's Word of the Day (July 10)
"Until now, you have asked nothing in My Name.
Ask, and you will receive, that your joy may be full."
(John 16:24)
Food for the Soul: Ask God to bless you with the joy He has planned for your life.
Blessed Mother, graciously intercede for us.
Holy Trinity, we adore You! Hear and answer our prayers.

Piña Colada Day (July 10)

Piña Colada Cheese Squares

The buttery crust, creamy cheese filling, and crunchy coconut topping is a winning combination for this summer dessert!

Crust Ingredients:
1 cup flour
1/2 cup sugar
1 stick unsalted butter, softened
1/4 cup sweetened coconut flakes (optional)

Cheese Filling Ingredients:
8 oz cream cheese, softened
2 Tbsps sugar
2 Tbsps half and half
1 tsp vanilla
1 large egg
8 oz crushed pineapple, drained

Topping Ingredients:
1 cup sweetened coconut flakes
1 Tbsp unsalted butter, melted

Glaze Ingredients: (Optional)
1/2 cup powdered sugar, sifted
3 - 4 tsps half and half, or vanilla creamer
1/4 tsp vanilla, coconut, or rum extract

Directions: Preheat oven to 350 degrees. Lightly oil a 9 x 9 inch pan. Set aside. Prepare crust. In a medium bowl, combine flour, sugar, butter, coconut. Pat evenly into bottom of pan. Bake for 10 minutes. Remove from oven. While crust is baking, prepare cheese filling. Using the same bowl, combine cream cheese, sugar, half and half, vanilla, and egg. Beat mixture until smooth. Stir drained crushed pineapple into the cheese mixture until combined. Pour cheese filling over the crust. In a small bowl, combine coconut and melted butter. Stir until flakes are coated in the butter. Sprinkle buttered coconut flakes over the top of the cheese filling. Bake for 18 - 20 minutes. Remove from oven. After the pan is out of the oven, if you desire, prepare the glaze. (The glaze will add a little more sweetness to the cheese squares. If you prefer them to be less sweet, omit the glaze.) In a small bowl, mix together the powdered sugar, cream, and extract. Mix until smooth. Drizzle the glaze over the cake. Cool completely. Refrigerate for an hour or two, then slice into squares and serve.

Piña Colada Cream Pie
Cool, creamy, fruity, refreshing!

Ingredients:
- 1 cup half and half
- 1/4 cup pineapple juice
- French Vanilla pudding mix
- 3/4 cup toasted coconut
- 3/4 cup pineapple tidbits (drained, 1/4 cup juice reserved)
- 1/2 container of cool whip
- Premade shortbread pie crust (can be found near the premade graham cracker crusts)

Directions: In a large nonstick skillet, toast 3/4 cup of coconut to a golden brown. Stir constantly. Be careful not to burn. Remove from heat and set aside to cool. In a medium bowl, combine half and half and pineapple juice with the pudding mix. Fold the cool whip into the pudding mixture. Add the toasted coconut to the pudding mixture, reserving a little to sprinkle on top of the finished pie. Add the pineapple tidbits into the pudding mixture and stir. Pour the mixture into the pie crust. Sprinkle with a little toasted coconut. Refrigerate for at least an hour or two before serving.

Feast of St. Benedict (July 11)
Patron saint of students and African Americans.
*"Prayer ought to be short and pure,
unless it be prolonged by the inspiration of Divine grace."*
**Food for the Soul: Pray short prayers to God throughout your day.
"God, I love You!" "Jesus, I adore You!" "Guide me, Holy Spirit."**
*St. Benedict, pray for us.
Blessed Mother, graciously intercede for us.
Holy Trinity, we adore You! Hear and answer our prayers.*

God's Word of the Day (July 12)
*"Consider it pure joy, my brothers and sisters, whenever you
face trials of many kinds, because you know that the
testing of your faith produces perseverance."*
(James 1:2-3)
**Food for the Soul: Be prepared to tell yourself the truth when you are
challenged in your faith: God is with you. He is your help and your
strength. Whatever God has spoken is truth. He does not lie.**
*Blessed Mother, graciously intercede for us.
Holy Trinity, we adore You! Hear and answer our prayers.*

Feast of St. Henry (July 13)
**Patron saint of the childless and the handicapped.
Established peace in Europe.**
"Blessed are the peacemakers, for they shall be called sons of God."
(Matthew 5:9)
Food for the Soul: Sow God's peace today, in all circumstances.
*St. Henry, pray for us.
Blessed Mother, graciously intercede for us.
Holy Trinity, we adore You! Hear and answer our prayers.*

God's Word of the Day (July 14)

"Clap your hands, all you nations; shout to God with cries of joy."
(Psalms 47:1)

***Food for the Soul: Allow your soul to
cry out to God with joy, throughout your day!***

*Blessed Mother, graciously intercede for us.
Holy Trinity, we adore You! Hear and answer our prayers.*

Hotdog Day (Third Wednesday in July)

Chicago Style Dogs on a Raft

Who says we always have to serve a hotdog on a bun? Let's try a different way! When I worked at a lunch counter grill in our local mall as a teenager, they used to serve a hotdog sandwich similar to this...

Ingredients:
- Hot dogs, cooked as you choose
- Brioche bread
- Cheese slices, your choice
- Honey mustard, or your choice of mustard
- Mayonnaise
- Tomato slices, lightly seasoned with celery salt
- Sweet onion, thinly sliced
- Sweet relish
- Sport peppers (optional)

Directions: Preheat a nonstick medium skillet on medium heat. Build the sandwich. Take 2 slices of bread. On each slice of bread, spread some mayo and mustard. Then, place a slice of cheese on top of the condiments. Then, on one cheese slice, add a slice of seasoned tomato. On the other side, add thin slices of sweet onion. Top the onion with some sweet relish. Slice the hot dog lengthways and place on the relish. Then, sandwich the two slices of bread together. Add 1 tablespoon of margarine or butter to the pan. Melt. Add the sandwich to the pan and grill each side until golden brown and the cheese is melty, adding more margarine or butter, as needed. Remove from pan. Cut sandwich on an angle. Serve with sport peppers, if desired.

Feast of St. Bonaventure (July 15)
Bishop and Doctor of the Catholic Church.
Patron saint of bowel disorders.
"If you learn everything except Christ, you learn nothing. If you learn nothing except Christ, you learn everything."
Food for the Soul: God is everything you will ever need.
St. Bonaventure, pray for us.
Blessed Mother, graciously intercede for us.
Holy Trinity, we adore You! Hear and answer our prayers.

Feast of Our Lady of Mount Carmel (July 16)
Patroness of the Carmelite Order.
"She (Blessed Mother) said to him, "Receive, my beloved son, this habit of thy order: this shall be to thee and to all Carmelites a privilege, that whosoever dies clothed in this shall never suffer eternal fire...It shall be a sign of salvation, a protection in danger, and a pledge of peace."
---The Blessed Mother, speaking about the brown scapular
Food for the Soul: Pray the Memorare today.
Our Lady of Mount Carmel, graciously intercede for us.
Holy Trinity, we adore You! Hear and answer our prayers.

God's Word of the Day (July 17)
"Go, eat your food with gladness, and drink your wine with a joyful heart, for God has already approved what you do."
(Ecclesiastes 9:7)
Food for the Soul: Enjoy the blessings God bestows upon you today, as you live your life for God!
Blessed Mother, graciously intercede for us.
Holy Trinity, we adore You! Hear and answer our prayers.

Feast of St. Camillus (July 18)
Patron saint of the sick, hospitals, nurses, and physicians.
"Commitment is doing what you said you would do,
after the feeling you said it in, has passed."
Food for the Soul: Honor the promises you make,
in the Name of Jesus Christ.
St. Camillus, pray for us.
Blessed Mother, graciously intercede for us.
Holy Trinity, we adore You! Hear and answer our prayers.

God's Word of the Day (July 19)
"The prospect of the righteous is joy,
but the hopes of the wicked come to nothing."
(Proverbs 10:28)
Food for the Soul: Following God's path for your life.
In it, you will find His amazing joy!
Blessed Mother, graciously intercede for us.
Holy Trinity, we adore You! Hear and answer our prayers.

Feast of St. Apollinaris (July 20)
Patron saint of faith and courage.
"Faith is the assurance of things hoped for, the conviction of things not seen."
(Hebrews 11:1)
Food for the Soul: Pray to the Holy Trinity for an increase in our faith.
St. Apollinaris, pray for us.
Blessed Mother, graciously intercede for us.
Holy Trinity, we adore You! Hear and answer our prayers.

God's Word of the Day (July 21)

"Though you have not seen Him, you love Him; and even though you do not see Him now, you believe in Him and are filled with an inexpressible and glorious joy, for you are receiving the end result of your faith, the salvation of your souls."
(1 Peter 1:8-9)

Food for the Soul: Live today for the salvation of your soul!
Blessed Mother, graciously intercede for us.
Holy Trinity, we adore You! Hear and answer our prayers.

Feast of St. Mary Magdalene (July 22)

Patron saint of converts, hairstylists, pharmacists, and contemplative life.

"There is no saint without a past, no sinner without a future."
— St. Augustine

Food for the Soul: Bring all of your past failures to the Holy Cross, and lay them down at the pierced Feet of our Savior.
St. Mary Magdalene, pray for us.
St. Augustine, pray for us.
Blessed Mother, graciously intercede for us.
Holy Trinity, we adore You! Hear and answer our prayers.

Feast of St. Christina the Astonishing (July 23)

Patron saint of autism, psychiatrists, and social workers.

"Do with me whatever you like, my dear father; you can take my life, but the faith of Christ, you have no power to tear out of my heart. My Savior will strengthen me to suffer patiently all that you have threatened."

Food for the Soul: Pray today, "God, I thank You for Your Strength."
St. Christina the Astonishing, pray for us.
Blessed Mother, graciously intercede for us.
Holy Trinity, we adore You! Hear and answer our prayers.

Feast of St. John Cassian (July 23)
Patron saint of teachers.

"Cherubim means 'knowledge in abundance'. They provide an everlasting protection for that which appeases God, namely, the calm of your heart, and they will cast a shadow of protection against all the attacks of malign spirits."
-- St. John Cassian

Food for the Soul: Call upon the cherubim to guard and protect you.
All you Cherubim, watch over and protect us.
All Angels of God, guide us.
St. John Cassian, pray for us.
Blessed Mother, graciously intercede for us.
Holy Trinity, we adore You! Hear and answer our prayers.

Peanut Butter and Chocolate Day (July 23)

Peanut Butter and Chocolate Bars
This recipe was shared with me by a friend I used to work with many years ago when I first began my career as a teacher. Her name was Bonnie, and she, too, loved to cook and bake. When I tasted these bars, they were better than any peanut butter cup I ever had! They still are!

Peanut Butter Candy Ingredients:
- 1 cup creamy peanut butter
- 2 sticks unsalted butter, melted
- 1 cup graham cracker crumbs
- 1 lb box powdered sugar
-

Chocolate Topping Ingredients:
- 12 oz chocolate chips of your choice
- 1 stick unsalted butter
-

Directions: In a medium bowl, mix together the peanut butter and the melted butter. Add the graham cracker crumbs to the peanut butter mixture. Stir until combined. Add in the powdered sugar. Stir until combined. Press the peanut butter mixture into a 9 x 13 inch pan. In a small bowl, prepare the chocolate topping. Melt the butter and chocolate chips. Stir until combined. Pour the chocolate mixture over the peanut butter mixture in the pan. Smooth topping. Refrigerate until set. Remove from the refrigerator and set on counter to allow to reach room temperature. Cut into bars. Store in a tin in the refrigerator. (Separate the layers using wax paper.)

Feast of St. Sharbel Makhlūf (July 24)
Patron saint of those who suffer in body and soul.
"The ignorant man clings to the dust until he becomes the dust; the wise and prudent man clings to heaven until he reaches heaven."
Food for the Soul: Raise your eyes, your heart, your prayers, to heaven.
St. Sharbel Makhlūf, pray for us.
Blessed Mother, graciously intercede for us.
Holy Trinity, we adore You! Hear and answer our prayers.

Feast of St. James the Great (July 25)
The first apostle to be martyred. Patron saint of pilgrims, soldiers, veterinarians, pharmacists, and people with arthritis.
"Every good and perfect gift is from above, coming down from the Father of the heavenly lights, Who does not change like shifting shadows."
Food for the Soul: God is steady in His gifts of love and mercy. We can rely on Him, anytime, anywhere.
St. James the Great, pray for us.
Blessed Mother, graciously intercede for us.
Holy Trinity, we adore You! Hear and answer our prayers.

Instant Pot Honey Chicken
Once again for dinner, the instant pot comes to the rescue! This time we have a honey soy sauce to top off our tender, juicy chicken thighs. Serve the chicken over some seasoned, buttered rice, combined with peas, corn, and carrots for a perfectly balanced meal!

Ingredients:
- 1/3 cup honey
- 4 cloves of garlic, minced
- 1/4 cup low sodium soy sauce
- 1/4 cup water
- 3/4 cup ketchup
- 2 Tbsps light brown sugar
- 1/2 tsp oregano
- 6 bone-in skinless chicken thighs

Garnish Ingredients:
- 1/2 Tbsp toasted sesame seeds
- 2 - 3 Tbsps thinly sliced green onions

Directions: In the instant pot, add honey, minced garlic, soy sauce, water, ketchup, brown sugar, and oregano. Mix until well combined. Add the chicken thighs to the pot. Spoon the sauce mixture over the chicken. Close, lock, and seal the lid. Set to the poultry cycle on high pressure for 20 minutes. After the cycle is finished, natural release for 15 minutes. Remove lid. Remove chicken and place on a platter. Spoon sauce over chicken. Garnish chicken with toasted sesame seeds and thinly sliced green onions. Serve over seasoned, buttered rice, combined with peas, corn, and/or carrots, if desired.

Sts. Joachim and Anne, Blessed Mother's Parents (July 26)
Patron saints of grandparents.
"The angel went to her (Mary) and said, 'Greetings, you who are highly favored! The Lord is with you."
(Luke 1:28)
Food for the Soul: Pray ten Hail Marys for your parents today.
St. Joachim, pray for us.
St. Anne, pray for us.
Blessed Mother, graciously intercede for us.
Holy Trinity, we adore You! Hear and answer our prayers.

God's Word of the Day (July 27)
"May the God of hope fill you with all joy and peace, as you trust in Him, so that you may overflow with hope by the power of the Holy Spirit."
(Romans 15:13)
Food for the Soul: God is abundant in His gifts to us.
Let us thank Him for His goodness!
Blessed Mother, graciously intercede for us.
Holy Trinity, we adore You! Hear and answer our prayers.

God's Word of the Day (July 28)
"I tell you that in the same way, there will be more rejoicing in heaven over one sinner who repents than over ninety-nine righteous persons who do not need to repent."
(Luke 15:7)
Food for the Soul: Turn back to God. Trust in His plan for your life.
Blessed Mother, graciously intercede for us.
Holy Trinity, we adore You! Hear and answer our prayers.

God's Word of the Day (July 29)
"Nehemiah said, "Go and enjoy choice food and sweet drinks, and send some to those who have nothing prepared. This day is holy to our Lord. Do not grieve, for the joy of the Lord is your strength."
(Nehemiah 8:10)
Food for the Soul: Celebrate this day! God, our joy, is with us!
Blessed Mother, graciously intercede for us.
Holy Trinity, we adore You! Hear and answer our prayers.

Feast of St. Peter Chrysologus (July 30)
Doctor of the Church and patron saint of homilists.
"The poor stretch out the hand, but God receives what is offered."
Food for the Soul: Give as if you are handing it to God's own Hand.
St. Peter Chrysologus, pray for us.
Blessed Mother, graciously intercede for us.
Holy Trinity, we adore You! Hear and answer our prayers.

Cheesecake Day (July 30)

Caramel Cheesecake Squares
Rich, creamy, decadent! Isn't that what a delicious dessert is all about?!

Crust Ingredients:
- 14 golden sandwich cookies, crushed in a food processor
- 2 Tbsps unsalted butter, melted
-

Cheese Filling Ingredients:
- 10 golden sandwich cookies, coarsely chopped
- 16 oz cream cheese (2 packages)
- 7 oz jar of marshmallow creme
- 1 large egg
-

Caramel Sauce Ingredients:
- 25 German brand caramels, unwrapped
- 2 Tbsp half and half
-

Serving Suggestion:
Top with whipped cream and some ground walnuts

Directions: Preheat oven to 350 degrees. Prepare a 9 inch cake pan, ungreased. In a medium bowl, combine crushed cookies with melted butter. Press crust firmly into an 9 inch cake pan. Bake 10 minutes until golden brown. Remove crust from oven and allow to cool for 10 minutes. Prepare the caramel sauce. In a medium saucepan, warm the caramels and the half and half on medium low heat, stirring constantly, until melted, creamy, and combined. Remove from heat and set aside. In the medium bowl, beat cream cheese and marshmallow creme until well blended. Add the egg to the cream cheese mixture and mix well. Stir the chopped cookies into the cream cheese mixture. Pour the cream cheese mixture onto the cooled crust. Drop spoonfuls of the caramel sauce over the cream cheese mixture. Swirl the caramel gently with a knife for a marble effect. Bake 20 - 25 minutes, or until center is set. Remove from oven and cool completely. Refrigerate for 4 hours or overnight. Store leftovers in a container in the refrigerator. Serving suggestion: Top with whipped cream and ground walnuts or peanuts to compliment the flavors!

Try this recipe another way...
+++By making it into a *Chocolate Caramel Cheesecake!* Simply swap the golden sandwich cookies with the chocolate sandwich cookies.
+++By making it into a *Chocolate Raspberry Cheesecake!* Swap the golden sandwich cookies with chocolate sandwich cookies, and, in place of the caramel sauce, use 1/2 cup slightly warmed raspberry preserves.

Churro Crescent Cheesecake Bars
The buttery cinnamon sugar topping gives these creamy bars a welcome crunch!

Cheesecake Ingredients:
- 1 can of crescent dough (8 crescent size)
- 8 oz cream cheese, softened
- 1/2 cup sugar
- 1/2 tsp vanilla
- 1/4 cup sour cream
- 1 large egg

Topping:
- 1/4 cup sugar
- 1/2 Tbsp cinnamon
- 1/4 cup unsalted butter, melted

Directions: Preheat oven to 350 degrees. Prepare an 8 x 8 inch glass pan, ungreased. In the prepared pan, unroll and press in half of the can of crescents. (If dough is perforated, press together to smooth out dough so it is one piece.). Bake in oven for 5 minutes. Remove from oven and set aside. In a medium bowl, mix together cream cheese, sugar, vanilla, sour cream, and egg until smooth. Pour cream cheese mixture onto the bottom crust in the pan. Cover the cream cheese mixture with the other half of the crescent dough. Pour the melted butter for the topping, over the crescent dough. In a small bowl, mix together the sugar and cinnamon for the topping. Sprinkle the cinnamon sugar completely over the melted butter. Bake for 30 minutes. Remove from the oven and cool for 20 minutes. Serve warm, if you would like, or, serve chilled from the refrigerator. Either way, it is wonderfully delicious! Makes 16 bars.

Try this recipe another way...
+++By making a ***Sweet Heat Churro Crescent Cheesecake!*** Add 1/4 tsp of chili powder to the cinnamon sugar topping for a little bit of warming heat.

Feast of St. Ignatius of Loyola (July 31)
Patron saint of soldiers, especially Catholic soldiers.
"If God sends you many sufferings, it is a sign that He has great plans for you, and certainly wants to make you a saint."
Food for the Soul: A disappointment sometimes leads to a spiritual breakthrough.
St. Ignatius of Loyola, pray for us.
Blessed Mother, graciously intercede for us.
Holy Trinity, we adore You! Hear and answer our prayers.

August

August Birthday Cake

Heavenly Swedish Flop Cake

Celebrating a Birthday this month? We are! Try making this Chicago favorite! It's a cream filled coffeecake topped with a buttery streusel topping. My Aunt Bernice used to love this cake! It many not look like a traditional birthday cake, but the taste is worthy of holding a few candles! Ha!

Dough Ingredients:
- 1/3 cup half and half
- 1/3 cup water
- 4 tablespoons unsalted butter, melted
- 1/4 cup sugar
- 1/2 teaspoon salt
- 2 large eggs, room temperature
- 1 teaspoon vanilla extract
- 2 cups all-purpose flour
- 1 package quick-rise yeast

Streusel Ingredients:
- 1/2 cup all-purpose flour
- 1/2 cup sugar
- 4 tablespoons unsalted butter, room temperature

Fluffy Buttercream Filling Ingredients:
- 1/4 cup all-purpose flour
- 1 cup half and half
- 1 cup sugar
- 1/4 teaspoon salt
- 2 sticks unsalted butter, softened, room temperature
- 1 teaspoon vanilla extract

Directions: Make dough in a bread machine on the dough setting. Add half and half, water, melted butter (cooled), sugar, salt, eggs, vanilla, and flour. Make a well in the flour and add the yeast to the well. Make sure to layer the ingredients as listed, adding the yeast last. Set on the dough cycle. Grease a 13x9-inch baking pan. When dough has finished its cycle in the bread machine with the first rising, transfer the dough to the prepared pan; cover with plastic wrap and let rise in a warm place until doubled in size, about 45 minutes. While dough is rising, prepare the fluffy buttercream base so it has time to cool....Whisk the flour, half and half, sugar, and salt in a large saucepan. Cook, whisking constantly, over medium heat until mixture thickens, about 1 - 2 minutes. Remove from heat and allow to cool completely. After the fluffy buttercream's flour mixture has completely cooled, beat 2 sticks of unsalted butter and the vanilla on high speed in a stainless steel bowl until fluffy, about 2 minutes. Add cooled flour mixture; beat until fluffy and mousse-like, another 5 minutes. Preheat oven to 350°. Meanwhile, prepare the streusel. In a bowl, combine flour, sugar and salt. Add softened butter and cut in until coarse crumbs form. After the dough has risen in the pan, remove the plastic wrap and sprinkle the streusel evenly over the dough. Bake on the center rack until edges start to lightly brown, about 25 minutes. Cool in pan. Cut cooled cake into 15 slices. Horizontally cut each slice in half. Thickly spread the fluffy buttercream in between the top and bottom slices. (At this point, you can even spread a little jam of your choice in between as well, if you so choose.) Gently sandwich top and bottom together layers together. Store cake slices covered, in the refrigerator. Keeps fresh for four days. Makes 15 slices.

Feast of St. Alphonsus Liguori (August 1)
Patron saint of confessors, moral theologians, and those who suffer from arthritis.

"He who trusts himself is lost. He who trusts in God can do all things."
Food for the Soul: What are you struggling with?
Trust that God sees you through it successfully!
St. Alphonsus Liguori, pray for us.
Blessed Mother, graciously intercede for us.
Holy Trinity, we adore You! Hear and answer our prayers.

Feast of St. Peter Julian Eymard (August 2)
Holy Saint of God devoted to Christ in the Blessed Sacrament.

"During the days of His mortal life, Jesus was present in one place only. He dwelt in one house only. Few persons were privileged enough to enjoy His presence and listen to His words. But today in the Blessed Sacrament, He is, we may say, everywhere at one and the same time. In a way, His humanity shares the prerogative of His divine immensity which fills all things. Jesus is present in His entirety in an infinite number of temples and in each one of them. Since all the Christians scattered throughout the world are members of His Mystical Body, it does seem necessary that He, as the soul of it, should be everywhere present throughout the whole body, giving it life, and sustaining it in each one of His members."

Food for the Soul: Jesus is everywhere. He is God with us.

St. Peter Julian Eymard, pray for us.
Jesus, in the Blessed Sacrament, have mercy on us.
Blessed Mother, graciously intercede for us.
Holy Trinity, we adore You! Hear and answer our prayers.

Mustard Day (August 2)

Instant Pot Pork Tenderloin Medallions with Honey Mustard Cream Gravy

Mustard is a wonderful complimentary flavor to pork. It's even better when added to a creamy gravy!

Dry Rub Ingredients:
- 1 tsp meat tenderizer
- 1 tsp onion powder
- 1 tsp garlic powder
- 1/2 tsp black pepper
- 1 Tbsp light brown sugar

Ingredients:
- 1 pound pork tenderloin
- 1 cup low sodium chicken broth
- 1 Tbsp unsalted butter, quartered

Honey Mustard Cream Gravy Ingredients:
- 1 Tbsp unsalted butter
- 1 Tbsp flour
- 1 cup half and half
- 2 Tbsps honey Dijon mustard
- 1 - 2 Tbsps honey
- 1/4 tsp garlic powder
- 1/4 tsp onion powder
- Pinch of salt

Pork Tenderloin Directions: Prepare the dry rub: In a small bowl, mix together meat tenderizer, onion powder, garlic powder, black pepper, and brown sugar. On a baking sheet, apply the dry rub to the pork tenderloin. Add the chicken broth to the instant pot. Add the butter cubes into the broth. Place the pork tenderloin in the chicken broth. Close, lock, and seal lid. Set to pressure cook cycle for 3. minutes. (Yes, you read that right! 3 minutes. Trust me, the pork will be cooked perfectly!). After cycle is finished, natural release for 15 minutes. (This is a great time to make the Honey Mustard Cream Gravy.). Then do a quick release for any remaining pressure. Remove lid. Remove pork and place on a platter. Allow pork to rest for 3 minutes. Slice pork into medallions. Spoon Honey Mustard Cream Gravy over the medallions.

Honey Mustard Creamy Gravy Directions: In a small saucepan, melt the butter on medium heat. Add flour to the butter. Mix together and cook for about a minute or two. Slowly add in 1/4 cup of the half and half to the roux, stirring constantly. When the roux is incorporated into the half and half, slowly add the rest of the half and half, stirring constantly. Once the cream sauce is thickened, turn off the heat. Add the mustard and honey to the sauce. Stir to combine. Taste. Add a pinch of salt, if needed. Add a bit more honey or mustard, to achieve desired taste. Pour sauce over the pork tenderloin medallions.

God's Word of the Day (August 3)
"For I know the plans I have for you", declares the Lord, "Plans to prosper you and not to harm you, plans to give you hope and a future."
(Jeremiah 29:11)
Food for the Soul: Digest this truth! Trust in God's plan for your life!
Blessed Mother, graciously intercede for us.
Holy Trinity, we adore You! Hear and answer our prayers.

Feast of St. John Vianney (August 4)
Patron saint of parish priests.
*"We are, each of us, like a small mirror in which
God searches for His reflection."*
Food for the Soul: God is alive within you. Have you encountered Him?
St. John Vianney, pray for us.
Blessed Mother, graciously intercede for us.
Holy Trinity, we adore You! Hear and answer our prayers.

Chocolate Chip Cookie Day (August 4)

My Favorite Chocolate Chip Cookies
*I rarely eat or make chocolate chip cookies,
but when I do, this is my go-to recipe!*

Ingredients:
- 2/3 cup unsalted butter, softened
- 2/3 cup sugar
- 1/2 cup brown sugar
- 1 large egg
- 1 tsp vanilla
- 1 1/2 cups flour
- 12 oz bag of semisweet or milk chocolate chips (or 1/2 bag of each)

Directions: Preheat oven to 325 degrees. Prepare a cookie sheet, lined with parchment paper. In a medium bowl, cream butter and sugars until light and fluffy. Beat in the egg and vanilla. Mix in the flour. Do not overmix. Stir in the chocolate chips. Drop by tablespoonfuls onto the lined cookie sheet. Leave room for the cookies to spread as they bake. Bake for 15 - 17 minutes. Serve warm or completely cooled. Best if eaten the same day!

Try this recipe another way...
+++By making **Walnut Chocolate Chip Cookies!** When adding the chocolate chips, add 3/4 cup chopped walnuts.

God's Word of the Day (August 5)
"But as for me, I watch in hope for the Lord,
I wait for God my Savior; my God will hear me."
(Micah 7:7)
Food for the Soul: God listens to us. Speak to Him.
Blessed Mother, graciously intercede for us.
Holy Trinity, we adore You! Hear and answer our prayers.

God's Word of the Day (August 6)
"Not only so, but we also glory in our sufferings, because we know that suffering produces perseverance; perseverance, character; and character, hope."
(Romans 5:3-4)
Food for the Soul: Try looking at your struggles
with the Light of Jesus shining on them.
Blessed Mother, graciously intercede for us.
Holy Trinity, we adore You! Hear and answer our prayers.

Feast of St. Sixtus II (August 7)
Patron saint of good prosperity of grapes.
"By the power of the Holy Spirit, help us to be quick to believe and unwavering in the profession of our Faith."
Food for the Soul: Christ is our firm foundation.
Let us be like Him, in this way, for those we love.
St. Sixtus II, pray for us.
Blessed Mother, graciously intercede for us.
Holy Trinity, we adore You! Hear and answer our prayers.

Feast of St. Mary MacKillop (August 8)
Patron saint of Australia and the Archdiocese of Brisbane.
*"My heart would sink but for the firm conviction t
hat God's Word can never fail."*
Food for the Soul: "God's Word can never fail." No exceptions.
St. Mary MacKillop, pray for us.
Blessed Mother, graciously intercede for us.
Holy Trinity, we adore You! Hear and answer our prayers.

Feast of St. Dominic (August 8)
Patron saint of astronomers and the Dominican Republic.
*"A man who governs his passions is master of his world.
We must either command them or be enslaved by them.
It is better to be a hammer than an anvil."*
Food for the Soul: Be the hammer. Be in control of you passions rather than be controlled by them. God is your strength!
St. Dominic, pray for us.
Blessed Mother, graciously intercede for us.
Holy Trinity, we adore You! Hear and answer our prayers.

Feast of St. Teresa Benedicta of the Cross (August 9)
**Known as Edith Stein. Patron saint of Europe
and those who have lost parents.**
"If anyone comes to me, I want to lead them to Him."
Food for the Soul: Lead those around you today to Christ.
St. Teresa Benedicta of the Cross, pray for us.
Blessed Mother, graciously intercede for us.
Holy Trinity, we adore You! Hear and answer our prayers.

Feast of St. Lawrence (August 10)
**Martyr. Patron saint of school children,
poor people, cooks, and comedians.**

"Learn, unhappy man, how great is the power of my God; for your burning coals give me refreshment, but they will be your eternal punishment."

Food for the Soul: Holy Martyrs of God, pray for us!

St. Lawrence, pray for us.
Blessed Mother, graciously intercede for us.
Holy Trinity, we adore You! Hear and answer our prayers.

God's Word of the Day (August 11)

"Acknowledge and take to heart this day, that the Lord is God in heaven above and on the earth below. There is no other."
(Deuteronomy 4:39)

**Food for the Soul: There is one Lord, one faith,
one Baptism. Jesus reigns!**

Blessed Mother, graciously intercede for us.
Holy Trinity, we adore You! Hear and answer our prayers.

Feast of St. Jane Frances de Chantal (August 12)
**Patron saint of forgotten people, widows,
and parents who are separated from their children.**

"In prayer, more is accomplished by listening than talking."

**Food for the Soul: Spend some time in silence today with God.
Listen as He speaks to your heart.**

St. Jane Frances de Chantal, pray for us.
Blessed Mother, graciously intercede for us.
Holy Trinity, we adore You! Hear and answer our prayers.

Feast of St. Pontian and St. Hippolytus (August 13)
Pope and martyr. Priest and martyr.

"Fly to the Catholic Church! Adhere to the only faith which
continues to exist from the beginning, that faith
which was preached by Paul and is upheld by the Chair of Peter."
-- St. Hippolytus

**Food for the Soul: Be Christ as a member of His Church.
Make it stronger in His Holy Name.**

St. Pontian, pray for us.
St. Hippolytus, pray for us.
Blessed Mother, graciously intercede for us.
Holy Trinity, we adore You! Hear and answer our prayers.

Feast of St. Maximilian Kolbe (August 14)
**Patron saint of amateur radio operators,
political prisoners, families, and journalists.**

"I prayed very hard to Our Lady to tell me what would happen to me.
She appeared, holding in her hand, two crowns, one white, one red.
She asked if I would like to have them – one was purity, the other for
martyrdom. I said, 'I choose both.' She smiled and disappeared."

Food for the Soul: Love God with all your heart.

St. Maximilian Kolbe, pray for us.
Blessed Mother, graciously intercede for us.
Holy Trinity, we adore You! Hear and answer our prayers.

Feast of the Assumption (August 15)

"We never give more honor to Jesus than when we honor His mother,
and we honor her simply and solely to honor Him all the more perfectly.
We go to her only as a way leading to the goal we seek – Jesus, her Son."
-- St. Louis de Montfort

**Food for the Soul: Through Mary to Jesus.
He listens to His mother's requests.**

St. Louis de Montfort, pray for us.
Mary, Mother of God, graciously intercede for us.
Holy Trinity, we adore You! Hear and answer our prayers.

Potato and Cheese Angel Dumplings

It's hard to find a recipe for feathery, light potato dumplings, but, here they are! I call them "angel" light! Pair them with melted butter and sour cream and you have a warm, comforting side dish or meal...

Ingredients:
- 1/2 cup mashed potatoes
- 1/2 cup whole milk ricotta cheese
- 2 large egg yolks
- 2 Tbsps of margarine, softened
- 1 packet of Splenda
- 1/2 tsp salt
- 1 tsp baking powder
- 3/4 cup flour
- 1/4 cup corn starch

Directions: Fill a medium sized pot two-thirds with water. Bring the water to a rolling boil. Meanwhile, in a medium bowl, combine potatoes and ricotta cheese. Mix in egg yolks, one at a time. Add margarine, Splenda, and salt to the potato/cheese mixture. Stir until combined. Add baking powder, flour and corn starch. Mix in gently. Do not over mix. Allow dumpling mixture to rest for five minutes. Drop dumplings into boiling water, about 2/3 teaspoonful at a time. Dumplings will drop to the bottom of the pot, then float to the top. Allow them to remain in the boiling water a little while longer to cook after they float to the top, before removing them with a slotted spoon. Place boiled dumplings on a wax paper lined platter. Do not pile them on top of each other, they may stick together, place wax paper in between them. After boiling the dumplings, warm them in melted unsalted butter on a frying pan, or store them in the refrigerator. Serve them with sour cream, or lightly sweetened sour cream, if desired. The dumplings will remain fresh in the fridge for a day or two.

Feast of St. Stephen of Hungary (August 16)
**Patron saint of Hungary, bricklayers,
parents who have lost a child, and kings.**

"Be humble in this life, that God may raise you up in the next. Be truly moderate and do not punish or condemn anyone immoderately. Be gentle, so that you may never oppose justice. Be honorable, so that you may never voluntarily bring disgrace upon anyone. Be chaste, so that you may avoid all the foulness of lust like the pangs of death."

Food for the Soul: Be better than you believe yourself to be, for God's glory.

St. Stephen of Hungary, pray for us.
Blessed Mother, graciously intercede for us.
Holy Trinity, we adore You! Hear and answer our prayers.

God's Word of the Day (August 17)

"For everything that was written in the past was written to teach us, so that through the endurance taught in the Scriptures, and the encouragement they provide, we might have our hope."
(Romans 15:4)

**Food for the Soul: Take time to learn God's Word.
He speaks only the Truth.**

Blessed Mother, graciously intercede for us.
Holy Trinity, we adore You! Hear and answer our prayers.

God's Word of the Day (August 18)

"And He that sat upon the throne said, 'Behold, I make all things new.' And He said unto me, "Write: for these words are true and faithful.""
(Revelation 21:5)

**Food for the Soul: Ask Jesus to make you new today;
to become who He wants you to be.**

Blessed Mother, graciously intercede for us.
Holy Trinity, we adore You! Hear and answer our prayers.

Feast of St. John Eudes (August 19)
Patron saint of missionaries.

"I ask you to consider, that our Lord Jesus Christ is your true head and that you are a member of His Body. He belongs to you as the head belongs to the body. All that is His is yours – breath, heart, body, soul, and all His faculties. All of these you must use, as if they belonged to you, so that in serving Him, you may give Him praise, love and glory."

Food for the Soul: Remember today, as we interact with others, we are all a part of the same God. Find His goodness within them.

St. John Eudes, pray for us.
Blessed Mother, graciously intercede for us.
Holy Trinity, we adore You! Hear and answer our prayers.

Feast of St. Bernard of Clairvaux (August 20)
Patron saint of beekeepers, candlemakers, the Knights Templar.

"In dangers, in doubts, in difficulties, think of Mary, call upon Mary. Let not her name depart from your lips, never suffer it to leave your heart. And that you may obtain the assistance of her prayer, neglect not to walk in her footsteps. With her for guide, you shall never go astray; while invoking her, you shall never lose heart; so long as she is in your mind, you are safe from deception; while she holds your hand, you cannot fall, under her protection you have nothing to fear; if she walks before you, you shall not grow weary; if she shows you favor, you shall reach the goal."

Food for the Soul: Pray to the Blessed Mother today. Tell her your worries, share with her your plans, ask for her intercession. And don't forget to tell her you love her.

St. Bernard of Clairvaux, pray for us.
Blessed Mother, graciously intercede for us.
Holy Trinity, we adore You! Hear and answer our prayers.

Bacon Day (August 20)

Fried Bacon

Sometimes I get very impatient when I am cooking bacon! I've tried baking it in the oven, cooking it on a sandwich grill...I kept thinking, there has to be an easier and quicker way! So recently, I bought some thick cut bacon and decided to fry it up in a deep fryer. I was extremely happy with the results!

Ingredients:
- 16 oz thick cut bacon (only use thick cut for best results)
- 1 cup rice flour
- Few tsps brown sugar, white sugar, or Splenda
-

Directions: Preheat the deep fryer to 375 degrees. Prepare a paper towel lined baking sheet. In a shallow bowl, mix together the rice flour and sugar. Cut the slices of bacon in half with kitchen shears. Coat each slice of bacon in the flour mixture. Place bacon on a plate. Add about 5 or 6 slices of bacon into the fryer. In about 20 - 30 seconds, turn the bacon over. Bacon will fry quickly! (Yay!) Watch carefully! When bacon slices are golden brown, remove from fryer and place on the prepared pan. Allow to cool slightly. Eat while still warm.

Feast of St. Pius X (August 21)
Patron saint of First Communicants and pilgrims.
"...nobody ever knew Christ so profoundly as the Blessed Mother did, and nobody can ever be more competent as a guide and teacher of the knowledge of Christ."
Food for the Soul: Ask the Blessed Mother to educate you in your faith. To show you how to pray. To teach you how to say, "Yes" to God.
St. Pius X, pray for us.
Blessed Mother, graciously intercede for us.
Holy Trinity, we adore You! Hear and answer our prayers.

Feast of the Queenship of the Blessed Virgin Mary (August 22)

*"Men do not fear a powerful hostile army,
as the powers of hell fear the name and protection of Mary."
-- St. Bonaventure*

Food for the Soul: Ask the Blessed Mother for her motherly protection.

St. Bonaventure, pray for us.
Mary, Queen of Heaven, graciously intercede for us.
Holy Trinity, we adore You! Hear and answer our prayers.

Feast of St. Rose of Lima (August 23)

Patron saint of Peru and South America.

*"Know that the greatest service that man can offer
to God is to help convert souls."*

**Food for the Soul: Be Christ to those around you. Change their world.
Change their hearts. Bring them to God.**

St. Rose of Lima, pray for us
Blessed Mother, graciously intercede for us.
Holy Trinity, we adore You! Hear and answer our prayers.

Swedish Meatball Day (August 23)

Swedish Meatballs

As I was growing up, I was surrounded by so much love and so much wonderful food! Of course, my Mom, and many of my aunts loved to cook and bake...Aunt Ann, Aunt Charlotte, Aunt Bernice, Aunt Helen, Aunt Jeanie. This meatball recipe is inspired by my Aunt Helen's recipe...

Meatball Ingredients:
- 1 lb ground beef
- 3 oz cream cheese, softened
- 2 Tbsps onion soup mix
- 1/4 tsp nutmeg
- I cup bread crumbs
- 1/4 cup half and half

Gravy Ingredients:

- 2 Tbsps unsalted butter
- 2 Tbsps flour
- 1/2 cup beef broth
- 1/2 cup half and half
- 1 tsp Worcestershire sauce
- 1/2 tsp garlic powder
- 1/2 tsp onion powder
- 1/4 tsp beef powder
- 4 Tbsps sour cream

Directions: Prepare the meatballs. Mix together the cream cheese, onion soup mix, half and half, breadcrumbs, and nutmeg until smooth. Add ground beef and mix until combined. Do not overmix. Shape meat mixture into small, round meatballs. In a large nonstick skillet, add 1 - 2 Tbsps canola oil. Heat on medium heat. Add the meatballs and cook until lightly browned and cooked through. Remove cooked meatballs from pan and place in a large bowl. Set aside. Prepare the gravy. Over medium heat, melt the butter in the same skillet. Add the flour and mix together to make a roux. Add in the beef broth, a little at a time, stirring until the roux is smoothly mixed in to the broth. Add in the half and half. Stir and cook until slightly thickened. Lower the heat to low. Add Worcestershire sauce, garlic powder, onion powder, and beef powder. Stir constantly and heat until well combined. In a small bowl, add the sour cream. Add a few tablespoons of the gravy into the sour cream to incorporate. Add a few more tablespoons of the gravy into the sour cream mixture. Then add the sour cream mixture to the gravy in the pan. Stir. Add in the cooked meatballs and cook on low heat for about 10 - 15 minutes, stirring frequently. Serve over buttered rice, mashed potatoes, or egg noodles.

Care for a light, Swedish Dessert?
*Make a batch of my **Crepes** (next recipe) ahead of time, warm them up in the microwave with some unsalted butter, spoon over some lingonberry preserves, and top with whipped cream! What a Swedish delight!*

Crepes ala Chris

Fluffy, light, thin, delicate pancakes that you can enjoy, savory or sweet, for breakfast, brunch, lunch, or dinner!

Ingredients:
- 1 cup pancake mix (my favorite is the "K" brand)
- 1 cup half and half
- 1/2 cup water
- 1 egg
- 2 Tbsp melted unsalted butter
- 1/2 tsp vanilla

Directions: Place all of the ingredients in a blender. Blend well. Allow crepe batter to rest for 10 - 15 minutes. Heat a 7 - 8 inch nonstick pan to medium heat. Before pouring the batter into the pan, spray it with a nonstick cooking spray. Continue to do this before each crepe. Pour a little less than 1/4 cup of batter into the center of the pan and swirl it in the pan until you have a thin layer of batter that reaches to the edge of the pan. Using a small silicone spatula, loosen the edges all around as the crepe cooks. Check the crepe underneath, and as it gets lightly browned, flip it carefully, so as to not tear it. Cook the crepe for about another 15 seconds, then remove from the pan. This side should only be very lightly cooked. Using wax paper or parchment paper squares in between each crepe (I get one hundred in a package at the dollar store), stack the crepes on a plate. Store in the fridge. Makes 12 - 14 crepes.

To reheat the crepes (I usually have three), I lightly butter them, roll them, and place in the microwave for about 40-60 seconds. For breakfast, I like them with butter, a few drops of lime juice, and sprinkled with some powdered sugar. Then I dip them in some sweetened sour cream. So simple and absolutely delightful! Or try with some jam or top them with your favorite syrup.

Try this recipe another way...
+++By making **Crepes with Scrambled Eggs!** For a hearty breakfast, scramble up some eggs, cheese, onion, and ham and fill the crepes.

+++By making **Chicken ala King Crepes!** For brunch, lunch, or dinner, make the recipe for the creamy chicken filling from my **Chicken Pot Pie (*January 23*)** to fill the crepes. Heat until warm. Top with some shredded cheese.

Feast of St. Bartholomew (August 24)
Patron saint of dermatology, farmers, and plasterers.

"You will be betrayed even by parents and brothers, relatives and friends; and they will put some of you to death. And you will be hated by all for My name's sake."
(Luke 21:16-17)

***Food for the Soul:** Sometimes those we love may betray us. Be mindful, they are not the enemy. They are under the influence of the fallen angel. Pray for them to find the Truth of God.*
St. Bartholomew, pray for us.
Blessed Mother, graciously intercede for us.
Holy Trinity, we adore You! Hear and answer our prayers.

Waffle Day (August 24)

Cinnamon Apple Waffles

Have a few extra apples in your kitchen? Then, whip up some of these waffles using your favorite boxed pancake mix. Easy and delicious!

Ingredients:
- 1 1/4 cups cold water
- 1/4 cup vanilla creamer
- 1 large egg
- 2 Tbsps canola oil
- 2 cups pancake mix
- 1 large apple, peeled and shredded
- 1/2 tsp cinnamon

Directions: Preheat waffle iron. In a medium bowl, add cold water, cream, egg, and oil. Mix together until well blended. Add pancake mix. Stir together until blended. Do not overmix. Add shredded apple and cinnamon. Stir until combined. Pour batter into a 2 cup measuring cup for easy pouring. Using a cooking spray, generously coat the waffle iron. Pour some of the batter onto the hot iron. Cook waffles until steaming stops or until golden brown. Remove from iron and serve, topped with butter and cinnamon sugar, or your favorite toppings/syrup/fruit.

Try this recipe another way...

+++By making *Cinnamon Apple Waffles ala Mode!* Serve these waffles as a special dessert by topping it with my *Cinnamon Apple Ice Cream (February 1)*, some whipped cream, and chopped walnuts.

Carrot Cake Waffles

The flavors of carrot cake in a waffle? That sounds amazing! Make this waffle day a special breakfast day! And don't forget to top them off with a cream cheese icing drizzle! Want to have them for dessert, instead? That's okay, too!

Ingredients:
- 1 1/4 cups cold water
- 1/4 cup vanilla creamer
- 1 large egg
- 2 Tbsps canola oil
- 2 cups pancake mix
- 3 Tbsps carrot baby food
- 2 Tbsps crushed pineapple, well drained
- 1 - 2 Tbsps chopped walnuts
- 3/4 tsp cinnamon

Cream Cheese Icing Drizzle Ingredients:
- 2 Tbsps unsalted butter, softened
- 2 oz cream cheese, softened
- 1/2 cup powdered sugar, sifted
- Vanilla creamer, to thin icing, if needed

Directions: Preheat waffle iron. Prepare cream cheese icing drizzle: In a small bowl, combined butter and cream cheese. Stir in powdered sugar. If needed, thin icing drizzle with just a touch of creamer. Stir until smooth. Set aside. In a medium bowl, add cold water, cream, egg, and oil. Mix together until well blended. Add pancake mix. Stir together until blended. Do not overmix. Add carrots, pineapple, walnuts, and cinnamon. Stir until combined. Pour batter into a 2 cup measuring cup for easy pouring. Using a cooking spray, generously coat the waffle iron. Pour some the batter onto the hot iron. Cook waffles until steaming stops or until golden brown. Remove from iron and serve, topped with some butter and the cream cheese icing drizzle.

God's Word of the Day (August 25)
"Blessed are they that mourn; for they shall be comforted."
(Matthew 5:4)
Food for the Soul: Comfort those who mourn. Be Christ to them.
Blessed Mother, graciously intercede for us.
Holy Trinity, we adore You! Hear and answer our prayers.

God's Word of the Day (August 26)
"Take My yoke upon you, and learn of Me; for I am meek and lowly in heart. And you shall find rest unto your souls. For My yoke is easy, and My burden is light."
(Matthew 11:29-30)
Food for the Soul: Find time to rest in the arms of the Lord today. He will lighten your burdens.
Blessed Mother, graciously intercede for us.
Holy Trinity, we adore You! Hear and answer our prayers.

Feast of St. Monica, Mother of St. Augustine (August 27)
Patron saint of widows, wives, alcoholics, and difficult children.
"Nothing is far from God."
Food for the Soul: God can do all. Everything is possible with Him.
St. Monica, pray for us.
St. Augustine, pray for us.
Blessed Mother, intercede for us.
Holy Trinity, we adore You! Hear and answer our prayers.

Feast of St. Augustine (August 28)
Patron saint of brewers, printers, and theologians.
"God loves each of us as if there were only one of us."
Food for the Soul: You are precious in His sight.
You are special and He loves you.
St. Augustine, pray for us.
St. Monica, pray for us.
Blessed Mother, graciously intercede for us.
Holy Trinity, we adore You! Hear and answer our prayers.

God's Word of the Day (August 29)
"The Spirit of the Lord is upon me, because the Lord has anointed me to proclaim good news to the poor. He has sent me to bind up the brokenhearted, to proclaim freedom for the captives, and a release from darkness for the prisoners."
(Isaiah 61:1)
Food for the Soul: The Spirit empowers us to do what God requires us to do, in His Name.
Blessed Mother, graciously intercede for us.
Holy Trinity, we adore You! Hear and answer our prayers.

God's Word of the Day (August 30)
"But in your hearts, revere Christ as Lord. Always be prepared to give an answer to everyone who asks you to give the reason for the hope that you have. But do this with gentleness and respect."
(1 Peter 3:15)
Food for the Soul: Share your faith with others. Gently.
Blessed Mother, graciously intercede for us.
Holy Trinity, we adore You! Hear and answer our prayers.

God's Word of the Day (August 31)

"To them, God has chosen to make known among the Gentiles, the glorious riches of this mystery, which is Christ in you, the hope of glory."
(Colossians 1:27)

Food for the Soul: It's like not knowing you have a super power when you do not know Jesus Christ. He has so many wonderful gifts for those who love, acknowledge, and worship Him.

Blessed Mother, graciously intercede for us.
Holy Trinity, we adore You! Hear and answer our prayers.

September

September Birthday Cake

Walnut Cinnamon Crunch Apple Cake

Are you celebrating a birthday this month? Then celebrate with this yummy cake! It's actually based on the old recipe for "Friendship Bread", but, without using a starter. I decided to add in a shredded apple, so there would be no worries about larger pieces of chopped apples not being tender. These flavors embrace the warming flavors of the upcoming fall. Apples, cinnamon, walnuts, unite together for a comforting dessert experience!

Cake Ingredients:
- 1/3 cup canola oil
- 1/3 cup half and half
- 1 large egg
- 1/4 tsp vanilla
- 3/4 cup sugar
- 1 1/3 cup + 2 Tbsps flour
- 3/4 tsp baking powder
- 1/4 tsp baking soda
- 1/4 tsp salt
- 1 tsp cinnamon
- 1 large apple, peeled and shredded

Crunch Topping Ingredients:
- 2 Tbsps unsalted butter, cold
- 1/4 cup light brown sugar
- 1/4 cup flour
- 1/3 cup ground walnuts
- 1/4 tsp cinnamon

Directions: Preheat oven to 350 degrees. Prepare pan: 8 x 8 inch glass pan, oiled. In a medium bowl, combine oil, half and half, egg, and vanilla. Add sugar, mix until blended. Add in flour, baking powder, baking soda, salt, and cinnamon. Mix until blended. Do not overmix. Stir in shredded apple. Pour batter into the prepared pan. Prepare the crunch topping: In a food processor, add the butter, flour, and sugar. Pulse until coarse crumbs. Place crumbs in a small bowl. Add in nuts and cinnamon. Stir until well combined. Top batter, evenly, with the crumb mixture. Bake for 30 minutes. Remove from oven and cool. Cut into 16 slices. Can be served warm or completely cooled. Top off a warm slice with my **Apple Cinnamon Ice Cream (February 1)** or a cooled slice with fresh, whipped cream and a sprinkle of cinnamon..

Labor Day
(First Monday of September)
"Whenever you begin any good work, you should first of all make a most pressing appeal to Christ, our Lord, to bring it to perfection."
-- St. Benedict
Food for the Soul: Sometimes we get so excited about our new plans, we forget to seek Jesus! Pray to Him about your endeavors. He loves to be included in your life.
St. Benedict, pray for us.
Blessed Mother, graciously intercede for us.
Holy Trinity, we adore You! Hear and answer our prayers.

God's Word of the Day (September 1)
"But seek first His kingdom and His righteousness, and all these things will be given to you, as well.
(Matthew 6:33)
Food for the Soul: Place God first in all you do today.
Blessed Mother, graciously intercede for us.
Holy Trinity, we adore You! Hear and answer our prayers.

God's Word of the Day (September 2)
"In the same way, let your light shine before others, that they may see your good deeds and glorify your Father in heaven."
(Matthew 5:16)
Food for the Soul: Shine with the Light of Jesus!
Blessed Mother, graciously intercede for us.
Holy Trinity, we adore You! Hear and answer our prayers.

Coconut Day (September 2)

Coconut Cream Pie

Paul and I, on occasion, do enjoy a great coconut cream pie! By using a premade shortbread pie crust, it makes it even easier to prepare!

Ingredients:
- 1 1/4 cup half and half
- French Vanilla pudding mix
- 1/2 tsp coconut extract
- 1 1/2 cups toasted coconut
- 1/2 container of cool whip
- Premade shortbread pie crust (can be found near the premade graham cracker crusts)

Directions: In a large nonstick skillet, toast 1 1/2 cups of coconut to a golden brown. Stir constantly. Be careful not to burn. Remove from heat and set aside to cool. In a medium bowl, mix half and half with pudding mix and coconut extract. Fold the cool whip into the pudding mixture. Add the toasted coconut to the pudding mixture, reserving a little to sprinkle on top of the finished pie. Pour the mixture into the pie crust. Sprinkle with a little toasted coconut. Refrigerate for at least an hour or two before serving.

Try this recipe another way...
+++By making ***Chocolate Coconut Cream Pie!*** Substitute the shortbread crust with a premade chocolate crust. Substitute the vanilla pudding mix with a chocolate pudding mix. Omit the coconut extract.

Feast of St. Gregory the Great (September 3)
Patron saint of teachers, musicians, and singers.

"If we are, in fact, now occupied in good deeds, we should not attribute the strength with which we are doing them to ourselves. We must not count on ourselves, because even if we know what kind of person we are today, we do not know what we will be tomorrow."

Food for the Soul: Take no credit for yourself.
Give all credit, and glory, to God.
St. Gregory the Great, pray for us.
Blessed Mother, graciously intercede for us. Holy Trinity, we adore You!
Hear and answer our prayers.

Feast of St. Rose of Viterbo (September 4)
Patron saint of people in exile.
"I die with joy, for I desire to be united to my God. Live so as not to fear death. For those who live well in the world, death is not frightening, but sweet and precious."
Food for the Soul: Live a life that seeks to be united with God.
This will be your joy, now and forever.
St. Rose of Viterbo, pray for us.
Blessed Mother, graciously intercede for us.
Holy Trinity, we adore You! Hear and answer our prayers.

Feast of St. Teresa of Calcutta (September 5)
Patron saint of World Youth Day, Missionaries of Charity, Archdiocese of Calcutta.
"Pain and suffering have come into your life, but remember pain, sorrow, suffering are but the kiss of Jesus – a sign that you have come so close to Him that He can kiss you."
Food for the Soul: Offer your struggles today to Jesus.
St. Teresa of Calcutta, pray for us.
Blessed Mother, graciously intercede for us.
Holy Trinity, we adore You! Hear and answer our prayers.

God's Word of the Day (September 6)
"Do unto others as you would have them do to you."
(Luke 6:31)
Food for the Soul: Be His hands. Be His feet.
Blessed Mother, graciously intercede for us.
Holy Trinity, we adore You! Hear and answer our prayers.

Coffee Ice Cream Day (September 6)

Coffee and Cream Dream
A refreshing ice cream beverage to make at home! It's a coffee lovers dream!

Ingredients:
- 1 cup coffee ice cream
- 1 cup cold coffee
- 1 can of whipped cream
- Cinnamon

Directions: In a blender, mix together the ice cream and the coffee. When smooth, add about 1/2 cup of the canned whipped cream. Pulse to combine. Pour mixture into a glass. Top with more whipped cream. Top with a sprinkle of cinnamon.

God's Word of the Day (September 7)
"The thief comes only to steal, kill, and destroy;
I have come that they may have life, and have it to the full."
(John 10:10)
Food for the Soul: Choose life. Choose Jesus.
Blessed Mother, graciously intercede for us.
Holy Trinity, we adore You! Hear and answer our prayers.

God's Word of the Day (September 8)
"I am the Good Shepherd. The Good Shepherd
lays down His life for the sheep."
(John 10:11)
**Food for the Soul: Thank Jesus today for
His protection, His Mercy, His love.**
Blessed Mother, graciously intercede for us.
Holy Trinity, we adore You! Hear and answer our prayers.

Feast of St. Peter Claver (September 9)
Patron saint of African missions and interracial justice.
"Seek God in all things and you shall find God by your side."
Food for the Soul: When we seek God, we will find Him.
St. Peter Claver, pray for us.
Blessed Mother, graciously intercede for us. Holy Trinity, we adore You!
Hear and answer our prayers.

God's Word of the Day (September 10)
"Jesus looked at them and said, 'With man, this is impossible, but with God, all things are possible.'"
(Matthew 19:26)
Food for the Soul: God does the impossible.
He does what no man can do.
Blessed Mother, graciously intercede for us.
Holy Trinity, we adore You! Hear and answer our prayers.

God's Word of the Day (September 11)
"Then Jesus declared, 'I am the Bread of Life. Whoever comes to Me will never go hungry, and whoever believes in Me, will never be thirsty.'"
(John 6:35)
Food for the Soul: Bread of Life, feed our hungry souls.
Blessed Mother, graciously intercede for us.
Holy Trinity, we adore You! Hear and answer our prayers.

God's Word of the Day (September 12)
"Do not judge, or you, too, will be judged."
(Matthew 7:1)
Food for the Soul: Lord, help me to withhold my judgement of others.
Blessed Mother, graciously intercede for us.
Holy Trinity, we adore You! Hear and answer our prayers.

Feast of St. John Chrysostom (September 13)
Patron saint of epileptics, lecturers, and preachers.
*"Let us not hesitate to help those who have died
and to offer our prayers for them."*
**Food for the Soul: Begin the habit to pray, each morning and each
night, for those who have died. They need our prayers.**
*St. John Chrysostom, pray for us.
Blessed Mother, graciously intercede for us.
Holy Trinity, we adore You! Hear and answer our prayers.*

Feast of the Exaltation of the Cross (September 14)
*"The Cross is the Father's Will, the glory of the Only Begotten,
the joy of the Spirit, the pride of the angels, the guarantee of the Church,
Paul's boast, the bulwark of the saints, and the light of the entire world."
-- St. John Chrysostom*
**Food for the Soul: Look for the image of the cross today in the most
ordinary places, and be reminded, each time, of the great love our
Lord Jesus Christ has for you! Rejoice in His victory!**
*St. John Chrysostom, pray for us.
Blessed Mother, graciously intercede for us.
Holy Trinity, we adore You! Hear and answer our prayers.*

Cream Filled Donut Day (September 14)

Easy Cream Filled Donuts

If you would like, you could use my Perfect Paczki dough recipe to make the dough for this recipe, but if you want to save a lot of time, use some canned biscuits instead! Just fill them up with my fluffy buttercream filling and enjoy!

Fluffy Buttercream Filling Ingredients:
- 1/4 cup all-purpose flour
- 1 cup half and half
- 1 cup sugar
- 1/4 teaspoon salt
- 2 sticks unsalted butter, softened, room temperature
- 1 teaspoon vanilla extract
- 1 can buttermilk biscuits

Directions: Prepare the buttercream filling so it has time to cool: Whisk the flour, half and half, sugar, and salt in a large saucepan. Cook, whisking constantly, over medium heat until mixture thickens, about 1 - 2 minutes. Remove from heat and allow to cool completely. After the flour mixture has completely cooled, beat 2 sticks of unsalted butter and the vanilla on high speed in a stainless steel bowl until fluffy, about 2 minutes. Add cooled flour mixture; beat until fluffy and mousse-like, another 5 minutes. Set aside. Preheat deep fryer to 360 degrees. Prepare pans: You will need one cookie sheet lined with paper towel and one cookie sheet lined with wax paper. Remove the biscuits from the can and place on the wax papered cookie sheet. Flatten biscuits slightly, so they are not too thick, especially in the middle, so they will cook through. One by one, place them in the fryer, no more than four at a time. Turn each biscuit over to fry the other side. Remove from fryer when they are golden brown. Place on paper towel lined baking sheet. Allow donuts to cool completely. Cut each horizontally, and fill with the buttercream. Place the donut top on top and sprinkle with some powdered sugar.

Serving suggestion:
You can also spread a thin layer of jam to each side of the donut before you add the buttercream filling!

Try this recipe another way...
+++By making **Jelly Donuts!** Substitute the buttercream filling for your favorite jam, jelly or preserves.

+++By making **Frosted Donuts!** Forget the filling and make some donuts. After you flatten the biscuit dough, cut out a small hole in the middle of the biscuit. Fry up the donuts and the donut holes. Dip the tops of the donuts into the **Donut Frosting** (2 Tbsps melted unsalted butter, 2 Tbsps vanilla creamer, 1 cup powdered sugar) and serve!

God's Word of the Day (September 15)
"No one can serve two masters. Either you will hate the one and love the other, or you will be devoted to the one and despise the other. You cannot serve both God and money."
(Matthew 6:24)
Food for the Soul: Are there other things that are the masters of our lives? See them as the distractions they are! Seek and honor God, and God alone.
Blessed Mother, graciously intercede for us.
Holy Trinity, we adore You! Hear and answer our prayers.

Feast of St. Cornelius (September 16)
Patron saint of earaches.
"God is One and Christ is One, His Church is One, His See is One, founded by the voice of the Lord on Peter."
Food for the Soul: Choose to live as one in the Lord.
St. Cornelius, pray for us.
Blessed Mother, graciously intercede for us.
Holy Trinity, we adore You! Hear and answer our prayers.

Feast of St. Robert Bellarmine (September 17)
Patron saint of religious education.

"Know that you have been created for the glory of God and your own eternal salvation. This is your goal; this is the center of your life; this is the treasure of your heart."

Food for the Soul: Do you ever wonder why you were born? Now you know. Place both of these goals as your life's focus.

St. Robert Bellarmine, pray for us.
Blessed Mother, graciously intercede for us.
Holy Trinity, we adore You! Hear and answer our prayers.

God's Word of the Day (September 18)

"Therefore, I tell you, do not worry about your life, what you will eat or drink; or about your body, what you will wear. Is not life more than food, and the body more than clothes?"

(Matthew 6:25)

Food for the Soul: Today, focus less on on the material and more on the spiritual.

Blessed Mother, graciously intercede for us.
Holy Trinity, we adore You! Hear and answer our prayers.

Feast of St. Januarius (September 19)
Patron saint of Naples. Bishop and martyr.

"But I tell you, love your enemies and pray for those who persecute you."

(Matthew 5:44)

Food for the Soul: Pray for those who may give you a difficult time today.

St. Januarius, pray for us.
Blessed Mother, graciously intercede for us.
Holy Trinity, we adore You! Hear and answer our prayers.

Feast of St. Andrew Kim Tae-Gôn (September 20)
Martyr. Patron saint of North Korea.
*"I am willing to lay down my life for the Lord.
Eternal life is about to begin for me."*
**Food for the Soul: Are you ready to lay down your life for God?
Is your soul ready to enter into eternal life?**
St. Andrew Kim Tae-Gôn, pray for us.
Blessed Mother, graciously intercede for us.
Holy Trinity, we adore You! Hear and answer our prayers.

Feast of St. Matthew (September 21)
Gospel writer and evangelist. Patron saint of financial matters and bankers.
"Afterward, Jesus went out and looked for a man named Matthew. He found him sitting at his tax booth, for he was a tax collector. Jesus said to him, 'Be My disciple and follow Me.' That very moment, Matthew got up, left everything behind, and followed Him."
(Luke 5:27-32)
**Food for the Soul: Are you ready to leave what
you have to follow Jesus?**
St. Matthew, pray for us.
Blessed Mother, graciously intercede for us.
Holy Trinity, we adore You! Hear and answer our prayers.

God's Word of the Day (September 22)
"For where your treasure is, there your heart will also be."
(Matthew 6:21)
**Food for the Soul: Meditate on what the treasure of your heart is.
Does your focus need to change?**
Blessed Mother, graciously intercede for us.
Holy Trinity, we adore You! Hear and answer our prayers.

Feast of St. Padre Pio da Pietrelcina (September 23)
Patron saint of civil defense volunteers and adolescents.

"Pray, hope, and don't worry. Worry is useless. God is merciful and will hear your prayer. Prayer is the best weapon we have; it is the key to God's heart."

Food for the Soul: Unite with God in prayer.
Know that God is listening and acting on your behalf.

St. Padre Pio da Pietrelcina, pray for us.
Blessed Mother, graciously intercede for us.
Holy Trinity, we adore You! Hear and answer our prayers.

First Day of Autumn
Pumpkin Spiced Biscuits

One day I had a taste for a treat with the flavors of pumpkin spice, but didn't have a lot of time. I thought, why not make some biscuits? So, I did! A great biscuit to welcome in the flavors of autumn.

Ingredients:
- 2 1/4 cups flour
- 6 Tbsps unsalted butter
- 1 Tbsp baking powder, heaping
- 1 tsp salt
- 3/4 cup canned pumpkin
- 1/2 cup sour cream
- 1/4 cup vanilla creamer, or half and half
- 3/4 cup powdered sugar
- 1 Tbsp pumpkin pie spice, heaping
- 1 tsp cinnamon

Directions: Preheat oven to 450 degrees. Prepare pan: Line a baking sheet with parchment paper. In a food processor, pulse together the flour and butter. Place in a medium bowl. Stir in baking powder and salt. Set aside. In a small bowl, mix together the pumpkin, sour cream, and creamer. Add powdered sugar, pumpkin spice and cinnamon. Stir together until well blended. Add pumpkin mixture to the flour mixture. Stir until well blended, but do not overmix. On a nonstick cookie sheet, pat the dough into a square. Cut into 9 squares. Place biscuits onto the parchment lined baking sheet. Place the biscuits in the fridge for 5 - 10 minutes. Remove from fridge. Brush the tops of the biscuits with some half and half or creamer, and top with cinnamon sugar. Place in the oven. Bake for 13 minutes. Remove from oven and allow to cool for about 5 minutes. Break biscuits open and serve warm with whipped butter, honey butter, or cinnamon sugar butter.

God's Word of the Day (September 24)

"Therefore, I tell you, whatever you ask for in prayer, believe that you have received it, and it will be yours."
(Mark 11:24)
Food for the Soul: Believe in the amazing power of God!
Blessed Mother, graciously intercede for us.
Holy Trinity, we adore You! Hear and answer our prayers.

God's Word of the Day (September 25)

"And when you stand praying, if you hold anything against anyone, forgive them, so that your Father in Heaven may forgive you your sins."
(Mark 11:25)
Food for the Soul: Forgive. It will set you free.
Blessed Mother, graciously intercede for us.
Holy Trinity, we adore You! Hear and answer our prayers.

Feast of St. Cosmas and St. Damian (September 26)
Brothers. Patron saints of physicians and surgeons.
"Contemplate how these brothers (Cosmas and Damian) imitated Christ by healing the whole person, both body and soul."
-- St. Pius X
Food for the Soul: Take care of those close to you, body and soul.
St. Pius X, pray for us.
St. Cosmas, pray for us.
St. Damian, pray for us.
Blessed Mother, graciously intercede for us.
Holy Trinity, we adore You! Hear and answer our prayers.

Feast of St. Vincent de Paul (September 27)
Priest and patron saint of charities and volunteers.

"However great the work that God may achieve by an individual, he must not indulge in self-satisfaction. He ought to be all the more humbled, seeing himself merely as a tool, which God has made use of."

Food for the Soul: How does God want to use you today? Allow Him to do so.

St. Vincent de Paul, pray for us.
Blessed Mother, graciously intercede for us.
Holy Trinity, we adore You! Hear and answer our prayers.

Feast of St. Wenceslaus (September 28)
**King of Bohemia, killed at age 22 by his brother.
Patron saint of Bohemia and former Czechoslovakia.**

"May God forgive you, brother."

Food for the Soul: Forgive those who have trespassed against you. Everyday.

St. Wenceslaus, pray for us.
Blessed Mother, graciously intercede for us.
Holy Trinity, we adore You! Hear and answer our prayers.

St. Michael, St. Gabriel and St Raphael (September 29)
St. Michael is the patron saint of the police,
grocers, bankers, and soldiers.
St. Gabriel is the patron saint of messengers,
communicators, and postal workers.
St. Raphael is the patron saint of the blind,
of happy meetings, nurses, physicians, and travelers.

Prayer to St. Michael
*St. Michael, the archangel, defend us in battle.
Be our protection against the wickedness and snares of the devil.
May God rebuke him, we humbly pray, and do thou,
O prince of the Heavenly Host, by the divine power of God,
cast into hell, Satan and all evil spirits
who roam about the world seeking the ruin of souls. Amen.*

Food for the Soul: The powers of God shine through His Angels. Seek their light! Call to them for help.
*St. Michael, the archangel, pray for us.
St. Gabriel, the archangel, pray for us.
St. Raphael, the archangel, pray for us.
All the Holy Angels of God, pray for us, guide us, and protect us.
Blessed Mother, graciously intercede for us.
Holy Trinity, we adore You! Hear and answer our prayers.*

Feast of St. Jerome (September 30)
Patron saint of translators and librarians.
"The Scriptures are shallow enough for a babe to come and drink, without fear of drowning, and deep enough for theologians to swim in, without ever reaching the bottom."
Food for the Soul: All are welcome to approach our God, to live in His light. He presents Himself to everyone.
*St. Jerome, pray for us.
Blessed Mother, graciously intercede for us.
Holy Trinity, we adore You! Hear and answer our prayers.*

October

October Birthday Cake

Carrot Pineapple Cake With Cream Cheese Frosting

Celebrating a Birthday this month? We are! This is one of Paul's favorite birthday cakes! It's moist, spiced, and bursting with flavor, covered in a tangy, not-too-sweet, smooth, cream cheese frosting.

Cake Ingredients:
- 3/4 cup canola oil
- 2 large eggs
- 1 tsp vanilla
- 1 cup light brown sugar, firmly packed
- 6 oz baby food carrots
- 1 small can of crushed pineapple, drained
- 1 cup flour
- Pinch of salt
- 1 tsp baking soda
- 1 tsp ground cinnamon
- 1/2 cup sweetened coconut flakes (optional)
- 1/2 cup chopped walnuts (optional)

Cream Cheese Frosting Ingredients:
- 4 oz cream cheese, softened
- 4 Tbsps unsalted butter, softened
- 1/2 tsp vanilla
- Between 1 1/2 cups and 2 cups of powdered sugar, sifted

Directions: Preheat oven to 350 degrees. Lightly oil a 9 inch round cake pan. In a medium bowl, combine oil, eggs, and vanilla. Add brown sugar. Mix well. Add carrots and pineapple. Stir well. Add flour, salt, baking soda, and cinnamon. Stir well. If you would like, stir in the optional ingredients, coconut flakes and chopped walnuts. Pour batter into prepared pan. Bake for 30 minutes. Remove from oven and cool for 10 minutes. Then, place a plate over the pan and invert pan to remove the cake. Cool cake completely. When cake is completely cooled, prepare the cream cheese frosting. In a small bowl, cream together the butter and cream cheese until smooth and creamy. Add vanilla. Mix well. Add 1 1/2 cups powdered sugar. Mix together well. Taste. Add more powdered sugar, little by little, if you prefer a sweeter frosting, up to a total of 2 cups. Frost the cake with the frosting. Refrigerate for an hour before serving. Store cake in refrigerator.

Octoberfest

__Instant Pot Brats__

*These are the most tender, juicy brats ever!
Cook plenty; your guests will be asking for more!*

Ingredients:
- 1 cup apple juice (adds a slightly sweeter taste), or beer (adds a slightly bitter taste), low sodium chicken broth, or water
- 1 package of Johnsonville brats

Directions: Add apple juice, beer, or low sodium chicken broth to the instant pot. Poke brats with fork several times before adding into the pot. Set instant pot to high heat on the "Meat" setting for 15 minutes. When cycle is finished, natural release for 15 minutes. Serve on bun with sautéed onions (try cooking the onions in a little apple juice or beer), mustard, and tangy **Instant Pot Onion Apple Kraut (next recipe).**

Instant Pot Onion Apple Kraut

This kraut has just enough sweet and sour to have you asking for another serving! Serve it beside some fresh Polish sausage, or use it as a topping for a brat or a hotdog!

Ingredients:
- One 14 ounce can of sweet Bavarian sauerkraut
- 1/2 cup of low sodium chicken broth
- 2 small Granny Smith apples, peeled and shredded
- One small onion, thinly sliced
- 1/4 tsp garlic powder
- 1/4 tsp onion powder
- 1 tsp brown sugar
- 1 Tbsp unsalted butter, before serving

Directions: Add all of the ingredients into the instant pot. Stir. Set the instant pot to "Pressure Cook" on high for fifteen minutes. Natural release for fifteen minutes. Strain most of the liquid from the kraut and serve. Add a tablespoon of unsalted butter. Stir until melted into the kraut. Serve

Apple Strudel

Don't forget to end your Octoberfest meal with some apple strudel! Crispy layers of buttery pastry wrapped around tender apples. I even add some ground walnuts and cinnamon sugar in between the layers for a little extra flavor.

Ingredients:
- 1 can of apple pie filling
- 1/4 cup golden raisins (optional)
- 10 sheets of phyllo dough, 5 per strudel
- 1 stick unsalted butter, melted, or more, if needed
- 1/3 cup ground walnuts
- 3/4 cup cinnamon sugar

Directions: Preheat the oven to 375 degrees. Prepare a large baking sheet with parchment paper. Keep a moist cloth over the phyllo dough while preparing the strudel, so the dough does not dry out. In a small bowl, pour in the apple pie filling. With some kitchen shears, cut the apples into small pieces. Then, add the raisins, if desired. Stir the filling. Set aside. In a small bowl, mix together the cinnamon sugar and the ground walnuts. Brush the parchment paper with melted butter. Place a sheet of the dough on the parchment paper. Brush the melted butter on the phyllo dough. Sprinkle some of the nut/sugar mixture onto the dough. Top with another sheet of dough. Brush with the butter, sprinkle with the nut/sugar mixture. Repeat with all the phyllo layers. Place the filling on the dough, on the first third side of the dough, lengthways, about 1 1/2 inches from the edge, using half of the amount of the filling. Roll the dough upwards, jelly roll style, using the parchment paper to help begin the roll up. Once rolled, place seam side down, and brush the top with melted butter. Top with nut/sugar mixture. Make the second strudel in the same way. Bake strudels for 20 minutes, until golden brown. Remove from oven. Cool completely. Slice with a serrated knife. Sprinkle powdered sugar on top.

Feast of St. Thérèse of Lisieux (October 1)
Patron saint of aviators, florists, illnesses, and missions.
"May you trust God that you are exactly where you are meant to be."
Food for the Soul: *At this moment, you are essential to God's plan, wherever you are.*
St. Thérèse of Lisieux, pray for us.
Blessed Mother, graciously intercede for us.
Holy Trinity, we adore You! Hear and answer our prayers.

Homemade Cookie Day (October 1)

Brandy Butter Cookie

As I was searching throughout my cookbooks, deciding on which recipes would be included in this book, I came across a recipe that I had never made. I had cut it out of a newspaper, probably about 30 - 40 years ago! As I read through the recipe, I was intrigued by two of the ingredients in this cookie -- brandy and cooked egg yolks. Curiosity got the best of me, and I knew it was finally time to give it a try! Paul and I were very happy with the result! It was soft in the center and a little crisp on the edges. Buttery, not too sweet, with a hint of that peach brandy flavor. Great with a cup of coffee.I dipped the tops in sugar, but I think the next time I make them, I will dip the tops in cinnamon sugar to compliment the brandy flavor more, adding some extra warmth....

Ingredients:
- 2 sticks of unsalted butter, warmed until almost melted
- 1 cup powdered sugar
- 1/4 cup peach brandy (or any brandy or rum you may have)
- 2 tsps lime juice
- 3 large egg yolks, cooked from boiled eggs, mashed
- 2 1/4 cups flour
- 1/2 tsp salt

Cookie Topping:
- Sugar or cinnamon sugar in a small bowl, your choice

Directions: Make the hard boiled the eggs. Cool. Peel. Place the yolks in a small bowl. Mash yolks and set aside. Preheat oven to 375 degrees. Prepare a cookie sheet with parchment paper. In a medium bowl, add in the butter. Warm until nearly melted. Add powdered sugar, brandy and cooked egg yolks. Stir until well combined. Add in flour and salt. Stir until combined. Spoon out a teaspoonful of dough and roll it into a ball. Dip the top of the ball into the cinnamon sugar. Place dough on cookie sheet, sugar side up. Press the dough down with three fingers. Continue forming and sugaring the rest of the cookies. (They do not spread on the pan very much.) Bake for 10 - 12 minutes, until edges are golden brown. Remove from oven. Place on wax paper to cool. Store in a cookie tin. Makes about 4 1/2 dozen.

Feast of the Holy Guardian Angels (October 2)
Guardian Angel Prayer
Angel of God, my guardian dear, to whom God's love commits me here, ever this day be at my side, to light and guard, rule and guide. Amen.
Food for the Soul: Pray to your guardian angel each morning and night.
Holy Angels of God, guard and protect us.
Blessed Mother, graciously intercede for us.
Holy Trinity, we adore You! Hear and answer our prayers.

Saint Quote of the Day (October 3)
"Our guardian angels are our most faithful friends, because they are with us, day and night, always and everywhere. We ought often to invoke them."
-- St. John Vianney
Food for the Soul: Throughout your day, call upon the Angels of God.
St. John Vianney, pray for us.
Holy Angels of God, watch over and protect us.
Blessed Mother, graciously intercede for us.
Holy Trinity, we adore You! Hear and answer our prayers.

Feast of St. Francis of Assisi (October 4)
Patron saint of animals, the environment, and merchants.
"Sanctify yourself and you will sanctify society."
Food for the Soul: Be holy. Bring holiness to wherever you go.
St. Francis of Assisi, pray for us.
Blessed Mother, graciously intercede for us.
Holy Trinity, we adore You! Hear and answer our prayers.

Cinnamon Roll Day (October 4)

<u>Pumpkin Cinnamon Rolls</u>

*Simply delightful in taste and texture!
How nice it would be to serve them for Halloween or Thanksgiving morning!*

Dough Ingredients:
- 1/4 cup sugar
- 3/4 tsp salt
- 1/4 cup melted butter, cooled
- 3/4 cup half and half
- 1 large egg
- 3/4 cup pumpkin purée
- 2 Tbsps pumpkin pie spice
- 4 cups bread flour
- 1 package of instant yeast

Cinnamon Filling Ingredients:
- 1/4 cup unsalted butter, softened
- 2/3 cup light brown sugar, firmly packed
- 1 1/2 Tbsps ground cinnamon

Cream Cheese Frosting Ingredients:
- 4 oz cream cheese, softened
- 3 Tbsps unsalted butter, softened
- 1/2 tsp vanilla
- 1/4 cup powdered sugar, sifted (to taste)

Directions: Using a bread machine, add roll ingredients; sugar, salt, melted butter, half and half, egg, pumpkin purée, pumpkin pie spice, and bread flour, in that exact order. Make a well in the bread flour. In the well, add the instant yeast. Set on "dough" cycle. In a small bowl, mix together the light brown sugar and cinnamon. Set aside. When bread dough cycle is finished, punch down dough. Place dough on a baking sheet and roll out into a rectangle. For the filling, spread softened butter on dough. Top butter with cinnamon mixture. Roll dough, jelly roll style. (Larger side up. Place seam side down.). Cut into 12 rolls. Place rolls, spirals facing upwards, in 2 rows of 6, on an oiled 9 x 13 inch glass pan. Cover pan with plastic wrap and allow rolls to rise for about an hour. About 50 minutes later, preheat oven to 350 degrees. When dough has risen, remove plastic wrap and place pan in the oven for 20 - 25 minutes. Remove from oven and cool rolls in pan for 10 minutes. While rolls are cooling, in a small bowl, combine cream cheese and butter until smooth. Add vanilla. Stir together. Add powdered sugar and combine until creamy. Taste. If not sweet enough, add a little more powdered sugar, adding a teaspoonful at a time. Top warm rolls with the cream cheese frosting. Serve while warm.

Cinnamon Roll Biscuits

Sometimes you just don't want to wait around for those delicious flavors!

Ingredients:
- 1/4 cup canola oil
- 3/4 cup half and half
- 2 cups flour, sifted
- 1 Tbsp baking powder
- 1 tsp salt
- 1/4 tsp baking soda

Filling Ingredients:
- 1 stick of unsalted butter, softened
- 3/4 cups brown sugar
- 1 tsp cinnamon

Icing Ingredients:
- 3 Tbsps unsalted butter, melted
- 3 oz cream cheese, softened
- 1 1/4 cup powdered sugar, sifted
- 1/4 tsp cinnamon
- 1/2 tsp vanilla

Directions: Preheat oven to 400 degrees. Oil a 9 inch cake pan. In a medium bowl, mix together the canola oil and the half and half. In another bowl, sift together the flour, baking powder, baking soda, and salt. Add the dry ingredients to the oil mixture. Combine. Do not overmix. In a small separate bowl, mix together the filling ingredients; butter, brown sugar, and cinnamon. Roll out the biscuit dough to a 15 x 8 inch rectangle. Spread the filling ingredients over the dough. Roll the dough, like a jelly roll, rolling up from the longer side of the dough. Cut slices, 1 1/2 inch thick. Place slices in the prepared pan. Bake at 400 degrees for 15 minutes. Mix the icing ingredients together while the biscuits are baking. Remove biscuits from oven. Top biscuits with icing immediately. Allow to cool for 5 minutes. Serve warm.

Feast of St. Faustina, Saint of Divine Mercy (October 5)

Apostle of Mercy. Patron saint of mercy and gratitude in the family.
"One thing alone sustains me and that is Holy Communion. From it I draw all my strength; in it is all my comfort. Jesus concealed in the Host is everything to me. I would not know how to give glory to God if I did not have the Eucharist in my heart."
Food for the Soul: The Holy Eucharist teaches us, directs us, embraces us, loves us.
St. Faustina, pray for us.
Jesus, our Redeemer, have mercy on us.
Blessed Mother, graciously intercede for us.
Holy Trinity, we adore You! Hear and answer our prayers.
Jesus, we trust in You.

Feast of St. Bruno (October 6)

Patron saint of exorcists and possessed persons.
"While the world changes, the Cross stands firm."
Food for the Soul: The Holy Cross, of simple wood, is our greatest source of strength.
St. Bruno, pray for us.
Blessed Mother, graciously intercede for us.
Holy Trinity, we adore You! Hear and answer our prayers.

Feast of Our Lady of the Holy Rosary (October 7)

"When the Holy Rosary is said well, it gives Jesus and Mary more glory and is more meritorious than any other prayer."
-- St. Louis de Montfort

Food for the Soul: Pray the Holy Rosary.
St. Louis de Montfort, pray for us.
Holy Mary, Mother of God, graciously intercede for us.
Holy Trinity, we adore You! Hear and answer our prayers.

Taco Day (October 7)

Taco Pan Pizza
Quick prep and easily customizable. Great for dinner or for a game day!

Ingredients:
- 1 can of refrigerated pizza dough or crescent dough
- 1 lb ground beef, cooked and drained
- 8 oz tomato sauce, garlic flavored
- 1 envelope of taco seasoning mix
- 1 cup cheddar or Colby jack cheese, freshly grated

Topping Suggestions:
- 1 small package of shredded lettuce
- 2 small vine tomatoes, diced
- 1 small sweet onion, diced
- 1-2 ripe avocados, diced
- Sour cream

Directions: Preheat oven to 425 degrees. Generously oil a 9 x 13 inch pan. Cook ground beef in a large nonstick skillet over medium heat. Brown lightly and drain. Add the tomato sauce and taco seasoning mix to the cooked beef. Stir until combined. Heat on medium low heat for 10 minutes, stirring occasionally. Press the pizza dough in to fit the pan. Make sure the dough comes up the sides a bit. Spoon the beef mixture on top of the dough. Sprinkle cheese on top of the beef mixture. (Add extra cheese, if you desire.). Bake in the oven for 15 - 20 minutes. Remove from the oven. Rest for a few minutes. Cut into large squares. Have everyone top their own slice with lettuce, tomato, onion, avocado, and/or sour cream.

Saint Quote of the Day (October 8)

"When tempted, invoke your angel. He is more eager to help you than you are to be helped. Ignore the devil and do not be afraid of him; he trembles and flees at the sight of your Guardian Angel."
-- St. John Bosco

Food for the Soul: Experiencing some difficulties? Call upon your Guardian Angel. He is close to your soul.

St. John Bosco, pray for us.
Angels of God, guard and protect us.
Blessed Mother, graciously intercede for us.
Holy Trinity, we adore You! Hear and answer our prayers.

Delicate Butter Cookies

Another version of the butter cookie, but this one is one of Paul's favorites! We may celebrate his October birthday with these, too!

Ingredients:
- 1 1/2 sticks unsalted butter, softened
- 3/4 cup powdered sugar, sifted
- 1 cup flour, sifted
- 1/2 tsp vanilla

Directions: Preheat oven to 325 degrees. Prepare cookie sheet, lined with parchment paper. In a medium bowl, sift together flour and powdered sugar. Add butter and mix until combined. Add vanilla and combine. Drop by teaspoonfuls onto cookie sheet. Cookies will spread, so leave an inch in between. Bake for 15 - 18 minutes, until edges are lightly browned. Carefully remove from pan when cool.

Feast of St. Denis (October 9)
**Bishop and Martyr. One of the Holy Helpers.
Patron of France and Paris.**
"If you are insulted because of the name of Christ, you are blessed, for the Spirit of glory and of God rests on you."
(1 Peter 4:14)
***Food for the Soul: Stand strong for the Holy Trinity.
Stand for Love, Peace, Joy, and Hope!***
*Blessed Mother, graciously intercede for us.
Holy Trinity, we adore You! Hear and answer our prayers.*

Saint Quote of the Day (October 10)
*"How great is the dignity of souls, that each person has, from birth, received an angel to protect it."
— St. Jerome*
***Food for the Soul: Your soul is precious to God.
Praise Him for His angels sent to protect it.***
*St. Jerome, pray for us.
Holy Angels of God, guard and protect us.
Blessed Mother, graciously intercede for us.
Holy Trinity, we adore You! Hear and answer our prayers.*

Feast of St. John XXII (October 11)
Patron saint of papal delegates and the Second Vatican Council
"Consult not your fears but your hopes and your dreams. Think not about your frustrations, but about your unfulfilled potential. Concern yourself not with what you tried and failed in, but with what is still possible for you to do."
Food for the Soul: Move forward. Hopes and dreams deal with the future. Unshackle yourself of the past.
*St. John XXII, pray for us.
Blessed Mother, graciously intercede for us.
Holy Trinity, we adore You! Hear and answer our prayers.*

Saint Quote of the Day (October 12)
"Make yourself familiar with the angels, and behold them frequently in spirit. Without being seen, they are present with you."
-- St. Francis de Sales

Food for the Soul: Speak with the angels throughout your day. They are near. They will do God's Will.

St. Francis de Sales, pray for us.
Holy Angels of God, guard and protect us.
Blessed Mother, graciously intercede for us.
Holy Trinity, we adore You! Hear and answer our prayers.

Saint Quote of the Day (October 13)
"Beside each believer stands an Angel as protector and shepherd, leading him to life."
-- St. Basil the Great

Food for the Soul: Angels of God, lead me to the path of Eternal Life.

St. Basil the Great, pray for us.
Holy Angels of God, guard and protect us.
Blessed Mother, graciously intercede for us.
Holy Trinity, we adore You! Hear and answer our prayers.

Feast of St. Callistus I (October 14)
Pope and martyr. Patron saint of cemeteries.

"Do not fear any of those things which you are about to suffer. Indeed, the devil is about to throw some of you in prison, that you may be tested, and you will have tribulation ten days. Be faithful until death, and I will give you the crown of life."
(Revelation 2:10)

Food for the Soul: You may be tested today. Hold firm in your faith. Stand on the Mighty Rock.

St. Callistus I, pray for us.
Blessed Mother, graciously intercede for us.
Holy Trinity, we adore You! Hear and answer our prayers.

Feast of St. Teresa of Avila (October 15)
Patron saint of headaches, migraines, those who are ill, and those who are ridiculed for their religious faith.
"Though you have recourse to many saints as your intercessors, go especially to St. Joseph, for he has great power with God."
Food for the Soul: Pray to St. Joseph often. Share your concerns with him. Ask him to intercede on your behalf.
St. Teresa of Avila, pray for us.
St. Joseph, pray for us.
Blessed Mother, graciously intercede for us.
Holy Trinity, we adore You! Hear and answer our prayers.

Feast of St. Hedwig (October 16)
Patron saint of the poor and those in debt.
"The greater one is by birth, the greater one must be in virtue, and the more distinguished we are in station, the more we must distinguish ourselves by our conduct, in order to be a bright example to others."
Food for the Soul: Much is expected of those who have been given many gifts of the Spirit. Use those gifts to bring others to God.
St. Hedwig, pray for us.
Blessed Mother, graciously intercede for us.
Holy Trinity, we adore You! Hear and answer our prayers.

Feast of St. Ignatius of Antioch (October 17)
Patron of spiritual retreats.
"I wish, not only merely to be called Christian, but to be Christian."
Food for the Soul: Be a follower of Christ. Act on God's behalf.
St. Ignatius of Antioch, pray for us.
Blessed Mother, graciously intercede for us.
Holy Trinity, we adore You! Hear and answer our prayers.

Feast of St. Luke (October 18)
Evangelist. Gospel writer. Patron saint of painters.
"Most Blessed are you among women, and blessed is the fruit of your womb."
(Verse about the Blessed Mother, found in the Gospel of St. Luke, 1:42)
Food for the Soul: Share the Good News today!
St. Luke, pray for us.
Blessed Mother, graciously intercede for us.
Holy Trinity, we adore You! Hear and answer our prayers.

Feast of St. Paul of the Cross (October 19)
Saint who promoted the memory of the Passion of Jesus Christ.
"As soon as we know the Will of God, we ought, without delay, to follow it."
Food for the Soul: Seek God to discover the plans He has for your life. It will lead you to peace and joy as you bring His plans to fruition.
St. Paul of the Cross, pray for us.
Blessed Mother, graciously intercede for us.
Holy Trinity, we adore You! Hear and answer our prayers.

Sweetest Day/Anniversaries

Flourless Chocolate Cake
If you are looking for a rich, decadent dessert to share with the one you love, you've found it! An incredibly smooth and creamy, chocolate delight!

Ingredients:
- 1 1/4 cup semisweet chocolate chips
- 1 stick unsalted butter
- 2/3 cup sugar
- 3/4 tsp salt
- 1 tsp vanilla
- 3 large eggs + 1 egg yolk
- 1/2 cup Dutch processed cocoa powder
- 1/2 cup heavy cream

Directions: Preheat oven to 350 degrees. Prepare a 9 inch round pan. Oil the sides and bottom. Place a parchment paper round on the bottom. Oil the parchment paper. Set aside. In a medium bowl, melt chocolate chips and butter together in the microwave, cooking at 30 second intervals and stirring until melted. Add salt, sugar, and vanilla. Cool slightly. Add in the eggs, one at a time, whisking after each. Add in cocoa powder. Whisk together again. In a small, cold, metal bowl, add in heavy cream. Beat cream with an immersion blender into medium peaks. Fold into chocolate mixture. Pour mixture into pan. Smooth the top. Bake for 25 - 30 minutes or until cake is a little puffed and edges are set. It's okay if the center is still a bit wobbly. Cool for 10 minutes. Loosen the edges. Cool completely. Cover and refrigerate for at least 6 hours before slicing and serving. Serve, topped with whipped cream. You can freeze slices, too!

Saint Quote of the Day (October 20)

"If you remembered the presence of your angel and the angel of your neighbors, would avoid many of the foolish things which slip into your conversations."
-- St. Josemaría Escrivá

Food for the Soul: Think before you speak.
Allow your angel to guide your conversations.

St. Josemaría Escrivá, pray for us.
Holy Angels of God, guard and protect us.
Blessed Mother, graciously intercede for us.
Holy Trinity, we adore You! Hear and answer our prayers.

Saint Quote of the Day (October 21)

"Apart from the Cross, there is no other ladder by which we may get to heaven."
-- St. Rose of Lima

Food for the Soul: Gaze upon the crucifix.
Unite with Jesus in His sufferings.

St. Rose of Lima, pray for us.
Holy Angels of God, guard and protect us.
Blessed Mother, graciously intercede for us.
Holy Trinity, we adore You! Hear and answer our prayers.

Feast of St. John Paul II (October 22)
Patron saint of families.

"It is Jesus that you see when you dream of happiness; He is waiting for you when nothing else you find satisfies you; He is the beauty to which you are so attracted; it is He who provoked you with that thirst for fullness that will not let you settle for compromise; it is He who urges you to shed the masks of a false life; it is He who reads in your hearts your most genuine choices, the choices that others try to stifle."
Food for the Soul: Jesus, You are my joy! You are my everything.
St. John Paul II, pray for us.
Blessed Mother, graciously intercede for us.
Holy Trinity, we adore You! Hear and answer our prayers.

Feast of St. John of Capistrano (October 23)
Priest and patron saint of military chaplains and jurists.

"Those who are called to the table of the Lord must glow with the brightness that comes from the good example of a praiseworthy and blameless life. They must learn from the eminent Teacher, Jesus Christ...
'You are the light of the world.' (Matthew 5:14). Now, a light does not illumine itself, but instead, it diffuses its rays and shines all around upon everything that comes into its view."
Food for the Soul: Be His Light! Shine for Jesus today!
St. John of Capistrano, pray for us.
Blessed Mother, graciously intercede for us.
Holy Trinity, we adore You! Hear and answer our prayers.

Feast of St. Anthony Mary Claret (October 24)
Patron saint of weavers.

"Whenever I see sinners, I grow restless, I cannot quiet down, I cannot be consoled, my heart goes out to them."
Food for the Soul: Pray for all sinners to find their way back to Christ.
St. Anthony Mary Claret, pray for us.
Blessed Mother, graciously intercede for us.
Holy Trinity, we adore You! Hear and answer our prayers.

Saint Quote of the Day (October 25)
"God is the brightest of lights, which can never be extinguished, and the choirs of angels radiate light from the divinity. Angels are pure praise without any trace of a bodily deed."
-- St. Hildegard of Bingen

Food for the Soul: God's radiant light shines to His angels. As His children, we are His light in the world. Let us shine brightly and lead all to Him.

St. Hildegard of Bingen, pray for us.
Holy Angels of God, guard and protect us.
Blessed Mother, graciously intercede for us.
Holy Trinity, we adore You! Hear and answer our prayers.

Feast of St. Alfred the Great (October 26)
Patron saint of learning, the arts, and literature.
"Ah, what shall I be at fifty, should nature keep me alive, if I find the world so bitter when I am but twenty-five?"

Food for the Soul: Bitterness will get us nowhere. Replace it with the Hope of the Lord.

St. Alfred the Great, pray for us.
Blessed Mother, graciously intercede for us.
Holy Trinity, we adore You! Hear and answer our prayers.

Chicken Alfredo Pizza
This is a great dinner to make when you have some leftover chicken...

Pizza Dough Ingredients:
- 1 cup water
- 1 Tbsp + 1 tsp sugar
- 1 tsp salt
- 2 Tbsps canola or olive oil
- 3 cups flour
- 1 package of instant yeast

Alfredo Sauce Ingredients:
- 2 cups heavy cream
- 1 stick unsalted butter
- 1 cup Parmesan cheese, freshly grated

Pizza Topping Ingredients:
- 2 cups shredded chicken
- 1 medium onion, thinly sliced, cooked in butter and a few tsps of water, until tender
- 2 sweet peppers, sliced into thin strips, oiled and cooked until tender in air fryer (optional)
- 1 1/2 cups of low moisture mozzarella cheese, freshly grated

Directions for Pizza Dough: Prepare dough for crust: Using a bread machine, add water, sugar, salt, oil, and flour, in that order, in the pan. Make a well in the flour. Place the yeast in the well. Set to the "dough" cycle. Dough will be ready to use as soon as the cycle is finished, no need to raise a second time.

Directions for Alfredo Sauce: Combined cream and butter in a medium saucepan. Stirring constantly, cook on medium heat until slightly thickened. Add Parmesan cheese to sauce. Stir constantly until cheese is melted and sauce is creamy.

Pizza Assembly Directions: Preheat oven to 415 degrees. Oil a 14 inch round pizza pan. Stretch the dough and press onto the pizza pan. With a fork, poke some holes in the bottom of the dough. Spread some Alfredo sauce onto the dough. Sprinkle a little mozzarella cheese on top of the sauce. Scatter on some cooked onion slices. Add the shredded chicken. Scatter some cooked sweet pepper slices and a few more onion slices on top of the chicken. Top with mozzarella cheese. Finish with a sprinkle of a little grated Parmesan cheese. Brush the crust with some melted salted butter. Bake for 20 - 22 minutes. Remove from oven and brush with melted butter. Allow pizza to rest for 5 minutes. Cut into slices and serve.

Try this recipe another way!
+++By making **Chicken Roasted Garlic Alfredo Pizza!** Substitute the traditional Alfredo Sauce for some **Roasted Garlic Alfredo Sauce**! Take a head of garlic and cut off the top so you can see the inside of the garlic cloves. Place the head of garlic in a piece of foil. Surround the head of garlic with the foil. Pour a tablespoon of canola oil, or more, over the head. Lightly salt and pepper. Wrap the head in the foil. Place in the air

fryer for 15 - 20 minutes at 370 degrees. Remove from the fryer, opening the foil carefully, being careful of any steam. Cool the garlic for 5 - 10 minutes. Squeeze the cloves of the garlic head into a small bowl and mash the garlic. Add the amazing, fragrant, roasted garlic to the Alfredo sauce.
+++By substituting the peppers for spinach (or in addition to!)
+++By substituting the chicken for turkey!
+++By using some sautéed spinach instead of the sweet peppers (or in addition to)!

World Series

Caramallow Salted Peanut Cups
"Take me out to the ballgame. Take me out with the crowd. Buy me some peanuts..."Get your peanuts! Everyone knows that peanuts go hand-in-hand with a great baseball game! These bite-sized cups are filled with marshmallow crème and silky caramel, then topped with chopped salted peanuts. They are based on one of my favorite candy bars from years gone by...but, by placing those candy flavors within that buttery crust, it's a thousand times better!

Crust Ingredients:
- 1 stick unsalted butter, softened
- 3 oz cream cheese, softened
- 1 cup flour

Filling Ingredients:
- 7 oz marshmallow crème
- 50 German caramels, unwrapped
- 3 Tbsps half and half
- 1 1/2 cups salted cocktail peanuts, finely chopped

Directions: Preheat oven to 350 degrees. Prepare mini muffin tins ready for 24 mini tarts. Prepare the crust: In a medium bowl, cream together the butter and 3 oz cream cheese. Stir the flour into the butter mixture. Do not overmix. Divide dough into 24 balls. Mold each ball into each of the 24 mini muffin tins. Bake tart crusts for 10 - 15 minutes, or until golden brown. Remove from oven. Cool tart crusts completely. Place a spoonful of marshmallow crème in each tart. In a medium saucepan, melt the caramels and the half and half. Stir until smooth and creamy. Place a spoonful of melted caramel sauce on top of the marshmallow crème. Top each tart generously with a spoonful of finely chopped peanuts. Store at room temperature.

Saint Quote of the Day (October 27)
"God is humanity's universal teacher and guardian, but his teaching to humanity is mediated by angels."
-- St. Thomas Aquinas
Food for the Soul: Angels of Heaven, teach us the ways of God.
St. Thomas Aquinas, pray for us.
Holy Angels of God, guard and protect us.
Blessed Mother, graciously intercede for us.
Holy Trinity, we adore You! Hear and answer our prayers.

Saint Quote of the Day (October 28)
"At the orders of the Queen, the angels frequently assisted the apostles in their travels and tribulations...The angels often visited them in visible shapes, conversing with them and consoling them in the name of the most blessed Mary."
-- St. Mary of Agreda
Food for the Soul: Mary, Queen of the Angels, come to our aid.
St. Mary of Agreda, pray for us.
Angels of God, guard and protect us.
Blessed Mother, graciously intercede for us.
Holy Trinity, we adore You! Hear and answer our prayers.

Chocolate Day (October 28)
Fabulous Fudge!
For me, this is the ultimate fudge recipe! It's like eating chocolate butter! Yum!

Ingredients:
- 12 oz semisweet chocolate chips
- 12 oz milk chocolate chips
- 26 large marshmallows
- 2 sticks unsalted butter
- 1 cup half and half
- 1 tsp vanilla
- 4 cups sugar

Directions: Oil a 12 x 15 inch foil pan, or, for thicker fudge, a 9 x 13 inch foil pan. Set aside. In a large pot, cook butter, milk, and sugar, and vanilla on medium heat to a rolling boil. Boil for 2 minutes, stirring constantly. Turn off heat. Add marshmallows. Stir until marshmallows are melted and well incorporated together with the milk mixture. Add chocolate chips. Stir until melted and well incorporated into the marshmallow mixture. Pour fudge mixture into the prepared pan. Refrigerate for 2 hours. Cut into 4 large squares. Wrap squares in plastic wrap and place squares in a gallon size freezer bag so fudge does not dry out. Cut smaller squares when you are ready to serve. Store fudge in the refrigerator.

Saint Quote of the Day (October 29)
"I have great reverence for St. Michael the Archangel; he had no example to follow in doing the will of God, and yet, he fulfilled God's Will faithfully."
-- St. Faustina Kowalska

Food for the Soul: Pray to St. Michael today.
He is our protector and defender.
St. Faustina Kowalska, pray for us.
Holy Angels of God, guard and protect us.
Blessed Mother, graciously intercede for us.
Holy Trinity, we adore You! Hear and answer our prayers.

Saint Quote of the Day (October 30)

"Those closest to God in heaven, the seraphim, are called the fiery ones because, more than the other angels, they take their fervor and ardor from the intense fire of God."
-- St. Robert Bellarmine

Food for the Soul: May we, too, be fiery for God!
Holy Angels of God, guard and protect us.
St. Robert Bellarmine, pray for us.
Blessed Mother, graciously intercede for us.
Holy Trinity, we adore You! Hear and answer our prayers.

Saint Quote of the Day (October 31)

"Let us be like the holy angels, now...If one day, we are to be in the angelic court, we must learn, while we are still here, the manners of the angels."
-- St. Vincent Ferrer

Food for the Soul: Learn how to pray. Learn God's Word. Learn about the saints and angels. Prepare now for your future life in Heaven.
St. Vincent Ferrer, pray for us.
Holy Angels of God, guard and protect us.
Blessed Mother, graciously intercede for us.
Holy Trinity, we adore You! Hear and answer our prayers.

Halloween (October 31)
Caramel Apples

Make these addictive, gourmet quality, gooey, creamy Caramel Apples with your choice of salty toppings from your own kitchen!

Ingredients:
- 6-7 medium sized Granny Smith apples (or your favorite kind of apple)
- 1 package of soft caramels, unwrapped (20 oz. package, German brand)
- 6 Tbsp of half and half
- 2 cups of assorted mixed salted nuts, roughly chopped (or crushed salted pretzels)
- 6-7 wooden popsicle sticks

Directions: Remove the stems from the apples. Insert the sticks into the apples. Heat 1 1/2 cups of water in a two cup measuring cup in the microwave, until boiling. One by one, swirl the apples in the boiling water for about twenty seconds. Wipe off and dry the apples well with a paper towel to remove the waxy coating and all of the water on the apples. Place the apples in the freezer for at least 15 minutes. Chop the nuts and place them in a medium sized bowl. Prepare a medium sized cookie sheet by lining it with parchment paper. Place it in the fridge. Unwrap the caramels and place them in a medium sized pot. Add in the half and half. Heat on medium low heat, until caramel is melted and a little bubbly. Stir constantly! Remove the pot from the heat and let the caramel cool slightly, for about three minutes.

Remove the apples, one at a time, from the freezer to dip. Tilt the pot of caramel and swirl the apple in the caramel, covering the whole apple with the caramel. Return the pot to the warm burner, with the heat still off. This will keep the caramel from cooling too much. Allow excess caramel to drip off the apple back into the pot. Then, hold the apple upside down, twirling the apple as you hold it. Wait about one minute before dipping the apple into the nuts, allowing the caramel on the apple to cool slightly. Lightly press the bottom of the apple into the nuts. With your hand, scoop and press the nuts up the sides of the apple until it is completely covered. Gently mold the nuts and caramel onto the apple. Place the apple on the parchment paper lined cookie sheet that you have in the fridge. Repeat the process with the other apples. If the caramel cools too much and becomes too thick, heat it up slightly once again. Allow to cool for three minutes. Continue dipping the rest of the apples. Allow the caramel apples to set for at least a half hour in the fridge. Then, slice 'em up and eat 'em up! They will keep fresh in the fridge for about two weeks, but I doubt if there will still be any left by then!

Try coating the Caramel Apples with crushed pretzels instead of nuts!

November

November Birthday Cake

Cranberry Orange Pound Cake

Celebrating a Birthday this month? We are!Orange and cranberry are definitely the stars of this cake, along with the addition of sour cream, which creates a perfectly moist crumb.

Ingredients:
- 1 1/2 cups unsalted butter, softened
- 2 1/2 cups sugar
- 1 tsp vanilla
- 1 tsp orange zest, freshly grated
- 6 large eggs
- 3 cups flour
- 1 tsp baking powder
- 1/2 tsp salt
- 8 oz sour cream
- 1 1/2 cups fresh cranberries, chopped

Directions: Preheat oven to 350 degrees. Generously oil and flour a 12 cup tube pan. (You can also use a Bundt pan, but they often only hold 10 cups; you can always make cupcakes or a small loaf with the extra batter.). In a large bowl, cream butter and sugar until light and fluffy. Add in vanilla and orange zest. Add in one egg at a time, beating well after each addition. In a medium bowl, combine flour, baking powder, and salt. Stir together with a fork to sift dry ingredients. Add flour mixture to butter mixture alternately with the sour cream. Mix well after each addition. Gently stir in cranberries. Pour batter into prepared pan(s). Bake for 65 - 75 minutes or until toothpick inserted in center comes out clean. Remove from oven. Cool for 15 minutes in the pan. Then, place a large plate over the cake and invert cake onto the plate. When completely cooled, dust with powdered sugar.

Try this recipe another way...

+++By making a **Blueberry Lemon Pound Cake!** Substitute the cranberries with whole blueberries, (coated in flour so they don't sink to the bottom). Instead of the orange zest, use lemon zest.

Feast of All Saints (November 1)
Food for the Soul: We are all called to become Holy Saints of God. Today, we celebrate those who have gone before us; those whom have achieved their heavenly goal!
We also take time to proclaim our belief. Our belief in God the Father, the Son, and the Holy Spirit. Our rejection of Satan, of all his works, and of all his empty promises. We acknowledge our belief in the Holy Catholic Church, the communion of the saints, the forgiveness of sins, the resurrection of the body, and life everlasting. Yes, Lord, we believe! And we believe that one day we shall see Your glorious Face and bask in Your most awesome presence. Yes, Lord, we believe!
"The saints are like the stars. In His providence, Christ conceals them in a hidden place that they may not shine before others when they might wish to do so. Yet, they are always ready to exchange the quiet contemplation for the works of mercy as soon as they perceive in their heart the invitation of Christ."
-- St. Anthony of Padua
Food for the Soul: Shine for God like a "hidden star" today.
St. Anthony, pray for us.
All the Holy Saints of God, pray for us.
Blessed Mother, graciously intercede for us.
Holy Trinity, we adore You! We thank You! Hear and answer our prayers.

All Souls' Day (November 2)

Pray for the Holy Souls in Purgatory everyday. They are grateful to those who pray for them, and when these souls arrive in heaven, they will pray for those who prayed for them.

"The blessed souls in purgatory are the Lord's eternal spouses."
— St. Alphonsus Maria de Liguori

Food for the Soul: Pray for the souls of all your family members and friends who have gone before you. They require your prayers now, more than ever.

Eternal rest, grant unto them, O Lord, and let Perpetual Light shine upon them. May the souls, and all the souls of the faithful departed, through the mercy of God, rest in peace. Amen.

O my Jesus, forgive us our sins. Save us from the fires of hell. Lead all souls to heaven, especially those who are most in need of Thy mercy. Amen.

St. Alphonsus Maria de Liguori, pray for us.
Blessed Mother, graciously intercede for us.
Holy Trinity, we adore You! We thank You! Hear and answer our prayers.

God's Word of the Day (November 3)

"Give thanks to the Lord, for He is good; His love endures forever."
(1 Chronicles 16:34)

Food for the Soul: Throughout your day, thank God for all His goodness!

Blessed Mother, graciously intercede for us.
Holy Trinity, we adore You! We thank You! Hear and answer our prayers.

Sandwich Day (November 3)

Monte Chris-to Sandwich

Patience and planning are required with this delectable sandwich...but it's well worth the wait! This sandwich delivers with crunchy, warm, melty goodness! My friend, Michelle, loves it!

Sandwich Ingredients:
- 6 slices of Brioche bread
- 6 slices of ham
- 6 slices of turkey
- 6 slices of American cheese (or your favorite)

About 3 hours before you want to eat, begin the sandwich preparation:
On each slice of bread, layer a slice of cheese, a slice of turkey, and a slice of ham. Put two together to form a sandwich. Press down on the sandwich with your hand to flatten the bread. Wrap each sandwich in some Saran Wrap and place in the fridge for about 3 hours. (Please don't skip this step! The sandwiches will fall apart in the fryer if you do.)
After three hours, prepare the batter and preheat your deep fryer to 360 degrees.
Batter Ingredients:
- 1 cup buttermilk pancake mix (I prefer the one that begins with "K")
- 2/3 cup water

Directions: Mix the pancake mix with the water. Feel free to add a little more water (but not too much!) until the batter has a consistency for a sandwich coating. One at a time, dip the sandwiches into the batter and completely coat the bread. Place carefully (the sandwiches will be heavy!) into the deep fryer, frying one at a time until golden brown. Place on a paper towel lined cookie sheet. Cut the sandwiches in fours on a diagonal. Sprinkle with powdered sugar. Serve with honey mustard and seedless raspberry jam. Makes 3 sandwiches.

Feast of St. Charles Borromeo (November 4)
Patron saint of bishops, cardinals, catechists, and seminarians.
"We must meditate before, during, and after everything we do. The prophet says: 'I will pray, and then I will understand.' This is the way we can easily overcome the countless difficulties we have to face day after day, which, after all, are part of our work. In meditation, we find the strength to bring Christ to birth in ourselves and in others."
Food for the Soul: Pray throughout your work day.
Understand what God requires of you.
St. Charles Borromeo, pray for us.
Blessed Mother, graciously intercede for us.
Holy Trinity, we adore You! We thank You! Hear and answer our prayers.

Election Day
(First Tuesday after the first Monday of the month)
Food for the Soul: Our pope was recently asked whom Americans should vote for president in this election year. He was rather vague and answered that we should vote for the "lesser evil". Of course, the candidates, and all of us, are imperfect. That is a given. We all do wrong things and say wrong things. How can we really calculate which of the two is the "lesser of two evils"? The more I prayed about it, God clarified to me how we should vote every Election Day:
Vote for the person whose policies do not encourage and promote others to sin.
"If anyone causes one of these little ones–those who believe in Me– to stumble, it would be better for them to have a large millstone hung around their neck and to be drowned in the depths of the sea."
(Matthew 18:6)
Holy Trinity, bless our country. Bless our world.
Bless our leaders. Guide them in Your Ways.
Blessed Mother, graciously intercede for us.
Holy Trinity, we adore You! We thank You! Hear and answer our prayers.

God's Word of the Day (November 5)
"Give thanks in all circumstances;
for this is God's Will for you in Christ Jesus." (1 Thessalonians 5:18)
Food for the Soul: Thank God for His presence in your life!
Blessed Mother, graciously intercede for us.
Holy Trinity, we adore You! We thank You! Hear and answer our prayers.

Feast of St. Theophane Venard (November 6)
A French Catholic missionary to Vietnam, martyred for the faith.
"Be merry, really merry. The life of a true Christian should be
a perpetual jubilee, a prelude to the festivals of eternity."
Food for the Soul: Be a joyful Christian! Celebrate God with your life!
St. Theophane Venard, pray for us.
Blessed Mother, graciously intercede for us.
Holy Trinity, we adore You! We thank You! Hear and answer our prayers.

God's Word of the Day (November 7)
"By Him, therefore, let us offer the sacrifice of praise to God continually,
that is, the fruit of our lips giving thanks to His name. But to do good and to
communicate, forget not, for with such sacrifices, God is well pleased."
(Hebrews 13:15-16)
Food for the Soul: Give thanks to God, simply, for Who He Is.
Blessed Mother, graciously intercede for us.
Holy Trinity, we adore You! We thank You! Hear and answer our prayers.

Feast of St. Elizabeth of the Trinity (November 8)
Patron saint of those who are sick and
those who have lost their parents.
"Receive every trial, every annoyance, every lack of courtesy in the light
that springs from the Cross; that is how we please God,
how we advance in the ways of love."
Food for the Soul: In any setbacks today, be mindful of the glory
and promises of the Holy Cross.
St. Elizabeth of the Trinity, pray for us.
Blessed Mother, graciously intercede for us.
Holy Trinity, we adore You! We thank You! Hear and answer our prayers.

God's Word of the Day (November 9)
"And whatever you do, whether in word or deed, do it all in the name of the Lord Jesus, giving thanks to God the Father through Him."
(Colossians 3:17)
Food for the Soul: Offer all you do today in the Name of Jesus, with a thankful and joyful heart.
Blessed Mother, graciously intercede for us.
Holy Trinity, we adore You! We thank You! Hear and answer our prayers.

God's Word of the Day (November 10)
"Devote yourselves to prayer, being watchful and thankful."
(Colossians 4:2)
Food for the Soul: Pray your way through your day!
Blessed Mother, graciously intercede for us.
Holy Trinity, we adore You! We thank You! Hear and answer our prayers.

Feast of St. Martin of Tours (November 11)
Patron saint of France and St. Martin's University.
"Lord, if your people need me, I will not refuse the work. Your Will be done."
Food for the Soul: Allow God to lead you to what He desires you to do.
St. Martin of Tours, pray for us.
Blessed Mother, graciously intercede for us.
Holy Trinity, we adore You! We thank You! Hear and answer our prayers.

Veteran's Day (November 11)
"Lord, if Your people still have need of my services, I will not avoid the toil. Your Will be done. I have fought the good fight long enough. Yet, if You bid me, continue to hold the battle line in defense of Your camp, I will never beg to be excused from failing strength. I will do the work You entrust to me. While You command, I will fight beneath Your banner."
-- *St. Martin of Tours*
Food for the Soul: Embrace the work God has set before you; embrace it with your whole heart.
St. Martin of Tours, pray for us.
Blessed Mother, graciously intercede for us.
Holy Trinity, we adore You! We thank You! Hear and answer our prayers.

Chris-py Oven Roasted Baby Potatoes

I've tried quite a few roasted potato recipes along the way, but none have ever given the crispy/creamy potato results like this recipe does!

Ingredients:
- 1 1/2 lbs baby red potatoes
- 1 tsp garlic powder
- 1 tsp onion powder
- 1 tsp salt
- 1/2 tsp black pepper
- Canola or olive oil

Directions: Preheat the oven to 425 degrees. Prepare the pan: A large, heavy rimmed baking sheet lined with foil. Place pan on the center rack of the 425 degree oven and leave there for 30 minutes. Prepare the seasoning mix for the potatoes. In a small bowl, combine garlic powder, onion powder, salt, and pepper. Mix thoroughly. Set aside. Prepare the potatoes. Scrub, rinse, and dry them. Cut each potato in half, and each half in quarters. Place these quarters in a large bowl. Toss the cut potatoes with enough oil to generously coat them. Toss seasoning mix with the potatoes. Toss until completely coated. Put on oven mitts!!! Quickly remove the hot pan in the oven and pour the potatoes onto the pan. Make sure the potatoes are in an even layer. Put oven mitts on!!! Place the hot pan back on the center rack of the oven and close the oven door. Roast potatoes for 15 minutes. Stir potatoes once. Roast for 15 more minutes, until the potatoes are well browned and tender when pierced with a fork. Remove from oven and serve immediately for the crispest results.

Feast of St. Josaphat of the Day (November 12)
Patron saint of the Ukraine.

"Lord Jesus Christ, Son of God, have mercy on me, a sinner."
Food for the Soul: Ask Jesus for His Divine Mercy to be upon you, everyday.
St. Josaphat, pray for us.
Blessed Mother, graciously intercede for us.
Holy Trinity, we adore You! We thank You! Hear and answer our prayers.

Feast of St. Frances Xavier Cabrini (November 13)
Patron saint of immigrants.
"We must pray without tiring, for the salvation of mankind does not depend on material success; nor on sciences that cloud the intellect. Neither does it depend on arms and human industries, but on Jesus alone."
Food for the Soul: Lean on Jesus and His victorious Cross!
St. Frances Xavier Cabrini, pray for us.
Blessed Mother, graciously intercede for us.
Holy Trinity, we adore You! We thank You! Hear and answer our prayers.

God's Word of the Day (November 14)
"Do not be anxious about anything, but in every situation, by prayer and petition, with thanksgiving, present your requests to God."
(Philippians 4:6)
Food for the Soul: Place all your needs before God.
Blessed Mother, graciously intercede for us.
Holy Trinity, we adore You! We thank You! Hear and answer our prayers.

Feast of St. Albert the Great (November 15)
Patron saint of scientists and philosophers.
"The greater and more persistent your confidence in God, the more abundantly you will receive all that you ask."
Food for the Soul: God is active in your life. He is providing His abundance to you. Understand and believe!
St. Albert, the Great, pray for us.
Blessed Mother, graciously intercede for us.
Holy Trinity, we adore You! We thank You! Hear and answer our prayers.

Feast of St. Elizabeth of Hungary (November 16)
Patron saint of bakers, the homeless, widows, and young brides.
"How could I wear a crown of gold when my Lord wears a crown of thorns and He wears it for me?"
Food for the Soul: Be humble before God. Leave your ego behind.
St. Elizabeth of Hungary, pray for us.
Blessed Mother, graciously intercede for us.
Holy Trinity, we adore You! We thank You! Hear and answer our prayers.

God's Word of the Day (November 17)

*"You will be enriched in every way so that you can be generous I
n every occasion, and through us, your generosity
will result in thanksgiving to God."*
(2 Corinthians 9:11)
**Food for the Soul: You will be blessed by God.
Share your blessings and God will be glorified.**
Blessed Mother, graciously intercede for us.
Holy Trinity, we adore You! We thank You! Hear and answer our prayers.

Fry Bread Day (November 17)

Fry Bread

*As I was nearing the end of writing this book, I decided to make some naan bread. I was going to try something new with it, by deep frying the naan to use it as a puffy flatbread base for some tacos. I placed all of the ingredients in the bread machine and let it work its magic! But, at the end of the hour and a half cycle, I looked inside and saw a disaster! The bread did not fully mix together, for whatever reason, let alone rise. Now what? Knowing I had to figure out a quicker alternative to save dinner, I came across this recipe. Instead of an hour and a half, it came together in about 15 minutes! And the fry bread was delicious! In the end, I had one fry bread left over, so I sprinkled it generously with some cinnamon sugar – Paul and I shared it, and we loved it! It was just like those elephant ears from the fairs!
Just goes to show, sometimes a great failure can
turn into an even greater success!*

Ingredients:
- 2 cups flour, plus an extra tablespoon set aside for working with dough
- 1 Tbsp baking powder
- 2 tsps sugar
- 1 cup chicken broth

Directions: Preheat deep fryer to 350 degrees. Prepare a paper towel lined baking sheet. In a medium bowl, combine flour, baking powder, sugar, and salt. Stir with a fork, sifting the ingredients together. Heat the broth in the microwave until hot, about a minute. Stir. Add the hot broth to the flour mixture. Stir until combined. The dough will be tacky. Allow dough to rest for 10 minutes. Divide dough into 8 portions Sparingly apply some flour to your hands, and roll each portion into a ball. Flatten into a thin disc. Place disc into the deep fryer. Fry each side until golden. Remove from fryer and place on prepared pan. Serve while warm.

Try this recipe another way...
+++By making **Elephant Ears!** Follow the recipe and generously sprinkle of cinnamon sugar immediately out of the fryer.
+++By making **Navajo Tacos!** Follow the recipe. Top with your favorite taco toppings and serve!

Feast of St. Rose Philippine Duchesne (November 18)
Patron saint of perseverance amid adversity.
"We may not understand His Will for us in time, but in eternity, the veil will be drawn and we shall see that He acted only for our happiness."
Food for the Soul: God knows what is best for you. Trust in Him.
St. Rose Philippine Duchesne, pray for us.
Blessed Mother, graciously intercede for us.
Holy Trinity, we adore You! We thank You! Hear and answer our prayers.

God's Word of the Day (November 19)
"For everything God created is good, and nothing is to be rejected, if it is received with thanksgiving, because it is consecrated by the Word of God and prayer."
(1 Timothy 4:4-5)
Food for the Soul: Let us praise God for all His creation!
Blessed Mother, graciously intercede for us.
Holy Trinity, we adore You! We thank You! Hear and answer our prayers.

Feast of St. Edmund (November 20)
Patron saint of kings, pandemics, and wolves.
"It is better to say one 'Our Father' fervently and devoutly than a thousand with no devotion and full of distraction."
Food for the Soul: Pray fervently and devoutly to God.
St. Edmund, pray for us.
Blessed Mother, graciously intercede for us.
Holy Trinity, we adore You! We thank You! Hear and answer our prayers.

Let us pray together the words our Savior taught us to pray:

Our Father, Who art in heaven, hallowed be Thy name.
Thy Kingdom come, Thy Will be done on earth, as it is in heaven.
Give us this day our daily bread, and forgive us our trespasses,
As we forgive those who trespass against us.
And lead us not into temptation, but deliver us from evil.
For Thine is the Kingdom, the power and the glory, for ever and ever.
Amen.

Feast of the Presentation of the Blessed Virgin Mary (November 21)
"You are my Mother, the Mother of Mercy,
and the consolation of the souls in Purgatory."
-- St. Bridget
Food for the Soul: Ask the Blessed Mother to console all those souls of our loved ones who have gone before us from this life.
St. Bridget, pray for us.
Blessed Mother, graciously intercede for us.
Holy Trinity, we adore You! We thank You! Hear and answer our prayers.

Feast of St. Cecilia (November 22)
Patron saint of musicians, composers, instrument makers, and poets.
"Arise, soldiers of Christ, throw away the works of darkness and put on the armor of light."
Food for the Soul: Put on your armor of light today! Be clothed in Christ!
St. Cecilia, pray for us.
Blessed Mother, graciously intercede for us.
Holy Trinity, we adore You! We thank You! Hear and answer our prayers.

Feast Day of St. Clement I (November 23)
Pope. Patron saint of marble workers.
"Let us fix our thoughts on the Blood of Christ and reflect how Precious that Blood is, in God's eyes, inasmuch, as its outpouring for our salvation, has opened the grace of repentance to all mankind."
Food for the Soul: Precious Blood of Christ, protect us.
St. Clement I, pray for us.
Blessed Mother, graciously intercede for us.
Holy Trinity, we adore You! We thank You! Hear and answer our prayers.

God's Word of the Day (November 24)
"I will praise God's name in song and glorify Him with thanksgiving."
(Psalm 69:30)
Food for the Soul: Turn to the music of the Lord and glorify Him through it.
Blessed Mother, graciously intercede for us.
Holy Trinity, we adore You! We thank You! Hear and answer our prayers.

Feast of St. Catherine of Alexandria (November 25)
Martyr and patron saint of students, teachers, philosophers, and unmarried women.

"O Jesus, good King, I await the sword for Thy sake; do Thou deign to receive my spirit, and to show mercy to those who honor my memory."

Food for the Soul: Martyrs of our faith, thank you for all you have done in love of Jesus Christ!

St. Catherine of Alexandria, pray for us.
Blessed Mother, graciously intercede for us.
Holy Trinity, we adore You! We thank You! Hear and answer our prayers.

Christ the King (Fourth Sunday of November)

"Jesus Christ, you have heard Him spoken of, indeed the greater part of you are already His – you are Christians. So, to you Christians, I repeat His name, to everyone I proclaim Him – Jesus Christ is the beginning and the end, the Alpha and the Omega. He is the King of the new world. He is the secret of history. He is the key to our destiny."
-- St. Paul VI

Food for the Soul: There is power in the Name of Jesus!

Jesus Christ, our King, our Joy, we adore You!
St. Paul VI, pray for us.
Blessed Mother, graciously intercede for us.
Holy Trinity, we adore You! We thank You! Hear and answer our prayers.

Thanksgiving Day (Fourth Thursday of November)

*"Get used to lifting your heart to God, in acts of
thanksgiving, many times a day."*
-- St. Josemaría Escrivá

*"Jesus does not demand great action from us,
but simply, surrender and gratitude."*
-- St. Thérèse of Lisieux

Food for the Soul: Jesus, I thank You. I surrender to You.

Holy Trinity, we thank You for all You are and for all You do in Your great goodness. We thank You for Your abundance and bounty.

Bless us, O Lord, in these, Thy gifts, which we are about to receive from Thy bounty, through Christ, our Lord. Amen.

*St. Josemaría Escrivá, pray for us.
St. Thérèse of Lisieux, pray for us.
Blessed Mother, graciously intercede for us.
Holy Trinity, we adore You! We thank You! Hear and answer our prayers.*

Sugar Top Cranberry Muffins

These muffins sure bring back some good memories! When I was a little girl, my Mom would make these for us for breakfast on Thanksgiving mornings. The contrast of the crunchy sugared tops and the tart cranberries inside make this recipe a true winner!

Ingredients:
- 1/2 cup unsalted butter, softened
- 1/3 cup sugar
- 1 large egg, well beaten
- 2 cups flour
- 1 Tbsp baking powder
- 1/4 tsp salt
- 1/2 cup half and half
- 1/4 cup vanilla creamer
- 1 cup fresh cranberries, cut in half
- Extra sugar for topping

Directions: Preheat oven to 400 degrees. Prepare muffin tins with cupcake liners. Mix together butter, sugar, and egg in a medium bowl. In a small bowl, combine flour, baking powder, and salt. Alternately, add some flour, then some half and half, then some more flour, then some more half and half into the butter mixture. Do not overmix. Add in cranberry halves. Fold in gently. Fill cups 2/3rds of the way. Generously sprinkle sugar on the tops. Bake for 20 - 30 minutes. Serve warm with unsalted butter.

Try this recipe another way...
+++By making ***Sugar Topped Blueberry Muffins!*** Substitute the cranberries with whole blueberries. When using blueberries, coat them in flour before you put them in the batter, so they do not sink to the bottom.

+++By making ***Sugar Topped Raspberry Muffins!*** Substitute the cranberries with whole raspberries. Coat them in flour.

Sous Vide Boneless Turkey Breast

With little preparation, tender, juicy turkey breast can be on your dinner table to delight the tastebuds of your guests!

Ingredients:
- 3 lb boneless frozen turkey breast, thawed
- 1-2 Tbsp olive oil
- 1 tsp meat tenderizer
- 1 tsp onion powder
- 1 tsp garlic powder
- 2 Tbsp unsalted butter

Directions: Prepare sous vide to 145 degrees. In the meantime, remove turkey breast from packaging. Leave on the netting. Place on a medium sized cookie sheet. In a small bowl, mix together a teaspoonful of each: meat tenderizer, onion powder, and garlic powder. Dry the turkey breast with some paper towel. Rub the olive oil all over the turkey, then rub the dry seasoning mix all over the turkey. Place the seasoned turkey breast, along with two, one tablespoon pats of unsalted butter, into a vacuum sealed bag. Place the bag into the sous vide container. Sous vide for 3 1/2 hours. Remove bag from sous vide bath. Remove turkey from sealed bag. Save the juices in a bowl to pour over the turkey slices later. That will make those slices extra flavorful and juicy! Remove netting. Slice and eat!

I like to cool the turkey (if we can wait!) overnight in the fridge before slicing. We invested in a reasonably priced electric meat slicer and it has definitely been worth the small investment. The slices come out perfectly!

Crispy Skinned Convection Oven Thanksgiving Turkey

Having made my Crispy Skinned Air Fryer Chicken throughout the year with amazing results, I decided to give my Thanksgiving Turkey the same delicious treatment! Ah, the joy of success!

Ingredients:
- 1 ten pound turkey
- 1 apple, cut in quarters
- 1 lemon, cut in quarters
- 1 onion, cut in quarters
- 1/4 cup water
- 3-4 Tbsp olive oil

Compound butter for under the skin:
- 1 stick unsalted butter, softened
- 1/2 tsp onion powder
- 1/2 tsp garlic powder
- 1/2 tsp meat tenderizer

Chris's Crispy Skinned Turkey Dry Rub
- 2 tsp baking powder
- 2 tsp onion powder
- 2 tsp garlic powder
- 2 tsp meat tenderizer
- 1 tsp black pepper

Directions:
Place the thawed turkey on the counter and remove from the store packaging. Drain juices from the turkey. Remove the neck bone and any packages of giblets, etc. Place turkey on a large cookie sheet. Use paper towels to totally dry the skin of the turkey. Set turkey to the side while you make other preparations. Prepare the compound butter. Mix seasonings with softened unsalted butter. Set to the side. Prepare the Crispy Skinned Turkey dry rub. Combine the seasonings with the baking powder. Mix. Set aside. (The baking powder is the key ingredient for crispy skin!)

Prepare a pan for the turkey. Line a large cookie sheet with foil. Pour a 1/4 cup of water on the foil. Place a baking rack on the sheet to keep the turkey off of the bottom of the cookie sheet so air can flow around the bird. Preheat the oven to 350 degrees on the "convection roast" setting.

Prepare the turkey. Double check the skin is nice and dry. Carefully lift the breast meat skin up, without tearing the skin. Then, stuff the compound butter under the skin. Rub the olive oil all over the skin of the turkey. Then, rub about three quarters of the dry rub seasoning all the turkey skin.
Coat the lemon and apple quarters with the extra dry rub. Stuff the lemon, apple and onion quarters into the bird. Having the fruit and onion inside the bird will help flavor and steam the inside of the bird, making the turkey meat juicy and moist. It will also provide delicious drippings from the bird! Cover the drumstick ends and the wing tips with foil. Place the turkey on the center of the baking racks on the large cookie sheet, breast side up. Carefully place the cookie sheet into the oven. The turkey should be on the second rack from the bottom in the oven. Roast at 350 for one hour.

After the first hour, check the turkey to see if the skin is getting too brown. If it is, place some foil securely over the turkey breast. Reduce the temperature to 325 degrees and continue roasting for one and a half more hours. Remove from the oven and check for an internal temperature of 170 degrees. When the bird is at this temperature, allow the turkey to rest for thirty minutes before carving. Remove all foil. Remove the crispy skin. Divide the skin among your guests and devour! Place the turkey on a large cookie sheet. Carve the turkey; as you carve the turkey, the juices will run out onto the pan. Soak the turkey slices/pieces in those delicious juices. Don't forget the juices from the original baking pan, as well. Remove the legs and wings. Give God thanks, serve, and eat!

Autumn Sweet Potato Crisp

Celebrate the warm, wonderful flavors of autumn with this holiday side dish!

Ingredients:
- 2 1/2 lbs baked sweet potatoes, removed from skins
- 8 oz cream cheese, softened
- 3 Tbsps orange juice
- 2 Tbsps unsalted butter, softened
- 1/4 cup brown sugar
- 1/4 tsp ground cinnamon
- 1/2 tsp salt

Fruit Topping Ingredients:
- 1 cup chopped apple, peeled and cored
- 2/3 cup fresh cranberries, chopped

Crisp Topping Ingredients:
- 1/2 cup flour
- 1/2 cup brown sugar
- 1/3 cup unsalted butter, cold
- 1/2 cup rolled oats
- 1/4 cup chopped pecans

Directions: Preheat air fryer to 400 degrees. Scrub the sweet potatoes clean. With a fork, poke several holes into each side. Rub some canola oil over the potato skins and place in air fryer. Bake for 25 minutes. Turn the potatoes over and spray with oil. Bake for another 25 minutes. Remove from air fryer. Allow to cool for 30 minutes. Cut sweet potatoes open and remove potatoes from skins. Place potatoes in a medium bowl. Allow potatoes to cool for 15 minutes. Preheat oven to 350 degrees. Oil a 1 1/2 quart casserole dish. Set aside. Prepare the crisp topping: In a food processor, pulse together the flour, brown sugar, and butter for the crisp mixture. Transfer those coarse crumbs into a medium bowl. Add oats and pecans. Stir together well. Set aside. Add cream cheese, orange juice, and butter to the sweet potatoes. Mix until well combined. Add brown sugar, salt, and cinnamon. Mix until well combined. Taste the mixture. Does it need a little more sweetness? Add a little more brown sugar. Need a little more salt? Add a tiny pinch. Want the warm cinnamon flavor to shine through? Add a bit more cinnamon. Spoon potato mixture into the oiled casserole dish. Top with chopped apples and cranberries. Top the fruit with the crisp topping mixture. Bake the sweet potato casserole for 35 - 40 minutes, until topping is golden brown. Remove from oven. Allow to set for 5 minutes. Spoon and serve alongside a sous vide turkey breast...or a convection oven turkey...Yum! Store leftovers in the refrigerator.

Pumpkin Custard Pie

When I was growing up, Mom and Dad would buy a frozen pumpkin pie to bake for Thanksgiving Day. But it wasn't just any pumpkin pie, it had to be a pumpkin custard pie. It was delicious! That pumpkin custard was so smooth and creamy. No other pumpkin pie every tasted the same.
So when I found a recipe for pumpkin custard pie filling many years later, I was so happy! It tastes so much better than that frozen store bought pie of years gone by.I paired it with my favorite buttery pie crust recipe and achieved a most delectable result. These two recipes were made for each other! I wish my Mom and Dad were here to enjoy it with Paul and I now...they would love it!

Crust Ingredients:
- 1 1/2 cups flour
- 1 package of Splenda
- 1/4 tsp salt
- 1 stick unsalted butter, melted
- 2 vanilla creamers

Pumpkin Custard Filling Ingredients:
- 15 oz can of pumpkin puree
- 3 large eggs
- 1/2 cup Splenda brown sugar blend
- 1/2 tsp salt
- 1 tsp cinnamon
- 1 Tbsp pumpkin pie spice
- 3/4 cup heavy cream

Directions: Preheat the oven to 375 degrees. Prepare the pie crust. Melt the butter in a medium bowl. Add in the flour, salt, Splenda, and creamers. Mix until combined. Do not overmix. Press the dough into an 8 x 8 inch square glass pan. Set aside. Prepare the filling. In the same medium bowl, add the pumpkin and eggs. Mix until eggs are incorporated into the pumpkin. Add the brown sugar, salt, cinnamon, and pumpkin pie spice. Mix until combined. Add the heavy cream and stir until combined. Pour the filling into the crust. Bake for 40 - 45 minutes, until center of pie is set. Remove from oven and cool. Cut into 16 squares. Serve warm or cool, with a dollop of whipped cream and a sprinkle of cinnamon. Refrigerate any leftovers. You can always warm up the slice in the microwave for about 15 seconds before adding the dollop of whipped cream.

Try this recipe another way...

***By making **Baked Pumpkin Custard!** Just follow the above recipe, but omit the crust. Pour the filling into an oiled 8 x 8 inch square glass pan and bake it at the same temperature, for the same amount of time.

***By making **Pumpkin Custard Pancakes or Waffles!** Add a slice of the pumpkin custard filling (no crust) to your pancake or waffle batter! It takes traditional pumpkin pancakes up, up, up to a whole new level!

God's Word of the Day (November 26)

"I will give thanks to the Lord with my whole heart; I will recount all of Your wonderful deeds. I will be glad and exult in You; I will sing praise to Your name, O Most High."

(Psalm 9:1-2)

Food for the Soul: Praise God. Thank Him. Adore Him.

Blessed Mother, graciously intercede for us.
Holy Trinity, we adore You! We thank You! Hear and answer our prayers.

God's Word of the Day (November 27)

"Enter His gates with thanksgiving, and His courts with praise! Give thanks to Him; bless His name!"

(Psalm 100:4)

Food for the Soul: Bless the Lord, my soul!

Blessed Mother, graciously intercede for us.
Holy Trinity, we adore You! We thank You! Hear and answer our prayers.

God's Word of the Day (November 28)
"Sing unto the Lord with thanksgiving; sing praise upon the harp unto our God..."
(Psalms 147:7)
Food for the Soul: Praise God in song!
Blessed Mother, graciously intercede for us.
Holy Trinity, we adore You! We thank You! Hear and answer our prayers.

God's Word of the Day (November 29)
"And be not drunk with wine, wherein is excess; but be filled with the Spirit; speaking to yourselves in psalms and hymns and spiritual songs, singing and making melody in your heart to the Lord; giving thanks always for all things unto God the Father, in the name of our Lord Jesus Christ..."
(Ephesians 5:18-20)
Food for the Soul: The Holy Spirit is the One Who will provide joy, calm our anxieties, and bring us the peace of Christ to our lives. Go to Him.
Blessed Mother, graciously intercede for us.
Holy Trinity, we adore You! We thank You! Hear and answer our prayers.

Feast of St. Andrew (November 30)
Apostle, brother of Simon Peter.
Patron saint of sore throats, singers, and fishmongers.
"The first thing Andrew did was to find his brother, Simon, and tell him, 'We have found the Messiah'!"
(John 1:41)
Food for the Soul: Imagine the joy Andrew felt when he spoke those words to his brother! Bring that same energy and joy when you speak of Christ to all!
St. Andrew, pray for us.
St. Peter, pray for us.
Blessed Mother, graciously intercede for us.
Holy Trinity, we adore You! We thank You! Hear and answer our prayers.

Advent Season

Four Weeks of Advent Cookies

Week 1 of Advent: Hope

*"At this Christmas when Christ comes, will He find a warm heart?
Mark the Season of Advent by loving and serving others
with God's own love and concern."*
-- St Teresa of Calcutta
***Food for the Soul: Examine your heart. Clean it out.
Decide what will go, what will stay. Make room for the Lord!***
St. Teresa of Calcutta, pray for us.
Blessed Mother, graciously intercede for us.
Holy Trinity, we adore You! Hear and answer our prayers.
Come, Lord Jesus, come! I have prepared a home for You in my heart.

Nut Cup Tarts
These nut cup tarts are like mini pecan pies...

Crust Ingredients:
- 1 stick unsalted butter, softened
- 3 oz cream cheese, softened
- 1 cup flour

Filling Ingredients:
- 1 large egg
- 1 Tbsp melted unsalted butter
- 3/4 cup light brown sugar, firmly packed
- 1/2 cup ground walnuts or pecans

Directions: Preheat oven to 350 degrees. You will use mini muffin tins for 24 mini tarts. Prepare the crust: In a medium bowl, cream together the butter and 3 oz cream cheese. Stir the flour into the butter mixture. Do not overmix. Divide dough into 24 balls. Mold the ball of dough into each of the 24 mini muffin tins so it looks like a little pie crust. In a small bowl, prepare the filling. Add egg, water, and melted butter. Stir well. Add brown sugar. Stir well. Add ground walnuts or pecans. Stir well. Add a heaping tablespoonful of nut filling on top of each crust in the muffin tins. Bake nut cups for 20 minutes at 350 degrees. Then lower the oven's temperature to 250 degrees and continue to bake for 10 minutes, until crust is golden brown. Remove from oven. Cool for 5 minutes. Carefully loosen the cups from the muffin tins, lifting the cups with a small fork. Place cups on a plate to cool. Store at room temperature in a cookie tins. Place wax paper in between layers.

Week 2 of Advent: Peace

"This time of Advent is a time for hope. These great horizons of our Christian vocation, this unity of life built on the presence of God our Father, can and ought to be a daily reality. Ask our Lady...to make it come true. Try to imagine how she spent these months, waiting for her Son to be born. And our Lady, Holy Mary, will make of you 'alter Christus, ipse Christus': another Christ, Christ Himself!"
-- St. Josemaría Escrivá

Food for the Soul: Invite the Blessed Mother into your heart. Keep her close to you.

Hail Mary, full of grace, the Lord is with thee. Blessed art thou among women, and blessed is the fruit of thy womb, Jesus. Holy Mary, Mother of God, pray for us sinners, now and at the hour of our death. Amen.

St. Josemaría Escrivá, pray for us.
Blessed Mother, graciously intercede for us.

Holy Trinity, we adore You! Hear and answer our prayers.
Come, Lord Jesus, come! I have prepared a home for You in my heart.

Helen's Polish Walnut Crescents

These traditional Polish cookies my Mom made were loved by us all, anytime of the year!

Ingredients:
- 2 sticks of unsalted butter, room temperature
- 1 cup confectioner's sugar
- 1 tsp vanilla
- 2 cups walnuts, finely ground (you can also use pecans)
- 2 1/4 cups of flour

Directions: Cream butter with a mixer, then add in confectioner's sugar and vanilla. Mix again. Add in flour alternately with the finely ground walnuts. Do not over mix. (If the dough is too sticky, you can add up to an extra 1/4 cup of flour; but the less flour you use, the more tender your cookie will be.) Scoop a heaping teaspoonful of dough and shape it into a crescent. (If you would rather not form them into a crescent shape, try what I do; roll that teaspoonful of dough into a ball and then flatten it between the palms of your hands. The result will be a crunchier cookie texture.) Place them on a parchment lined cookie sheet. Bake at 350 degrees for 15-20 minutes, until golden brown. Remove the cookies from the pan while still warm and dip them in confectioner's sugar. Makes 60 cookies.

Week 3 of Advent: Joy

"In Advent, we await an event which occurs in history, and at the same time, transcends it. As it does, every year, this event will take place on the night of the Lord's Birth. The shepherds will hasten to the stable in Bethlehem; later the Magi will arrive from the East. Both, the one and the other, in a certain sense, symbolize the entire human family... 'Let us go joyfully to meet the Lord' spreads to all countries, to all continents, among every people and nation."
-- St. John Paul II

Food for the Soul: Have you prepared your journey to Christmas? Have you prepared yourself to greet the Newborn King?

St. John Paul II, pray for us.
Blessed Mother, graciously intercede for us.
Holy Trinity, we adore You! Hear and answer our prayers.
Come, Lord Jesus, come! I have prepared a home for You in my heart.

Buttery Christmas Snowballs

I discovered these cornstarch cookies when my family and I were visiting my Mom's sister, Aunt Charlotte, one afternoon. As we were gathered around her table, she brought out these powdered sugared wonders. They were so light and buttery! You can be sure I asked her for the recipe... thank you, Aunt Charlotte!

Ingredients:
- 2 sticks of unsalted butter, softened
- 3/4 cup cornstarch
- 1/3 cup of powdered sugar
- 1 cup flour

Directions: Cream the softened butter until fluffy in a medium sized bowl. Add the cornstarch and the powdered sugar. Beat until fluffy. Add the flour and mix until blended. Preheat the oven to 350 degrees. Roll the dough into small balls and place them on a parchment lined cookie sheet, leaving a little space in between each cookie. Bake for 10-15 minutes. While the cookies are still warm, roll the them completely in powdered sugar. Allow them to cool on wax paper before storing them in a cookie tin.

Week 4 of Advent: Love

"Open wide your door to the One Who comes. Open your soul, throw open the depths of your heart to see the riches of simplicity, the treasures of peace, the sweetness of grace. Open your heart and run to meet the Sun of Eternal Light that illuminates all..."
-- St. Ambrose of Milan

Food for the Soul: Throw open the doors of your heart for all the spiritual gifts the Christ Child brings! Race to His Light!

St. Ambrose of Milan, pray for us.
Blessed Mother, graciously intercede for us.
Holy Trinity, we adore You! Hear and answer our prayers.
Come, Lord Jesus, come! I have prepared a home for You in my heart.

Oatmeal Butterscotch Thin Crisps

This cookie, by far, is my favorite oatmeal cookie!
My Mom was the one who came up with chopping up the butterscotch chips, so the butterscotch flavor would be tasted more evenly throughout the whole cookie. What a genius idea! I wish I could tell her now how proud I was of her! Love you, Mom!

Ingredients:
- 1 1/2 sticks unsalted butter, softened
- 1/2 cup light brown sugar, firmly packed
- 1/2 cup sugar
- 1 large egg, slightly beaten
- 1 Tbsp water
- 1/2 tsp vanilla
- 3/4 cup flour
- 1/2 tsp baking soda
- 1 1/2 cups quick cooking oatmeal
- 12 oz butterscotch chips, chopped or ground

Directions: Preheat oven to 350 degrees. Prepare cookie sheets, lined with parchment paper. In a medium bowl, cream butter and sugars. Beat in egg, water, and vanilla. Mix in flour and baking soda. Add in oatmeal. Stir well. Add in ground butterscotch chips. Stir well. Drop by large teaspoonfuls onto cookie sheet. They will spread as they bake, so leave some room in between each cookie. Bake for 10 minutes, until golden brown. Remove from oven. Cool cookies slightly on pan. Remove them carefully from the pan. Store in cookie tins. Place wax paper in between layers.

Try this recipe another way...
+++By making **WCCP Oatmeal Thin Crisps!** What is WCCP? White Chocolate, Cranberry, Pecans! Substitute the butterscotch chips for 1/2 cup dried chopped cranberries, 1/2 cup chopped white chocolate chips, and 1/2 cup ground pecans.

+++By making **Cinnamon Apple Walnut Oatmeal Thin Crisps!** Substitute the butterscotch chips for 3/4 cup chopped dried apple and 3/4 cup ground walnuts. Also, add 1/2 tsp of ground cinnamon to the cookie dough when you add in the flour.

December

December Birthday Cake

Raspberry Continental Cake

*Celebrating a Birthday this month? We are!
This was my Mom's birthday month, and she often requested me to make this cake for her birthday, which was also on New Year's Eve day.
This cake is creamy, fruity, deliciousness!*

Cake Ingredients:
- 1 box of yellow cake mix, or white cake mix

Buttercream Filling Ingredients:
- 1 stick unsalted butter, softened
- 1 1/2 cup powdered sugar, sifted
- 1 large egg

Raspberry Filling Ingredients:
- 1/4 cup sugar
- 2 Tbsps cornstarch
- 10 oz package of frozen raspberries, undrained, thawed (or frozen strawberries packed in juice would be great, too)

Whipped Cream Topping:
- 1 cup heavy cream
- 3 Tbsps powdered sugar
- 1 Tbsp vanilla pudding mix (to stabilize whipped cream)
- 1/2 tsp vanilla

Directions: Prepare the cake batter according to the box instructions. Pour the cake batter equally into two oiled 9 inch round cake pans. Bake as box directs. Remove from oven and cool in pan for 10 minutes. After 10 minutes, place a plate over the cake pan and invert cake onto plate. Continue to cool cakes. We will only use one 9 inch cake, so you can freeze the other cake if you so desire. After cake is cooled, begin preparing buttercream filling. In a medium bowl, cream butter. Add sugar and cream well. Add egg. Beat until light and fluffy. Set aside. Prepare the raspberry filling. In a small saucepan, combine sugar, cornstarch, and raspberries. Cook over medium heat until thick and clear. Cool completely. Refrigerate for 30 minutes. Take the completely cooled 9 inch cake round and cut the cake in half horizontally with a very sharp knife, making two layers. On bottom layer, spread buttercream filling. On top of the buttercream filling, spread the raspberry filling. Top raspberry filling with the second layer of cake. Prepare the whipped cream topping. In a small cold metal bowl, beat heavy cream, powdered sugar, vanilla pudding, and vanilla until thick. Spread whipped cream topping over the cake, including on the sides. Smooth out the cream. Refrigerate for several hours or overnight.

Try this recipe another way...
+++By making a **Black Forest Cherry Continental Cake!** Substitute the yellow cake mix for a chocolate cake mix. Instead of making a fruit filling, use a cherry pie filling. (You probably won't use the whole can of filling...).

+++By making a **Caramel Apple Cinnamon Continental Cake!** Substitute the yellow cake mix for a cinnamon cake mix. Instead of making the fruit filling, use an apple pie filling. (You probably won't use the whole can of filling...). Add 1/2 tsp caramel extract to the buttercream filling.

God's Word of the Day (December 1)
*"The people walking in darkness have seen a great light;
on those living in the land of deep darkness, a light has dawned."*
(Isaiah 9:3)
Food for the Soul: Look for the Light of Christ in your life today.
*Blessed Mother, graciously intercede for us.
Holy Trinity, we adore You! Hear and answer our prayers.
Come, Lord Jesus, come! I have prepared a home for You in my heart.*

God's Word of the Day (December 2)
"A voice of one calling: In the wilderness, prepare the way for the Lord; make straight in the desert a highway for our God. Every valley shall be raised up, every mountain and hill made low..."
(Isaiah 40:3)
Food for the Soul: Prepare the way of the Lord in your life. Straighten the paths. Raise the valleys. Lower the mountains.
Blessed Mother, graciously intercede for us.
Holy Trinity, we adore You! Hear and answer our prayers.
Come, Lord Jesus, come! I have prepared a home for You in my heart.

Feast of St. Francis Xavier (December 3)
Patron saint of Roman Catholic missions.
"Speak to them of the great mercy of God... Sometimes, people are helped by your telling of your own lamentable past."
Food for the Soul: Share your faith with those around you. Start out small. Be gentle. Be humble. Be loving.
St. Francis Xavier, pray for us.
Blessed Mother, graciously intercede for us.
Holy Trinity, we adore You! Hear and answer our prayers.
Come, Lord Jesus, come! I have prepared a home for You in my heart.

Feast of St. John of Damascus (December 4)
Patron saint of pharmacists, theology students, and philosophers.
"The whole earth is a living icon of the face of God."
Food for the Soul: See God's beauty in these wintry days. Glorify His Name.
St. John of Damascus, pray for us.
Blessed Mother, graciously intercede for us.
Holy Trinity, we adore You! Hear and answer our prayers.
Come, Lord Jesus, come! I have prepared a home for You in my heart.

Cookie Day (December 4)

Creamy Toffee Nut Shortbread

With an extra creamy, crunchy topping, this shortbread is something else!

Ingredients:
- 1 cup unsalted butter, softened
- 1 cup sugar
- 1 large egg yolk
- 1/4 tsp vanilla
- 2 cups flour
- 1/2 cup walnuts, chopped (or pecans, or almonds)

Topping Ingredients:
- 3/4 cup (or more, to taste) toffee or brittle bits
- 8 oz cool whip

Directions: Preheat oven to 350 degrees. Oil a 15 x 10 x 1 inch pan. In a medium bowl, mix butter, sugar. Blend well. Add egg yolk and vanilla. Mix well. Add flour. Blend until combined. Do not overmix. Press dough into prepared pan. Sprinkle chopped walnuts over dough, then press walnuts into dough. Bake for 15 - 20 minutes, until lightly golden brown. Remove from oven. Cool completely. Prepare the topping. In a medium bowl, add cool whip. Fold in toffee or brittle bits. Cut the shortbread into squares. Top each serving with the creamy brittle topping.

God's Word of the Day (December 5)

*"And the glory of the Lord will be revealed,
and all the people will see it together."*
(Isaiah 40:5)

Food for the Soul: See the glory of the Lord in the people around you. Glorify His Name.

Blessed Mother, graciously intercede for us.
Holy Trinity, we adore You! Hear and answer our prayers.
Come, Lord Jesus, come! I have prepared a home for You in my heart.

Feast of St. Nicholas of Myra (December 6)

Patron saint of sailors, merchants, archers, repentant thieves, children, toymakers, students, and unmarried people.

"The Giver of every good and perfect gift, has called upon us to mimic God's giving, by grace, through faith, and this is not of ourselves."

Food for the Soul: Humble yourself in your deeds and give all glory to God!

St. Nicholas of Myra, pray for us.
Blessed Mother, graciously intercede for us.
Holy Trinity, we adore You! Hear and answer our prayers.
Come, Lord Jesus, come! I have prepared a home for You in my heart.

Candy Cane Chip Cookies

Since I am allergic to mint, I don't ever bake or cook anything that has mint in it...but, here is an exception to the rule! The salty potato chips and sweet candy canes nestled in a buttery cookie creates a unique flavor combination. How could I not use the candy cane, the symbol of St. Nicholas, in my cookie for today?!

Ingredients:
- 4 sticks of unsalted butter, softened
- 1 cup sugar
- 2 tsp vanilla
- 1 cup crushed potato chips (choose a light, crisp brand of chips, not kettle chips)
- 3 cups flour
- 2/3 cup crushed candy cane bits

Directions: Preheat oven to 350 degrees. Prepare the cookie sheets, lined with parchment paper. In a large bowl, cream together butter, sugar, and vanilla. Add potato chips to butter mixture. Combine. Add flour. Combine. Do not overmix. Stir in crushed candy cane bits. Drop by teaspoonfuls onto parchment papered sheets, about an inch apart. Bake for 10 - 15 minutes, until golden brown. Remove from cookie sheet and cool completely. Dust with powdered sugar.

Try this recipe in another way...
+++By making **Peppermint Bark Chip Cookies!** Substitute the candy bits for peppermint bark mix-ins, or some chopped peppermint bark.

+++By making **Festive Cherry Walnut Chip Cookies!** Substitute the candy cane bits for 1/3 cup of chopped red and green glazed cherries and 1/3 cup of chopped walnuts.

Feast of St. Ambrose (December 7)
Patron saint of Milan and beekeepers.
"No one heals himself by wounding another."
Food for the Soul: Be loving. Be Christ to all.
St. Ambrose, pray for us.
Blessed Mother, graciously intercede for us.
Holy Trinity, we adore You! Hear and answer our prayers.
Come, Lord Jesus, come! I have prepared a home for You in my heart.

Feast of the Immaculate Conception (December 8)
"The 'Hail Mary' is dew falling from heaven to make the soul fruitful. It is a pure kiss of love we give to Mary."
-- St. Louis de Montfort
Food for the Soul: Offer many "kisses" to the Blessed Mother today. Show her your love for her Son.
St. Louis de Montfort, pray for us.
Blessed Mother, graciously intercede for us.
Blessed Mother, graciously intercede for us.
Holy Trinity, we adore You! Hear and answer our prayers.
Come, Lord Jesus, come! I have prepared a home for You in my heart.

God's Word of the Day (December 9)

"Surely, God is my salvation; I will trust and not be afraid. The Lord, the Lord Himself, is my strength and my defense; He has become my salvation."
(Isaiah 12:2)

Food for the Soul: Continue to prepare your heart for the Christ Child. Our Mighty Savior, our Holy Redeemer, is coming to set us free!
Blessed Mother, graciously intercede for us.
Holy Trinity, we adore You! Hear and answer our prayers.
Come, Lord Jesus, come! I have prepared a home for You in my heart.

Pastry Day (December 9)

Chocolate Eclair Pastries
Light pastries filled with a custard cream and topped with chocolate.

Pastry Shell Ingredients:
- 1 cup water
- 1 stick unsalted butter
- 1 cup flour
- 4 large eggs

Filling Ingredients:
- 1 small box of instant vanilla pudding mix
- 1 1/4 cups half and half
- 1/2 tsp cornstarch
- 1 cup heavy cream
- 2 1/2 tsps powdered sugar
- 1 tsp vanilla

Chocolate Topping Ingredients:
- 1/2 cup semisweet chocolate chips
- 2 Tbsps unsalted butter
- 2 Tbsps water
- 2/3 cup powdered sugar

Directions: Preheat oven to 400 degrees. Prepare a large baking sheet by lining it with parchment paper. Set aside. Prepare the pastry shells: In a medium saucepan, heat water and butter until boiling. Remove saucepan from heat. Add flour and mix. Beat in eggs, one at a time. Drop shell batter, by tablespoonfuls, onto the baking sheet, leaving an inch between the pastry shells. You can also make a longer eclair shell, if you choose, by connecting two or three tablespoonfuls together. Bake shells for 20 minutes. Remove them from the oven and prick each shell several times with a toothpick. (This will make them a bit hollow in the center.) Return shells to the oven to bake for 5 more minutes. Remove shells from oven and cool completely.

Prepare the filling: In a medium mixing bowl, combine the pudding mix, half and half, and cornstarch until smooth. In a small metal bowl, beat the heavy cream, powdered sugar, and vanilla into whipped cream peaks. Do not over whip. Fold the whipped cream into the pudding mixture. When shells are completely cooled, slice horizontally, so you have a top and a bottom of the shell. Place a heaping spoonful of the filling onto the bottom of the shell. Place the top of the shell over the filling. Prepare the chocolate topping: Melt 1/2 cup chocolate chips with the butter and water. Stir until smooth. Add in the powdered sugar. Stir until smooth. If too thin, add a little more powdered sugar. Frost the tops of the shells. Store eclairs in a container in the refrigerator.

Try this recipe another way...
+++By making an ***Eclair Christmas Wreath!*** Instead of making individual pastry shells, make a circular wreath shape out of the pastry dough. Then continue on with the same directions. After the wreath is frosted, decorate with chopped green and red glazed cherries (do not use maraschino cherries).
+++By making ***Chocolate Filled Eclairs!*** Substitute the vanilla pudding mix for instant chocolate pudding mix in the filling.
+++By making ***Banana Pudding Eclairs!*** Substitute the vanilla pudding mix for instant banana cream pudding mix. To each eclair, add a thin slice of banana on top of the filling for even more banana flavor. Top with a sprinkle of powdered sugar instead of the chocolate topping, if desired.

+++By making **Banana Split Eclairs!** For this version, you can use either the vanilla pudding mix or the banana cream pudding mix. As you assemble the eclair, start with a thin slice of banana on the bottom pastry, followed by a spoonful of pudding, then some thinly sliced strawberries. Place the pastry "cap" on and frost with the chocolate topping. Top with a dollop of whipped cream and a maraschino cherry.

Feast of Our Lady of Loreto (December 10)

*"Love Mary! She is loveable, faithful, constant.
She will never let herself be outdone in love, but will remain supreme."
-- St. Alphonsus Liguori*
**Food for the Soul: Love the Holy Trinity.
Love Mary, and all the Saints of Heaven. Love each other.**
*St. Alphonsus, pray for us.
Our Lady of Loreto, graciously intercede for us.
Blessed Mother, graciously intercede for us.
Holy Trinity, we adore You! Hear and answer our prayers.
Come, Lord Jesus, come! I have prepared a home for You in my heart.*

God's Word of the Day (December 11)

"Sing to the Lord, for He has done glorious things; let this be known to all the world. Shout aloud and sing for joy, people of Zion, for great is the Holy One of Israel among you."
(Isaiah 12:5-6)
Food for the Soul: Spread the good news that Jesus is coming!
*Blessed Mother, graciously intercede for us.
Holy Trinity, we adore You! We thank You! Hear and answer our prayers.
Come, Lord Jesus, come! I have prepared a home for You in my heart.*

Feast of Our Lady of Guadalupe (December 12)

"Let not your heart be disturbed... Am I not here, who is your Mother? Are you not under my protection? Am I not your health? Are you not happily within my fold? What else do you wish? Do not grieve nor be disturbed by anything."
-- Our Lady of Guadalupe to St. Juan Diego

Food for the Soul: The Blessed Mother is our calm, as we rush around this season. Take time, throughout your day, to be with her, to pray to her.

St. Juan Diego, pray for us.
Our Lady of Guadalupe, graciously intercede for us.
Holy Trinity, we adore You! Hear and answer our prayers.
Come, Lord Jesus, come! I have prepared a home for You in my heart.

Feast of St. Lucy (December 13)
Patron saint of those with eye illnesses.

"Those whose hearts are pure are temples of the Holy Spirit."

Food for the Soul: Lord, purify our hearts, so the Holy Spirit may dwell within us!

St. Lucy, pray for us.
Blessed Mother, graciously intercede for us.
Holy Trinity, we adore You! Hear and answer our prayers.
Come, Lord Jesus, come! I have prepared a home for You in my heart.

God's Word of the Day (December 14)

"And Mary said: 'My soul glorifies the Lord and my spirit rejoices in God my Savior, for He has been mindful of the humble state of His servant. From now on, all generations will call me blessed, for the Mighty One has done great things for me – Holy is His Name."
(Luke 1:46-49)

Food for the Soul: Holy is Your Name, O God!

Blessed Mother, graciously intercede for us.
Holy Trinity, we adore You! Hear and answer our prayers.
Come, Lord Jesus, come! I have prepared a home for You in my heart.

God's Word of the Day (December 15)
"His Mercy extends to those who fear Him, from generation to generation He has performed mighty deeds With His Arm; He has scattered those who are proud in their inmost thoughts."
(Luke 1:50-53)
Food for the Soul: How great are You, O God! We adore You!
Blessed Mother, graciously intercede for us.
Holy Trinity, we adore You! Hear and answer our prayers.
Come, Lord Jesus, come! I have prepared a home for You in my heart.

God's Word of the Day (December 16)
"He has brought down rulers from their thrones, but has lifted up the hungry with good things, but has sent the rich away empty."
(Luke 1:54)
Food for the Soul: You are magnificent, my Lord!
Blessed Mother, graciously intercede for us.
Holy Trinity, we adore You! Hear and answer our prayers.
Come, Lord Jesus, come! I have prepared a home for You in my heart.

God's Word of the Day (December 17)
"He has helped His servant, Israel, remembering to be merciful to Abraham and His descendants forever, just as He promised our ancestors."
(Luke 1:55)
Food for the Soul: Fulfill Your promises to Your people, O Lord.
Blessed Mother, graciously intercede for us.
Holy Trinity, we adore You! Hear and answer our prayers.
Come, Lord Jesus, come! I have prepared a home for You in my heart.

God's Word of the Day (December 18)

"You who bring good news to Zion, go up on a high mountain. You who bring good news to Jerusalem, lift up your voice with a shout, lift it up, do not be afraid; say to the towns of Judah, "Here is your God!"
(Isaiah 40:9)

Food for the Soul: Proclaim to the world, "Our God is with us!"
Blessed Mother, graciously intercede for us.
Holy Trinity, we adore You! Hear and answer our prayers.
Come, Lord Jesus, come! I have prepared a home for You in my heart.

Bake Cookies Day (December 18)

Helen's Polish Kolacky

Since this is bake cookies day, I thought we would indulge ourselves with the queen of Polish cookies, kolacky! This was my Mom's recipe. Make sure you are able to dedicate most of the day to this project. My sisters and I always helped Mom to fill and fold them, so enlist some helpers to make this a memorable family experience. Making kolacky is a labor of love, but, oh, the delicious reward!

Ingredients:
- 4 sticks unsalted butter, softened
- 2 Tbsps sugar
- 1 package of instant yeast
- 1/2 cup warm milk
- 3 large egg yolks
- 4 cups flour

Filling:
- Cans of different Solo fillings in a variety of flavors; cherry, apricot, almond, poppyseed, etc. (If you use jam or jelly, it will spill out of the kolacky while baking. Solo filling is a little thicker. Preserves will also work pretty well.)

Directions: In a large bowl, cream together butter and sugar. In a small bowl, melt yeast in milk. Add yeast mixture to the butter mixture. Combine. Add egg yolks. Combine. Add flour. Combine. Do not overmix. Refrigerate dough for 1/2 hour. After 30 minutes has passed, prepare a cookie sheet, lined with parchment paper. Preheat the oven to 375 degrees. Remove some of the dough from the refrigerator. Roll dough out like pie crust on a dusted powdered sugared surface. (Use powdered sugar to roll out sweet doughs, instead of flour, to keep dough more tender!). Using a pastry cutter (or a knife, or a pizza cutter), cut dough into 2 1/2 inch squares. Place about a teaspoonful of filling in the center of the square. Fold the two opposite corners inward, to the middle, overlapping, and lightly press. Place kolacky on the prepared cooking sheet, about 1/2 inch apart. Bake for 20 - 25 minutes. Remove from pan. Cool. Sprinkle with powdered sugar when completely cooled. Store in metal tins. Place a piece of wax paper in between layers so they don't stick to each other.

God's Word of the Day (December 19)

"He tends His flock like a shepherd: He gathers the lambs in His arms and carries them close to His heart; He gently leads those that have young."
(Isaiah 40:11)
Food for the Soul: Shepherd me, O Lord! Guard and protect me.
Blessed Mother, graciously intercede for us.
Holy Trinity, we adore You! Hear and answer our prayers.
Come, Lord Jesus, come! I have prepared a home for You in my heart.

God's Word of the Day (December 20)

"How beautiful on the mountains are the feet of those who bring good news, who proclaim peace, who bring good tidings, who proclaim salvation, who say to Zion, 'Your God reigns.'"
(Isaiah 52:7)
Food for the Soul: God reigns among us! Rejoice!
Blessed Mother, graciously intercede for us.
Holy Trinity, we adore You! Hear and answer our prayers.
Come, Lord Jesus, come! I have prepared a home for You in my heart.

God's Word of the Day (December 21)

"Listen! Your watchmen lift up their voices; together they shout for joy. When the Lord returns to Zion, they will see it with their own eyes."
(Isaiah 52:8)
Food for the Soul: Together we shall see the goodness of the Lord. Rejoice!
Blessed Mother, graciously intercede for us.
Holy Trinity, we adore You! Hear and answer our prayers.
Come, Lord Jesus, come! I have prepared a home for You in my heart.

God's Word of the Day (December 22)

"Burst into songs of joy together, you ruins of Jerusalem, for the Lord has comforted His people, He has redeemed Jerusalem."
(Isaiah 52:9)
Food for the Soul: Our Redeemer arrives! Rejoice!
Blessed Mother, graciously intercede for us.
Holy Trinity, we adore You! Hear and answer our prayers.
Come, Lord Jesus, come! I have prepared a home for You in my heart.

God's Word of the Day (December 23)

"I will sing of the Lord's great love forever; with my mouth I will make Your faithfulness known through all generations. I will declare that Your love stands firm forever, that You have established Your faithfulness in heaven itself."
(Psalms 89:1-2)
Food for the Soul: Love arrives to warm the coldest of hearts. Rejoice!
Blessed Mother, graciously intercede for us.
Holy Trinity, we adore You! Hear and answer our prayers.
Come, Lord Jesus, come! I have prepared a home for You in my heart.

Christmas Season
Christmas Eve (December 24)

"Arise, all you nobles and peasants; Mary invites us all, rich and poor, just and sinners, to enter the cave of Bethlehem, to adore and to kiss the Feet of her newborn Son...let us enter; let us not be afraid."
-- St. Alphonsus Liguori

"My prayer for you is that when Christ comes to you in Christmas, He may find in you a warm home, warm love like that of a heart full of love, like that of a simple shepherd, who was the first one chosen to see Christ."
-- St. Teresa of Calcutta

"Glory to God in the highest, and on earth peace, goodwill toward men!"
(Luke 2:14)

Food for the Soul: Peace arrives! Rejoice!
All glory to the Newborn King!

Christmas Eve (December 24)

Maria's Sugar Cookies

My Mom used to make sugar cookies in cookie molds every Christmas Eve. My sister and I would help her shape them into the molds and decorate them. Since then, I've switched to a different recipe for the cookies, a recipe my friend, Maria, shared with me a long time ago, but I still use those same cookie molds with the shapes of Santa, a bell, a star, and a tree... no other food says "Christmas" to me like these cookies do!

Ingredients:
- 1/2 cup sugar
- 1/2 cup powdered sugar
- 1 stick unsalted butter, softened
- 1/2 cup canola oil
- 1 egg white
- 1 tsp brandy
- 1 tsp vanilla
- 2 1/4 cups flour
- 1/2 tsp cream of tartar
- 1/2 tsp baking soda

Directions: Preheat oven to 350 degrees. Prepare a parchment lined cookie sheet, or a cookie mold. In a large bowl, add sugar, powdered sugar, butter, and oil. Cream together until well blended. Add the egg white, brandy and vanilla. Blend together. In a small bowl, stir together flour, cream of tartar, and baking soda with a fork to sift. Add to butter mixture and mix until blended. Do not overmix. Mold dough into cookie molds, or roll a teaspoonful into a ball and flatten. Sprinkle decorative sugars, sprinkles on the top of cookies. You can also leave off the sugar and sprinkles and bake without any topping. Then, once the cookies are baked and cooled, use icing to decorate, or drizzle some melted candy wafers over the cookies. Bake for 10 - 12 minutes. Remove from oven. Allow cookies to cool for 2 minutes, then, remove from pan and place on wax paper. After completely cooled, store in tins.

Easy Potato Pierogi

Pierogi are wonderful, tender Polish dumplings that can be filled with your favorite fillings, topped with bread crumbs, fried up in lots of butter, and maybe with some diced onion, and served with sour cream! Comfort food at it's best! My Mom used to make pierogi from scratch, but then she found this easy recipe in a local newspaper. Once she tried making them this way, she never looked back! Mom always made pierogi for Christmas Eve, along side some fried fish, or shrimp, and peas... Maybe that is why those are some of my favorite foods!

Ingredients:
- 1 can of buttermilk layered biscuits
- Leftover mashed potatoes (my favorite filling!)
- Breadcrumbs
- Butter or margarine
- Sour cream

Directions: Fill a large pot with water, about 2/3rds of the way. Cover the pot and heat the water to boiling. Bring the leftover mashed potatoes to room temperature. If you don't have any leftover mashed potatoes, I usually make some instant butter flavored mashed potatoes, the brand that comes in red packaging. I add a few tablespoons of unsalted butter, sour cream, and cream cheese, and mix it in the cooked potatoes. Quick and easy! You can also add some of your favorite shredded cheese if you would like a potato cheese pierogi. Either way, allow the potato mixture to cool for a bit before spooning it onto the dough.

Open the tube of biscuits. Take a biscuit and divide it in half, so you have two round pieces of biscuit from the one biscuit. Take one of the rounds and flatten it so you have a thin round. Take a teaspoonful of mashed potatoes and place it on one half of the round, placing it more toward the center of the round so the filling doesn't ooze out when you seal the pierog closed. Fold the other half over the potatoes. Take a small fork and seal the edges of the biscuit dough together. Continue to do that for the rest of the dough rounds. Prepare a plate for the cooked pierogi...line a large paper plate with some wax paper. Put a thin layer of breadcrumbs on the wax paper.

Once the water is boiling and the pierogi and ready to be boiled, place about five pierogi at a time into the boiling water. They will float when you place them in there. Allow them to boil for about 2-3 minutes, then, with a slotted spoon, turn them over so the other side can cook, about two more minutes. You will notice as they cook, they will get puffier, that's a good sign! If they still look a little doughy, turn them again, but for a smaller amount of time. You don't want to cook them so long that they begin to disintegrate into the water. With a slotted spoon, remove the pierogi and place on the plate. Top the pierogi with a thin layer of breadcrumbs. Place another sheet of wax paper on top of those pierogi and add another layer of bread crumbs on the wax paper for the next group of five pierogi.

Continue cooking the rest of the pierogi in batches of five. At this point, you can cool the pierogi and place them in a gallon plastic bag and store them in the fridge until you are ready to fry and serve them. If you want to fry and serve them now, melt some butter or margarine into a frying pan. Place the pierogi into the pan and fry them up. Some people like them softer, like I do. Some people like them fried until crispy. Fry them as you like. Remove from pan, pour some of the melted butter from the pan onto the pierogi. Serve with a dollop or two of sour cream. If you would like a slightly sweeter topping, add a 1/2 packet of Splenda to the sour cream dollops. Dobry! (That's "good" in Polish!)

Feast of the Nativity of Our Lord: Christmas Day (December 25)

"For unto us a Child is born, to us a Son is given; and the government shall be upon His shoulder, and His Name shall be called Wonderful Counselor, Mighty God, Everlasting Father, Prince of Peace."
(Isaiah 9:6)

Food for the Soul: Glory to God in the Highest! Rejoice!
All glory to the Newborn King!

Polish Cheese Kowatz

Taste the rich, European flavor of a not-too-sweet cheese coffeecake to celebrate this Christmas morning!

Coffeecake Ingredients:
- 1 stick unsalted butter, softened
- 8 oz package of cream cheese, softened
- 1 1/4 cup sugar
- 2 eggs
- 1 tsp vanilla
- 1/2 cup half and half
- 3 Tbsp sour cream
- 2 cups flour
- 2 tsp baking powder
- 1/2 tsp baking soda
- 1/2 tsp salt

Cheese Filling Ingredients:
- 24 oz of ricotta cheese
- 2 egg yolks
- 3 Tbsp sour cream
- 1/3 cup of sugar
- 1/4 tsp vanilla

Streusel Topping Ingredients:
- 1/2 stick unsalted butter, softened
- 1/2 cup flour
- 1/2 cup sugar (or brown sugar)

Directions: Prepare the batter. In a large bowl, cream together butter, cream cheese, and sugar. Add eggs and beat well. Add vanilla, half and half, and sour cream. Mix well. Add flour, baking powder, baking soda, and salt. Mix until blended. Set aside. Grease a 13 x 9 inch glass pan. Set aside. Preheat oven to 350 degrees. Prepare cheese filling. In a medium bowl, mix cheese filling ingredients together until creamy. Set aside.

Prepare streusel topping. In a small bowl, cut butter into flour and sugar or use a food processor to mix it together until it is crumbly. Set aside. Pour coffeecake batter into the pan. Top with the cheese filling. Sprinkle the streusel over the filling. Bake at 350 degrees for 45 - 50 minutes, until cheese filling is set in the middle. Cool in pan. Cut into 24 squares. Store in refrigerator.

Santa Hat Mini Cheesecakes
These mini cheesecakes are adorable! Delicious, too!

Ingredients:
- 24 red velvet or golden sandwich cookies
- Three 8 oz packages of cream cheese, softened (24 oz total)
- 3 Tbsps sour cream
- 1 cup sugar
- 3 large eggs
- 1 tsp vanilla
- 24 plump, medium strawberries
- White candy wafers for melting

Directions: Preheat oven to 325 degrees. Line 24 muffin tins with paper or foil liners. Place one red velvet sandwich cookie in each of the liners. In a large bowl, beat cream cheese and sugar until smooth. Beat in the eggs, one at a time. Add the vanilla. Combine. Pour cream cheese mixture into each liner, filling 2/3rds full. Bake for 20 minutes, or until set. Remove from oven. Cool completely. Wash and hull strawberries. Make sure the wide end of the strawberry is cut flat. Melt the candy wafers. Dip the wide end of the strawberries, and the tip, into the melted wafers to make a Santa's hat. Immediately place the flat side of the strawberries onto the cheesecakes, before the candy cools and hardens. Store cheesecakes, covered, in the refrigerator.

Feast of St. Stephen (December 26)
Patron saint of bricklayers and stonemasons.
"You have power over your mind, not outside events. Realize this, and you will find strength."
Food for the Soul: Christ is born! Rejoice!
All glory to the Newborn King!
St. Stephen, pray for us.
Blessed Mother, graciously intercede for us.
Holy Trinity, we adore You! Hear and answer our prayers.

Saucy Meatloaf

Adapted from one of my Mom's favorite recipes, and, our friend, Fr. Marc loves it, as well! The thing I enjoy about this meatloaf is that it's made in a 9 x 13 inch pan instead of a traditional loaf pan, which allows more of the meatloaf to be covered in that delicious, saucy topping.

Meatloaf Ingredients:
- 1 cup (2 - 3 slices) garlic bread, thawed, or fresh white bread, torn into small pieces
- 1 cup half and half
- 2 Tbsps onion soup mix or minced onion
- 1/2 tsp garlic powder
- 1/2 tsp onion powder
- 1/2 tsp dried parsley
- 1/4 tsp black pepper
- 1 large egg, beaten
- 3 Tbsps Worcestershire sauce
- 1 1/2 lb ground beef

Saucy Topping Ingredients:
- 1/2 cup ketchup
- 1/2 cup water
- 1 Tbsp yellow mustard
- 3 Tbsps brown sugar

Directions: Preheat the oven to 300 degrees. Oil a 9 x 13 pan. Prepare the meatloaf. In a large bowl, add the half and half, onion soup mix, garlic powder, onion powder, parsley, pepper, egg, and Worcestershire sauce. Stir until combined. Add the garlic bread pieces into the mixture. Allow bread to soak in the mixture for a few minutes. Add the ground beef to the bread mixture. Gently combine. Do not overmix. Place the meatloaf mixture in the pan. Pat the mixture lightly into the pan so it is an even thickness. In a small bowl, mix together the sauce ingredients. Microwave the sauce for about 20 - 30 seconds so the brown sugar dissolves into the sauce. Pour the sauce on top of the meatloaf. Bake in the oven for 1 hour - 1 hour 10 minutes. Slice and serve.

Try this recipe another way...
+++By making a *Meatloaf Sandwich!* Place a slice of meatloaf between two slices of fresh white bread. Then add on some sliced raw sweet onion, or even some cooked sweet peppers to your sandwich, or both, for a tasty veggie crunch addition!

+++By making a *Saucy Turkey Meatloaf!* Substitute the ground beef for ground turkey.

Quote of the Day (December 27)
"A stable would be the last place in the world where one would have looked for Him. Divinity is always where one least expects to find it."
--Venerable Fulton Sheen
Food for the Soul: Hope arrives! Rejoice!
All glory to the Newborn King!
Blessed Mother, graciously intercede for us.
Holy Trinity, we adore You! Hear and answer our prayers.

Fruitcake Day (December 27)
I don't know about you, but I am usually not a big fan of fruitcake! Sometimes they are dry. Sometimes the flavors, and even the fruit in the cake, just taste a little bit unusual to me. With that said, be warned, the following three recipes do not share those same traditional fruitcake characteristics! So, if you, too, are not a fan of the traditional fruitcake, you may thoroughly enjoy these untraditional fruitcake recipes.
Maybe I should call them "Un-Fruitcake"! Ha!

Holiday Fruitcake Scones

This version of the English biscuit is at its best! Quick and easy, rich and tender. The perfect holiday breakfast treat for this joyous Yuletide season!

Ingredients:
- 2 cups + 2 Tbsps flour
- 1/3 cup + 2 Tbsps sugar
- 1 Tbsp baking powder
- 1/2 tsp salt
- 6 Tbsps unsalted butter, cold
- 1/4 cup glazed red and green cherries, chopped (or red maraschino cherries, chopped)
- 1/4 cup dried pineapple, chopped
- 3 Tbsps pecans, chopped
- 1 cup heavy cream
- 2 tsps apricot brandy (optional)
- extra sugar, for topping

Directions: Preheat oven to 400 degrees. Prepare baking sheet, parchment paper lined. In a food processor, add flour, sugar, baking powder, salt and cold butter. Pulse until coarse crumbs. Place flour/butter crumbs Into a medium bowl. Stir cherries, pineapple, and pecans into the crumb mixture. Gently stir in heavy cream and brandy. Do not overmix. Let stand for 2 minutes. On a lightly powdered sugared surface, press out dough, 1/2 inch thick. Cut into scones, whatever shape you desire. Place scones on a parchment paper lined baking sheet. Sprinkle tops with sugar. Bake for 15 minutes. Remove from oven and serve while warm.

Helen's Apricot Brandied Fruitcake

You say you don't like fruitcake? Then you haven't tried this one yet! It was one of my Mom's favorite recipes, so you know it's going to be good! This cake is a delicious, indulgent, nutty, fruity, brandied pound cake, embodying so many of the warm flavors of the holiday season.
Be sure to make it a few days before serving, so the brandy will have a chance to "settle in"...then sit back and enjoy a slice with a cup of coffee or, perhaps, with a cup of hot peach tea, in a loving nod to my Mom, "Peaches"... maybe top your slice with a dollop of real whipped cream?
After all, it is the holidays...calories don't count! Ha!

Ingredients:
- 1 stick unsalted butter, softened
- 1 1/2 cup sugar
- 3 large eggs
- 1/2 tsp orange extract
- 1/4 tsp salt
- 1/2 cup sour cream
- 1/4 tsp rum extract
- 1/8 tsp almond extract
- 1/4 tsp lemon extract
- 1/2 tsp vanilla
- 1/4 cup brandy
- 1 1/2 cups flour
- 1/8 tsp baking soda
- 1/2 cup chopped candied cherries, green and red
- 1/4 cup chopped dried pineapple
- 1/2 cup chopped walnuts, lightly dusted in flour so they won't sink to the bottom

Directions: Preheat oven to 350 degrees. Use some shortening to grease a Bundt cake pan and get into all of the crevices. Cream together butter and sugar in a large mixing bowl. Add eggs, one at a time, beating after each addition. Add flour and baking soda alternately with sour cream. Beat together. In a small bowl, mix together brandy and all of the extracts. Add brandy and extracts to the batter and mix. Stir in dried cherries, dried pineapple, and lightly floured walnuts. Pour batter into

Bundt pan. Bake for 1 hour and 10 minutes. Cool in pan for 10 minutes. Invert cake on a plate to release cake from pan. (Rap gently on pan bottom to help release the cake, if needed.) Using a skewer, poke holes into the cake. Pour 1/4 cup of brandy slowly over the cake to seep into the holes. Use a pastry brush and brush the whole cake with the brandy. Wrap the entire cake in Saran Wrap. Keep overnight for the flavors to develop. The next day, pour another 1/4 cup of brandy slowly over the cake to seep into the holes. Use a pastry brush and brush the whole cake with some brandy. Wrap the whole cake again in Saran Wrap. Keep overnight for the flavors to develop. Cut and serve the following day. Top with a dollop of whipped cream, if desired. Wrap leftovers in Saran Wrap to keep fresh and moist.

Fruitcake Cookies

Chewy, nutty, fruity, and oh, so good! Plus, this batch makes 7 dozen cookies so they will go a long way! Tip: Use oiled kitchen shears and snip away to easily "chop up" those sticky fruits!

Ingredients:
- 2 sticks unsalted butter, softened
- 3/4 cup light brown sugar, firmly packed
- 1 large egg
- 1 3/4 cup flour
- 1/2 tsp baking soda
- 1/2 tsp salt
- 8 oz chopped dates (1 1/2 cups)
- 1 cup dried pineapple, chopped
- 1/2 cup glazed red cherries, chopped
- 1/2 cup glazed green cherries, chopped
- 1 1/2 cups pecans or walnuts, chopped

Directions: Preheat oven to 350 degrees. Prepare a cookie sheet lined with parchment paper. In a large bowl, cream butter and brown sugar until light and fluffy. Beat in the egg. Add flour, baking soda, and salt. Mix well. Stir in dates, pineapple, cherries, and nuts. Drop by teaspoonfuls onto cookie sheets. Bake for 10 - 12 minutes. Cool cookies on sheet for 1 minute. Remove from cookie sheet. Cool completely. Store in cookie tins. Makes 7 dozen cookies.

Feast of The Holy Innocents (December 28)
Infant martyrs who died for baby Jesus by the hand of Herod and his soldiers. Patron saints of babies and children.

"The precious death of any martyr deserves high praise because of his heroic confession; the death of these children is precious in the sight of God because of the beatitude they gained so quickly. For already, at the beginning of their lives, they pass on. The end of the present life is, for them, the beginning of glory."
-- St. Augustine

Food for the Soul: Pray for all the unborn babies today. Place them in the tender care of our Blessed Mother.

Precious Holy Innocents of God, pray for us.
Mary, Mother of God, graciously intercede for us.
Sweet Jesus, Our Newborn King, have mercy on us.
Holy Trinity, we adore You! Hear and answer our prayers.

Feast of the Holy Family (Sunday after Christmas)
Let us pray to Jesus, the Blessed Mother, and St. Joseph for our own families today.

"It is easy to love the people far away. It is not always east to love those close to us. It is easier to give a cup of rice to relieve hunger than to relieve the loneliness and pain of someone unloved in your own home. Bring love into your home, for this is where our love for each other must start."
-- St. Teresa of Calcutta

Food for the Soul: Love arrives! Rejoice! All glory to the Newborn King!

Jesus, Son of the Most High, hear our prayers.
Mary, holy mother of God and to us all, pray for us.
St. Joseph, foster father to us all, pray for us.
St. Teresa, pray for us.
Holy Trinity, we adore You! Hear and answer our prayers.

Porcupine Meatballs

A comforting dinner of tomato sauce, ground beef, and rice.
An old favorite with a few new twists!

Rice Ingredients:
- 1 boil in the bag rice
- Beef broth
- 1/4 tsp garlic powder
- 1/4 tsp onion powder

Red Sauce Ingredients:
- 2 cans of tomato bisque condensed soup
- 1 Tbsp vanilla creamer
- 1/2 tsp garlic powder
- 1/2 tsp onion powder
- 2 - 3 packages of Splenda
- Salt, to taste

Meatball Ingredients:
- 1 lb ground beef
- 1 tsp garlic powder
- 1 tsp onion powder
- 1/2 tsp meat tenderizer
- 1 Tbsp Worcestershire sauce
- 1 large egg
- 1 cup of the cooked rice
- 3 Tbsps of prepared red sauce

Directions: Prepare the rice. In a medium saucepan, add beef broth, garlic powder and onion powder. Stir. Add bag of rice, and boil for 10 minutes. Shut off heat and allow rice to absorb broth for about another 15 minutes. Preheat the oven to 350 degrees. Prepare the red sauce. In a 2 1/2 quart casserole dish, add tomato bisque soup, creamer, garlic powder, onion powder, and Splenda. Heat until warm on stovetop, stirring often. Salt to taste. In a medium bowl, add the ground beef, garlic powder, onion powder, meat tenderizer, egg, Worcestershire sauce, 1 cup of the cooked rice, and 3 Tbsps of the prepared red sauce. Mix lightly together. Do not overmix. Divide into about 12 meatballs. Place the meatballs in the casserole dish, on top of the sauce. With a spoon, pour some of the sauce on top of the meatballs. Cover the dish with the casserole dish cover or tightly, with foil. Place in oven and bake for 50 minutes. Carefully remove from oven. Serve over mashed potatoes.

Try this recipe another way by...

+++By making **Unstuffed Cabbage Rolls!** Add 1 1/2 cups thinly chopped Napa cabbage when preparing the tomato sauce. Cook for 5 minutes. Proceed with the recipe.

+++By making **Unstuffed Sweet Peppers!** Add 1 1/2 cups of thinly sliced sweet peppers when preparing the tomato sauce. Cook for 5 minutes. Proceed with the recipe.

God's Word of the Day (December 29)

"But the angel said to them, 'Do not be afraid. I bring you good news that will cause great joy for all the people.'" (Luke 2"10)

Food for the Soul: Joy arrives! Rejoice! All glory to the Newborn King!

Blessed Mother, graciously intercede for us.

Holy Trinity, we adore You! Hear and answer our prayers.

God's Word of the Day (December 30)

"She will give birth to a Son, and you are to give Him the name 'Jesus', because He will save His people from their sins." (Matthew 1:21)

Food for the Soul: Our Savior arrives! Rejoice! All glory to the Newborn King!

Blessed Mother, graciously intercede for us.

Holy Trinity, we adore You! Hear and answer our prayers.

God's Word of the Day (December 31)

"The Word became flesh and made His dwelling among us. We have seen His glory, the glory of the one and only Son, Who came from the Father, full of grace and truth."

(John 1:14)

Food for the Soul: Jesus lives among us! Rejoice! All glory to the Newborn King!

Blessed Mother, graciously intercede for us.

Holy Trinity, we adore You! Hear and answer our prayers.

New Year's Eve (December 31)

Mexican Sopes

You might be wondering, why sopes for a New Year's Eve celebration? Because it was on that day in 2015, Paul proposed to me! It's a story you'll have to read in my first book.That evening, before Paul proposed, we had our favorite sopes at a Mexican restaurant... they have a very special place in our hearts!

Sope Shell Ingredients:
- 3 cups masa harina
- 3 cups warm low sodium chicken broth
- 2 tsps salt

Sope Topping Ingredients:
- 1 lb burrito beef (beef sliced into small pieces)
- 1 can of refried beans
- Shredded lettuce
- 1/2 small sweet onion, diced
- 1 small tomato, diced
- 1 cup shredded cheese
- 1 avocado, diced, salted and tossed in lime juice
- Sour cream
- Salsa, if desired

Directions: Marinate the beef: In a medium bowl, tenderize the beef with a tenderizer. Add some canola oil, garlic powder, onion powder, and meat tenderizer. Add a splash of lime juice. Stir well until meat is covered in the marinade. Set aside while you make the sope shells. In a large bowl, mix together masa, broth, and salt. (I put the salt into the broth and stir before adding it to the masa, so it is evenly distributed.) Divide the dough into 12 pieces. Shape each of those pieces into a ball. Prepare two sheets of wax paper and a shallow bowl. Place the dough ball in between the wax paper sheets and use the bowl to press down on the ball to flatten into circles that are roughly 1/4 inch thick. Place dough discs on wax paper squares. (I buy them at the dollar store, 100 in a pack. Very handy!) Heat an 8 inch nonstick pan to medium heat. Place a dough disc on the pan and cook for 1 minute on each side. Remove sope from pan and place on a plate. Immediately pinch the sides upward, so it forms a cup with about 1/2 inch sides. The sope will be hot! Use a paper towel to protect your fingers. Preheat the deep fryer to 375 degrees. Continue with the rest of the dough balls. Once all of the sopes are shaped, fry two at a time in the fryer until golden brown. Remove from fryer and place, upside down, on a paper towel lined baking sheet. Set aside. Cook the beef in a large skillet, until browned, Don't overcook. Heat the refried beans. Top the sope shells with the beans, beef, tomato, onion, lettuce, cheese, avocado and sour cream. Then enjoy the Mexican tower of goodness!

Fried Lobster

Each year, Paul and I celebrate with some lobster, either on New Year's Eve or New Year's Day. Here is a lobster dish we originally discovered during a trip to Las Vegas a few years ago. It's a "Wow"!

Ingredients:
- 4 oz lobster tails, as many as you like
- Rice flour
- Melted unsalted butter

Directions: Prepare the deep fryer to 375 degrees. Cut the lobster tail meat out of the shell. (If you don't know how to do this, find a YouTube video that will show you how. It's not difficult, at all. You will need a good pair of kitchen shears.) Once the lobster is out of the shell, cut the lobster meat in half, lengthwise. In a medium bowl, add in rice flour. Take each piece of lobster and coat in the rice flour. Immediately, place floured lobster pieces into the fryer. Fry until golden. (It won't take very long.). Place fried lobster on a paper towel lined baking sheet. Serve. Dip in melted unsalted butter.

Perfectly Poached Lobster Tails
Traditional. Simple. Elegant. Delicious.

Ingredients:
- 4 oz lobster tails, as many as you like
- Celery salt
- Melted unsalted butter

Directions: Boil a medium or large pot of water on medium high heat. Season water with 1/4 - 1/2 tsp celery salt. (You can decide if you want to remove the lobster meat from the shell or cook in the shell. Either is fine.) Once the water comes to a boil, set the heat on low. Add in the lobster tails. Poach for 8 minutes. Remove tails from the water and place on a towel lined baking sheet to allow the tails to drain. Serve with melted unsalted butter. Or try with some **Seasoned Butter**...directions on how to make it is in the next recipe!

Sous Vide Filet Mignon with Seasoned Butter
Sous vide cooking allows you to cook your steaks to perfection! This recipe makes two medium rare steaks. You can adjust the cooking temperature for your steaks to your temperature liking. (See my notes below.) Then, sear steaks in a pan, and top with seasoned butter when serving. Magnifique!

Ingredients:
- 2 beef tenderloin filets
- 2 Tbsps canola oil in the pan, to sear steaks

Seasoned Butter Ingredients:
- 4 Tbsps unsalted butter, softened
- 1/4 tsp meat tenderizer
- 1/4 tsp garlic powder
- 1/4 tsp onion powder
- 1/8 tsp black pepper

Directions: Prepare the sous vide. Set to 134 degrees for medium rare filets. Tenderize the filets, then season both sides of the steaks with a few shakes of meat tenderizer, garlic powder, and onion powder. Spray some canola oil on them. Massage into the meat. Place filets in vacuum sealed bags. Place the bags into the sous vide bath. Sous vide for 2 hours. Remove filets from bags. Place on a paper towel and pat dry. Prepare the seasoned butter. Add the seasonings to the butter. Mix well. Set aside. In a medium nonstick frying pan, add 2 Tbsps oil. Heat to medium high heat. Add filets in pan. Cook until a sear on each side. Do not overcook. Serve filets hot, topped with seasoned butter.

For rare tenderloin filets, set sous vide to 128 degrees.
For medium rare tenderloin filets, set sous vide to 134 degrees.
For medium tenderloin filets, set sous vide to 144 degrees.
For medium well tenderloin filets, set sous vide to 155 degrees.

Rum Cake

A deliciously moist cake saturated with a rum glaze to celebrate the New Year!

Cake Ingredients:
- 1 cup chopped pecans
- 4 large eggs
- 1/2 cup cold water
- 1/2 cup canola oil
- 1/2 cup rum
- 1 yellow cake mix
- 1 instant vanilla pudding mix
- **Rum Glaze Ingredients:**
- 1 stick unsalted butter
- 1/4 cup water
- 1 cup sugar
- 1/2 cup rum

Whipped Cream Topping Ingredients:
- 1 cup heavy cream
- 3 Tbsps powdered sugar
- 1 Tbsp vanilla pudding mix (to stabilize whipped cream)
- 1/2 tsp vanilla

Directions: Preheat oven to 325 degrees. Prepare pan: Well oil and flour a Bundt pan. Sprinkle chopped pecans in pan. Set aside. In a large mixing bowl, add in eggs, cold water, oil, and rum. Mix together. Add in cake mix and pudding mix. Mix until well combined. Pour batter over nuts in pan. Bake for 1 hour. Remove cake from oven. Allow to cool in pan for 10 minutes. While cake is cooling in the pan, prepare the glaze. In a medium saucepan, melt butter. Add water and sugar to the melted butter. Bring to a boil. Boil for 5 minutes, stirring constantly. Remove saucepan from heat. Stir in the rum. Place a plate over the cake pan and invert cake onto the plate. With a metal or wooden skewer, poke holes into the cake, all over. As you poke the holes, try making the hole a little wider by wiggling the skewer a bit. Drizzle the warm glaze over the warm cake, into the holes, so the glaze is well absorbed. Wrap cake in plastic wrap to keep moist. Store at room temperature. Prepare the whipped cream topping. In a small cold metal bowl, beat heavy cream, powdered sugar, vanilla pudding, and vanilla until thick. Store whipped cream in refrigerator until ready to serve. Slice and serve the rum cake slice with a dollop of whipped cream.

Try this recipe another way...
*By making a **Brandy Cake!** Substitute the rum with brandy.
*By making an **Irish Cream Cake!** Substitute the rum with Irish cream. Omit the nuts.
*By making an **Amaretto Cake!** Substitute the rum with amaretto. Substitute the pecans with chopped slivered almonds.
*By making a **Rum ala Baba Cake!** How I used to love the rum babas filled with custard at the local bakery! We can enjoy those same flavors once again by adding a large dollop of of custard onto the rum cake slice and then topping it off with the fresh whipped cream. Here is the recipe for stovetop custard...

Stovetop Custard

*Serve by itself or with a slice of Rum Cake.
Can be used as a filling for pastry shells, too!*

Ingredients:
- 1/3 cup sugar
- 2 Tbsps cornstarch
- 1/8 tsp salt
- 2 large egg yolks
- 1 cup half and half
- 1/2 Tbsp unsalted butter
- 1 tsp vanilla

Directions: In a medium saucepan, add the sugar, salt, and cornstarch. Whisk to combine. Add the egg yolks and half and half to the mixture and whisk until well combined. Set to medium low heat. Cook the mixture for 10 - 12 minutes or until thickened, stirring constantly. Remove from heat. Add the vanilla. Stir until combined. Pour into a bowl. Place a piece of plastic wrap right on top of the custard so a skin does not form. Refrigerate for 3 - 4 hours before serving. Overnight is best.

*"Remember that everything soon comes to an end...
and take courage. Think of how our gain is eternal."
–– **St. Teresa of Avila***

*St. Teresa, pray for us.
Blessed Mother, graciously intercede for us.*

Holy Trinity, we adore You! Thank You for all of Your blessings this past year. We pray for Your continued blessings. Hear and answer our prayers.

***Paul and I wish you and yours,
A Happy and Blessed New Year!***

Lenten Season

Fat Tuesday or Mardi Gras
(Can occur in February or March)

Perfect Polish Paczki!

This was my Mom's recipe for Polish paczki, and I think it's the best! I've always called it the "perfect paczki recipe". So many times, paczki dough is very heavy and doughy, but these are lighter in texture. Fill them with your favorite fillings. They are best eaten the day you make them, so gather 'round your family and friends! You can be sure, I will be making them on Paczki Day, also known as Fat Tuesday, the day before Ash Wednesday, before we begin our Lenten fast...

Ingredients:
- 3/4 cup of milk
- 1/2 cup sugar
- 3 egg yolks
- 1/2 tsp salt
- 1/2 tsp vanilla
- 4 Tbsp unsalted butter, melted
- 2 Tbsp brandy
- 3 cups of flour
- 1 packet of instant yeast

Directions: In the bread machine, add milk, sugar, egg yolks, salt, vanilla, melted butter, brandy. Then add the flour on top. Make a small well in the middle of the flour. Pour the instant yeast into that well. (It is very important to add the ingredients in that specific order so the yeast does not come in contact with the sugar and salt right away.). Set the machine to the "dough" cycle and start the cycle. When the cycle is finished and the dough has risen during that cycle in the machine, remove the dough from the machine and place it in a bowl. Punch down the dough. Shape the dough into walnut size pieces, or slightly larger. (Keep them relatively small, so their centers will cook through when we fry them later.). Flatten them slightly and place the pieces, (leaving space in between them so they can rise), in a 9 x 13 glass pan sprayed with cooking spray. Cover the pan with Saran Wrap and place in a warm area for the dough to rise. (To prepare a nice, warm environment for the dough to rise, I usually turn the oven on to its lowest setting. When it gets to about 200 degrees, I shut the oven off, crack the oven door open, and then place the pan with the dough on the stovetop. You just don't want to make it too hot for the dough. That will kill the yeast.) If you run out of space in that one pan, you can use a cookie sheet lined with parchment paper and place a clean, warm kitchen towel over them. (Warm your kitchen towel in the microwave for a minute or so!) Allow the dough to rise for one hour.

After the paczki have risen, preheat the oil to 365 degrees. (I've used canola oil or crisco. Both have worked out just fine. I put about two inches of oil in an electric skillet that has temperature control.). Place a few paczki at a time in the fryer. Don't put too many in at once. That will lower the temperature of the oil. You will notice them puff up as they float in the oil. If they begin to brown too quickly, lower the temperature a little bit. Once the first side is cooked, carefully flip them over and fry the other side. Remove the paczki from the fryer and place on a cookie sheet lined with a layer of paper towel to absorb any oil. Continue to fry the rest. When you are ready to eat and serve, cut the paczki horizontally and add your filling. My favorite fillings are apricot and raspberry! You can also fill them with fresh strawberries and whipped cream... pudding....or the heavenly cream filling I used for my Swedish Flop cake... the possibilities are endless!

Polish Paczki Coffeecake

If you don't feel like frying paczki, this coffeecake captures the rich European flavors of the popular dessert!

Ingredients:
- 3/4 cup half and half
- 2 tsp sour cream
- 1/2 cup sugar
- 3 egg yolks
- 1/2 tsp salt
- 1/2 tsp vanilla
- 4 Tbsps melted unsalted butter, cooled
- 2 Tbsps brandy
- 3 1/4 cups flour
- 1 package instant yeast

Coffeecake Filling:
1 can Solo filling of your choice (apricot, poppyseed, almond, cherry, etc)

Directions: Using the bread machine, add half and half, sour cream, sugar, egg yolks, salt, vanilla, cooled melted butter, brandy, and flour into the pan. Make a well in the flour. Pour the yeast into the well. Set the cycle to "dough". When the cycle is finished, remove the dough from the pan. Place on a cookie sheet. Punch down the dough. Divide the dough into two equal pieces. Flatten one of the dough pieces into a rectangle. Spread half of the solo filling on the rectangle, within 1/2 inch of the edges. Roll the dough, from the longer side, up, like a jelly roll. Place the roll, seam side down, on a parchment paper lined cookie sheet.Do the same for the second piece of dough. You may use a different flavor filling, if you would prefer. Cover the coffeecakes lightly with a kitchen towel or with Saran Wrap. Allow to rise for 35 minutes. After 30 minutes, preheat oven to 350 degrees. Brush tops of coffeecakes with melted unsalted butter. Bake for 20 - 25 minutes, until tops are golden. Remove from oven. Rub a knob of unsalted butter over the tops. Cool for 10 - 15 minutes. Slice and serve warm, slathered with room temperature unsalted or whipped butter.
Try this recipe another way...

+++By making **Cheese Filled Paczki Coffeecake!** Instead of using a solo filling, make a cream cheese filling.

Cream Cheese Filling Ingredients:
- 8 oz cream cheese, softened
- 1/2 cup sugar
- 1/2 tsp vanilla
- 1/4 cup sour cream
- 1 large egg yolk

Mix ingredients together. Spread cream cheese mixture over dough rectangles. Roll dough like a jelly roll and continue with the original recipe.

Ash Wednesday
(The Lenten Season can begin in February or March)

"Lent is like a long 'retreat' during which we can turn back into ourselves and listen to the voice of God, in order to defeat the temptations of the evil one. It is a period of spiritual 'combat' which we must experience alongside Jesus, not with pride and presumption, but using the arms of faith: prayer, listening to the Word of God, and penance. In this way, we will be able to celebrate Easter in truth, ready to renew the promises of our Baptism."
-- Pope Benedict XVI

**Food for the Soul: Prepare your heart
so you may celebrate Easter in truth.**

Precious Jesus, Savior of the world, have mercy on us.
Blessed Mother, graciously intercede for us.
Holy Trinity, we adore You! Hear and answer our prayers.
For the sake of His Sorrowful Passion,
have mercy on us and on the whole world.

Lenten Friday, Week 1:

"Jesus said to all: 'If any man will come after me, let him deny himself, and take up his cross daily, and follow Me.'" (Luke 9:23)

Food for the Soul: See your cross as a light, guiding you, and others, to Jesus.

Precious Jesus, Savior of the world, have mercy on us.
Blessed Mother, graciously intercede for us.
Holy Trinity, we adore You! Hear and answer our prayers.
For the sake of His Sorrowful Passion,
have mercy on us and on the whole world.

Fish Fry Day

Fish Fry Tacos

Imagine a soft, warm, corn tortilla enveloping nuggets of cod in a light, crunchy batter, topped with shredded radishes, thin slices of onion, diced avocado, and shredded cheese, then crowned with a homemade chipotle mayo sauce. Sounds oh, so good!

Cod Batter Ingredients:
- 1/2 cup flour
- 1/2 cup rice flour
- 2 Tbsps baking powder
- 1 1/2 tsp lemon pepper
- 1 tsp garlic powder
- 1 tsp onion powder
- 1 tsp paprika
- 1/2 cup half and half
- 1/2 cup water or beer

- 1 lb cod, patted dry, cut into nuggets
- Extra small bowl of flour

- 1 package corn tortillas, warmed

Taco Topping Ingredients:
- 1/2 cup shredded radishes
- 1/2 cup thinly sliced sweet or red onion
- 1 avocado, diced, tossed in lime juice and lightly salted
- 1 cup (or more) shredded quesadilla cheese, or your choice

Chipotle Mayo Ingredients:
- 1 small can of chipotle peppers in adobo sauce
- 1/2 cup mayo

Directions: Shred the radishes and onion. Set aside. Prepare the mayo. Place the chipotle peppers in a food processor. Pulse until smooth. Take about 1 Tbsp of the chipotle sauce and add it to the mayo. Adjust the amount of chipotle sauce to your taste preference. Preheat the deep fryer to 375 degrees. Prepare a baking sheet lined with paper towels. Prepare the cod. Cut the cod into nuggets. Pat the cod dry. Coat the cod in the flour. Place nuggets on a platter. Set aside. Prepare the batter. In a medium bowl, combine the dry ingredients; flour, rice flour, baking powder, lemon pepper, garlic powder, onion powder, paprika. Stir together with a fork. Add in the half and half and the water. Stir until combined. Add additional half and half or water to the batter to thin it out to a coating consistency, if needed. Dip the nuggets into the batter and then place into the fryer, about 6 nuggets at a time. Turn the nuggets over in the fryer to fry both sides, until golden brown. Place on the prepared baking sheet. Continue the process until all nuggets are fried. Prepare the avocado. Dice and toss in lime juice. Salt lightly. Set aside. Warm the tortillas in a cloth tortilla warmer in the microwave. Build your fish taco! Layer your tortilla with cod, radish, onion, avocado, chipotle mayo, cheese. Store cod leftovers in refrigerator. You can warm up leftover cod nuggets in the air fryer to retain that crispness. They will taste just as good as freshly made!

Lenten Friday, Week 2

"Apart from the Cross, there is no other ladder by which we may get to heaven."
—— St. Rose of Lima

Food for the Soul: See your cross as a ladder;
With every rung bringing you closer to Jesus.

St. Rose of Lima, pray for us.
Precious Jesus, Savior of the world, have mercy on us.
Blessed Mother, graciously intercede for us.
Holy Trinity, we adore You! Hear and answer our prayers.
For the sake of His Sorrowful Passion,
have mercy on us and on the whole world.

Crispy Shrimp Tacos with Pineapple Salsa

I started making these tacos after I married Paul. A Polish girl's twist on a Mexican favorite! My homemade pineapple salsa is slightly sweet with a mild kick. The shrimp are light and crispy with my use of the rice flour coating. A tasty variety of ingredients makes this recipe one, you and your family will come back to, time and time again!
My sister-in-law, Celia, gives them a thumbs up!

Crispy Shrimp Ingredients:
- 12 oz of large raw shrimp, peeled and deveined, tails removed
- 3 Tbsp, heaping, rice flour

Pineapple Salsa:
- 1 can of mild green chiles, 4 oz., drained
- 4-5 pineapple rings, drained, cut into tidbits, depending on your taste
- 1 small onion, diced
- 2 Tbsp chipotle mayo
- 1 packet of Splenda

Taco Toppings:
- 1 bag of shredded, sweetened coconut, 8 oz.
- Sliced Almonds
- Quesadilla cheese, shredded

- 6 corn tortillas

Directions: Prepare the Pineapple Salsa. Dice the small onion, add to a medium sized bowl. Add the drained green chiles, and the pineapple tidbits. Stir. Add the chipotle mayo and the packet of Splenda. Mix thoroughly. Taste. Adjust to your taste. Set aside. Prepare the toasted coconut. Pour the coconut into a medium sized frying pan. Heat on medium heat, stirring the coconut constantly until the coconut turns golden brown. Remove the coconut from the pan and store in a container. Set aside. (You can store any extra toasted coconut at room temperature in a closed container or ziplock bag for the next time you make these tacos.)

Prepare the shrimp. Preheat your deep fryer. Cut the shrimp into bite sized pieces. Toss the shrimp in the rice flour right before you are ready to throw them in the fryer. Fry the shrimp pieces for a minute or two, until golden brown. Remove from the fryer. Place on a paper towel to drain.

Warm the corn tortillas in a tortilla warmer. Have your guests assemble the tacos....tortillas, shrimp, heaping spoonfuls of salsa, toasted coconut, sliced almonds and cheese. Olé!

Lenten Friday, Week 3

"Show me your hands. Do they have scars from giving? Show me your feet. Are they wounded in service? Show me your heart. Have you left a place for divine love?"
-- Venerable Fulton Sheen

Food for the Soul: See your cross as a gift for others, providing them with inspiration, drawing them ever closer to Jesus.
Precious Jesus, Savior of the world, have mercy on us.
Blessed Mother, graciously intercede for us.
Holy Trinity, we adore You! Hear and answer our prayers.
For the sake of His Sorrowful Passion,
have mercy on us and on the whole world.

Velvety, Creamy Corn and Shrimp Chowder

A thick, velvety, rich chowder full of sweet corn. Simply delicious!

Ingredients:
- 4 Tbsps unsalted butter
- 1/2 cup mixture of sweet onion, celery, and carrots, diced
- 1/4 cup flour
- 1 can of low sodium chicken broth
- 1 can extra sweet corn, undrained
- 1 cup half and half
- Another 4 Tbsps unsalted butter, cut into 8 pieces
- 1 cup tiny cooked shrimp, thawed
- Salt and pepper to taste

Directions: In a medium saucepan, melt 4 Tbsps of unsalted butter. Add the diced onion, celery, and carrots mixture and sauté until softly cooked. Add 1/4 cup of flour cook until combined. Heat the can of chicken broth. Add slowly to the veggie mixture and stir until well combined. Add an undrained can of extra sweet corn to the broth and veggie mixture. Heat for a few minutes. Add one cup of half and half and cook on medium heat for a few minutes, stirring constantly so the chowder does not catch and burn. Add 4 Tbsps of unsalted butter that is cut into eight pieces, a piece or two at a time, stirring constantly. Add salt and pepper to taste. Add a handful of tiny shrimp into each bowl. Pour the chowder over the shrimp. Stir together. Serve with **Colby Jack Cheese Bread (April 12)** or some **Garlic Cheddar Scones (February 14)**.

Lenten Friday, Week 4

*"Let the mouth fast from foul words and unjust criticism,
for what good is it if we abstain from birds and fishes,
but bite and devour our brothers?"
-- St. John Chrysostom*
**Food for the Soul: Be kind and gentle with others.
Control any anger or spite.**
St. John Chrysostom, pray for us.
Precious Jesus, Savior of the world, have mercy on us.
Blessed Mother, graciously intercede for us.
Holy Trinity, we adore You! Hear and answer our prayers.
For the sake of His Sorrowful Passion,
have mercy on us and on the whole world.

Four Cheese Veggie Egg Noodle Lasagna

I make my lasagna using egg noodles to keep it light. Plus, each layer is full of delicious flavor. Those layers combine together to create a tantalizing treat for the tastebuds!

Sauce with Veggies Layer Ingredients:
- One 24 ounce jar of your favorite pasta sauce
- 2 cups of your favorite veggies, diced and cooked (you can always switch out the veggies for one pound of Italian sausage, cooked, oil drained)

Noodle Layer Ingredients:
- Six ounces of medium size egg noodles, cooked
- 4 Tbsp unsalted butter, cut into eight pieces
- 4 Tbsp sour cream
- Sprinkle of garlic powder, to taste
- Sprinkle of onion powder, to taste
- Light sprinkle of salt, to taste

Cheese Layer Ingredients:
- 7 1/2 ounces of whole milk ricotta cheese
- 8 ounces of cream cheese, softened
- 1 large egg yolk
- 2 Tbsp sour cream
- 2 packets of Splenda
- 1/2 cup shredded mozzarella
- 2 1/2 Tbsp Parmesan cheese, from the jar
- Sprinkle of dried parsley

Directions: Preheat the oven to 375 degrees. Oil a 9 x 5 inch non-stick loaf pan. Set aside. Cook the diced veggies for the sauce. (Why cook them? The veggies have water in them. By cooking them, we remove most of that water. This way, our sauce, and lasagna, will not turn into a soupy, watery mess!) When cooked, add them to the sauce. Set aside. Cook the noodles. Drain the water. Add the butter to the noodles and stir until the butter is melted. Stir in the sour cream. Sprinkle in the onion and garlic powder. Add a light sprinkle of salt. Taste. Adjust flavors, if needed. Set aside. In a microwave safe medium sized bowl, place the cream cheese. Microwave for about 30-40 seconds until the cream cheese is very soft, soft enough to stir. Add the ricotta cheese to the cream cheese. Stir until completely combined. Stir in the egg yolk and sour cream. Add the Splenda. Add the mozzarella and the Parmesan cheeses. Add a pinch or two of the dried parsley. Stir until combined. (You may be thinking, why not use regular Parmesan cheese? Why use the Parmesan from the jar? It's because the Parmesan cheese in the jar ends up thickening the cheese mixture. I find, it holds the cheese mixture together nicely.)

Once all of the layers have been prepared, take your oiled loaf pan and begin the layering process. First, add a layer of the veggie sauce into the pan to cover the bottom of the pan. Next, add a layer of the noodle mixture, about a 1/2 inch thick. Then, add a layer of the cheese mixture, about a 1/2 inch thick. Repeat the layers in the same order. Lastly, add a thin layer of the veggie sauce on the top. Cover the lasagna with non-stick aluminum foil. Place the loaf pan on a cookie sheet covered with non-stick foil (to catch any drips) and bake covered for 25 minutes. After

25 minutes, carefully remove the foil from the loaf pan and bake uncovered for another 25 minutes. Remove the lasagna from the oven. Allow the lasagna to rest for 15 minutes.

At this point, I would cool the lasagna on the counter and then put it in the refrigerator so we can have it for dinner the next day. (I usually make it the evening before we want to eat it.) Why? Because if I cut it right now, the layers will not hold together as well. Chilling the lasagna will help the layers to set, allow the flavors to meld, and it will make it easier to cut and remove from the pan. The layers will hold together perfectly! When you are ready to eat it, slice the lasagna, place the slice on a plate, cover the slice with a damp paper towel, and heat it up in the microwave for 2-3 minutes. Grab some warm Italian bread, softened butter or oil, and "mangia"!

Try this recipe in another way...
+++By making **Italian Sausage Egg Noodle Lasagna!** Just swap out the veggies for 1 pound of ground Italian sausage, cooked, with oil drained. If I can't find the sausage in bulk, I buy the links, cut them open, and remove the casing...

Lenten Friday, Week 5

"Fasting is directed to two things; the deletion of sin,
and the raising of the mind to heavenly things."
-- St. Thomas Aquinas

Food for the Soul: Meditate on the Lord throughout your day.
Allow your meditation to crowd out any thoughts
that will lead you to sin.

Precious Jesus, Savior of the world, have mercy on us.
Blessed Mother, graciously intercede for us.
Holy Trinity, we adore You! Hear and answer our prayers.
For the sake of His Sorrowful Passion,
have mercy on us and on the whole world.

Savory Cheese Flan Cups

This dish is similar to quiche, but the filling is a little richer. And the crust of these cups will melt in your mouth! Serve them as an appetizer or an entree. Wonderful served for breakfast, too!

Crust Ingredients:
- 2 cups of flour
- 2 sticks of unsalted butter, melted
- 6 oz of cream cheese, softened

Flan Ingredients:
- 10 ounces of half and half
- 3/4 cup of your favorite shredded cheese
- 2 large eggs

Pan:
Two muffin tins, one twelve count and one six count

Directions: In a medium saucepan, heat half and half and cheese until the cheese is melted. Remove from heat and add the eggs, one at a time. For the crust, in a medium bowl, mix together the butter and the cream cheese. Add the flour and mix until combined. Do not over mix the dough, so it will remain tender and flaky. Preheat the oven to 325 degrees. Divide the crust dough into eighteen pieces. Place each piece into a each muffin tin cup. Line each muffin cup with the dough for the crust. If you have a little extra shredded cheese on hand, sprinkle a little on the bottom of each cup of crust. Then, pour the flan filling into each crust. Do not overfill. Bake for twenty-five to thirty minutes, until flan is set. Remove pan from the oven and allow to rest for a few minutes. Remove the flan cups from each tin, carefully, with the tip of a knife sliding between the crust and the pan. Serve.

Try this recipe another way...
+++By making ***Savory Ham and Cheese Flan Cups!*** Add some shaved or diced ham with some shredded cheese to the cups before pouring in the flan filling, for another delicious variation.

+++By making **Savory Tuna and Cheddar Flan Cups!** Add some flaked canned albacore tuna with some shredded cheddar cheese to the cups before pouring in the flan filling.

+++By making **Savory Veggie and Cheese Flan Cups!** Add some sautéed diced onions, slivers of cooked sweet peppers, and shredded cheese to the cups before pouring in the flan filling.

Holy Week

"The tragedy of the Passion brings to fulfillment our own life and the whole of human history. We can't let Holy Week be just a kind of 'commemoration'. It means contemplating the mystery of Jesus Christ as something which continues to work in our souls."
-- St. Josemaría Escrivá

Food for the Soul: Walk alongside Jesus throughout this week. May His Passion come alive in all of your senses. See. Feel. Hear.
St. Josemaría Escrivá, pray for us.
Precious Jesus, Savior of the world, have mercy on us.
Blessed Mother, graciously intercede for us.
Holy Trinity, we adore You! Hear and answer our prayers.
For the sake of His Sorrowful Passion,
have mercy on us and on the whole world.

Palm Sunday

"Hosanna! -- which means, 'Save!' 'Hosanna to You Who are in the highest.' O Almighty, save those who are humbled. Have mercy on us, in consideration of our palms, may the palms we wave move Your Heart, You Who come to call Adam..."
-- St. Romanus the Melodist

Food for the Soul: Save Your people, O Lord! Have mercy on us.
St. Romanus, pray for us.
Precious Jesus, Savior of the world, have mercy on us.
Blessed Mother, graciously intercede for us.
Holy Trinity, we adore You! Hear and answer our prayers.
For the sake of His Sorrowful Passion,
have mercy on us and on the whole world.

Holy Thursday

"The washing of the feet and the sacrament of the Eucharist: two expressions of one and the same mystery of love entrusted to the disciples, so that, Jesus says, 'as I have done...so also must you do.'"
-- St. John Paul II

Food for the Soul: Ask Jesus to show you how He desires you to serve others.

St. John Paul II, pray for us.
Precious Jesus, Savior of the world, have mercy on us.
Blessed Mother, graciously intercede for us.
Holy Trinity, we adore You! Hear and answer our prayers.
For the sake of His Sorrowful Passion,
have mercy on us and on the whole world.

Naan Bread

Pillowy soft, buttery flatbread, ready to be topped with whatever your hungry heart desires. Even though I know this bread has yeast in it and Jesus shared unleavened bread at the Last Supper, I can imagine Jesus passing some naan bread around to everyone around His table. Make some naan for your Holy Thursday supper and pass it to all those gathered around your table. Meditate on the sacred words Jesus spoke to His disciples that night: "Do this in remembrance of Me."

Ingredients:
- 2 tsp sugar
- 1 tsp salt
- 1/2 cup sour cream
- 1/2 cup water
- 1 Tbsp olive oil
- 2 1/4 cups flour
- 1 package instant yeast

For Pan and Finishing:
- 2 1/2 Tbsp unsalted butter, melted
- 2 1/2 Tbsp salted butter, melted

Directions: Add the sugar, salt, sour cream, water, olive oil, and flour in order in the bread machine. Make a well in the middle of the flour and fill it with the yeast. Choose the dough setting cycle. Before removing the dough from the bread machine, melt the unsalted and salted butter together. You will use the melted butter when cooking the naan. After dough rises in the machine, remove dough and place it on a cookie sheet. Shape dough into a cylinder. Cut into 8 equal pieces. Heat a small sized nonstick pan to medium high heat. With a pastry brush, brush pan lightly with melted butter. With your palm, flatten one piece of dough into a thin disc. Place on heated pan. Lightly apply melted butter with a pastry brush on the uncooked side. Dough will begin to puff up. Flip when underside is browned. Remove from pan when both sides have a few browned "spots". Place cooked naan on a platter and apply more melted butter to both sides of each piece of naan with a pastry brush. Repeat the same process with the other pieces of dough. Store in a gallon size plastic bag. May be stored at room temperature or in the fridge. To reheat, use a cloth tortilla warmer to warm the naan for a soft texture, or you may warm the naan in an air fryer for a lightly crispy texture. Delicious either way! Makes 8 naan.

Try this recipe another way...
+++By making **Garlic Butter Green Onion Naan!** Substitute garlic butter for the butter. As you are shaping the dough into a cylinder, add 2 Tbsps of thinly sliced green onions to the dough. Continue with the recipe.

Friday of Lent, Week 6:
Good Friday (Begin the Divine Mercy Novena)

We adore You, O Christ, and we praise You.
Because by Your Holy Cross, You have redeemed the world.

"Through a tree we were made debtors to God;
so through a tree we have our debt canceled."
-- St. Irenaeus

"Yesterday, Christ raised Lazarus from the dead; today, He is going to His own death. Yesterday, He tore off the strips of cloth which bound Lazarus; today, He is stretching out His Hand to those who want to bind Him. Yesterday, He tore that man from darkness and the shadow of death. And the Church is celebrating. She is beginning the feast of Feasts, for she is receiving her King as a Spouse, for her King is in her midst."
-- St. Ephrem

Food for the Soul: We love You, Jesus. Have mercy on us, O Lord. Graciously, hear us.

Eternal Father, I offer You, the Body and Blood,
Soul and Divinity of Your dearly beloved Son, our Lord Jesus Christ,
for the atonement of our sins, and those of the whole world.

For the sake of His Sorrowful Passion,
have mercy on us, and on the whole world.
Holy God, Holy Mighty One, Holy Immortal One,
have mercy on us and on the whole world.
-- Prayers from the Chaplet of Divine Mercy
St. Irenaeus, pray for us,
St. Ephrem, pray for us.
St. Faustina, pray for us.
Mother, Most Sorrowful, graciously intercede for us.
Jesus, our Lord and Savior, have mercy on us.
Holy Trinity, we adore You! Hear and answer our prayers.

Hot Cross Buns

These buns are traditionally baked by many Catholics for Good Friday or Easter morning breakfasts.

Ingredients:
- 3/4 cup half and half
- 1/4 cup canola oil
- 1 tsp sugar
- 1/2 cup light brown sugar
- 2 large eggs
- 1 tsp vanilla
- 1/2 tsp ground cinnamon
- 1 tsp salt
- 3 1/2 cups flour
- 1 package of instant yeast

Bread Add-Ins:
- 3/4 cups of raisins, currants, or dried cranberries, plumped in hot water for 5 minutes, drained and patted dry

Cross Mixture Ingredients:
- 1/2 cup flour
- 6 - 8 Tbsps water

Glaze. Ingredients:
- 2 Tbsps apricot jam
- 2 tsps water

Directions: Using a bread machine, add half and half, oil, sugar, brown sugar, eggs, vanilla, cinnamon, salt, and flour (in that order) to the pan. Make a small well in the center of the flour and add yeast into that well. Set on the "dough" cycle. When add-in beeps are heard during the dough cycle, add in the plumped raisins or dried cranberries. Prepare by oiling a 9 x 13 inch glass cake pan. Once the cycle is complete, remove the dough from the bread machine pan. Punch down dough. Shape into 14 - 16 balls of dough. Place buns in prepared pan. Cover the pan lightly with a kitchen towel or plastic wrap. Allow to rise for 1 hour. Prepare the cross mixture of the flour and water, in a small bowl. Use between 6 and 8 Tbsps of water so the consistency of the mixture will pipe easily onto the buns. Place cross mixture into a small plastic bag. Snip corner to pipe mixture. Preheat oven to 350 degrees. Meanwhile, slowly pipe the cross mixture onto the risen buns, going straight across the center of all of the buns in a single line, and then a single line down the center of the buns. This will result in a cross on top of each bun. Bake buns for 20 - 25 minutes, until golden brown on top. If buns are browning too quickly, loosely place some aluminum foil over the top of the pan. Remove from the oven. In a small bowl, lightly heat up the apricot jam and the water. Stir until combined. Brush the glaze over the buns with a pastry brush. Allow to cool for about 10 minutes. Serve buns warm.

Note: If you would rather not use the flour mixture to pipe crosses onto the buns before baking, you can omit that part and, instead, use some powdered sugar icing (1/2 cup powdered sugar mixed with a tablespoon of half and half) and pipe the crosses onto the baked buns after the buns have completely cooled.

Tuna Pot Pie

This pot pie recipe is for an open faced pie, with no crust on top. You can top it with 1 cup of freshly shredded cheese of your choice for the last 5 minutes of baking time, or until the cheese topping is melted. Or you can make another batch of pie crust and top the open faced pie with the top crust before baking. Just be sure to cut a few slits in the top crust to allow the steam to release while baking...

Pie Crust Ingredients:
- 1 1/2 cups flour
- 1/4 tsp salt
- 1 stick unsalted butter, melted
- 2 vanilla creamers

Tuna Filling Ingredients:
- 1/2 stick unsalted butter
- 3 Tbsps flour
- 1/2 tsp salt
- 1/8 tsp pepper
- 1/2 tsp onion powder
- 1/2 tsp garlic powder
- 1 cup vegetable broth
- 1 cup half and half
- 2 cups flaked canned albacore tuna
- 3/4 cups cooked vegetables (peas, corn, carrots, etc)

Directions: In a large nonstick skillet, melt butter. Stir in flour, salt, pepper, onion powder and garlic powder. Stir in broth on low heat. Stir in cream. Cook, stirring constantly, until sauce begins to thicken. Then cook 2 additional minutes. Add tuna and cooked vegetables. Combine. Prepare the pie crust. Combine the melted butter, salt, creamers, and flour. Do not overmix. Press the dough into an 8 x 8 inch square pan or 8 or 9 inch pie pan. Add tuna filling to pie crust. Bake at 385 degrees for 30 minutes, until crust is golden brown. Remove pot pie from oven. Allow pie to sit for 5 minutes before cutting and serving.

Try this recipe another way...
+++By making ***Creamy Tuna ala Biscuits!*** Instead of making the tuna filling in a pie crust, serve it over some fresh, hot, homemade biscuits. You can use the recipe for ***Whipped Cream Vanilla Biscuits (January 5)*** by changing it into a savory biscuit recipe. Omit the vanilla and omit sugaring the biscuit tops before baking. You can even add 1/2 cup of freshly shredded cheese (cheddar or colby jack) to the dough. Then, just break open those fresh baked biscuits and top with the warm, comforting, creamy, tuna and veggie goodness!

Easter Vigil

"...He slept, so that we might be awakened. He died, so that we might live."
-- St. Augustine

Food for the Soul: Death cannot hold Jesus Christ, our Lord!
We adore You, O Christ, and we praise You. Because by Your Holy Cross, You have redeemed the world!

St. Augustine, pray for us.
Blessed Mother, graciously intercede for us.
Holy Trinity, we adore You! Hear and answer our prayers.
Jesus Christ, have mercy on us.

Easter Season

Easter Sunday
Jesus Christ is risen today! Hallelujah!
"Yes, Christ is truly risen, and we are witnesses of this. We proclaim this witness to the world, so that the joy, which is ours, will reach countless other hearts, kindling in them the light of the hope which does not disappoint."
-- St. John Paul II

Food for the Soul: Proclaim to all you know, Jesus is risen from the dead! Hallelujah!

We adore You, O Christ, and we praise You. Because by Your Holy Cross, You have redeemed the world! Hallelujah!
St. John Paul II, pray for us.
Blessed Mother, graciously intercede for us.
Holy Trinity, we adore You! Hear and answer our prayers.
Jesus Christ is risen today! Hallelujah!

Citrus Pull Apart Bread

Breads are popular to make around Easter time because they are symbolic. The breads we raise are a tribute to our dear Lord Jesus, as we celebrate His rising from the dead!

Growing up, my Mom was always searching to find new recipes, especially for breads, coffeecakes, and desserts. I loved her adventurous spirit! She wasn't afraid to try any recipe! I guess I definitely take after her in that respect. I, too, enjoy finding and trying new recipes. When I recently found this recipe, it sounded so good. The fresh flavors of oranges and lemons. The rich, buttery dough. Layers upon layers of comfort. And then to top it off, literally, a glaze that would be baked on to the crust of the bread! That was something new! I made this bread the very next day. I was initially worried that the dough would not rise with so much butter, but it rose very well. The aroma of the citrus was heavenly as it baked. Then, the taste test... outstanding! We took a loaf over to our friends, Ellen and Greg, and they ranked it as the best thing I have ever made! Thank you! Those words certainly say a lot!

Bread Ingredients:

- 1/4 cup water
- 1 stick unsalted butter, slightly melted
- 1/2 cup sugar
- 1 tsp salt
- 2 large eggs, lightly beaten
- 1 cup half and half
- 1 Tbsp fresh lemon juice
- 4 1/2 cups bread flour
- 1 (1/4-oz.) envelope instant yeast
-

Citrus Filling Ingredients:

- 3/4 cup sugar
- Zest from 2 oranges
- Zest from 2 large lemons
- 4 Tbsp of unsalted butter, softened, divided in half, for spreading on each of the two loaves, two tablespoonfuls of butter for each loaf

Citrus Filling Directions:

1. Stir together sugar, orange zest, and lemon zest until combined. (Divide in half; half for each loaf). Set aside.

Glaze Topping Ingredients: (use only for sweet breads)

- 1/4 cup butter, melted
- 2 tablespoons honey
- 1 large egg white
- 2/3 cup powdered sugar

Directions: Using the bread machine, add water, melted butter (cooled), sugar, salt, eggs, half and half, lemon juice, and bread flour. Make a well in the flour and add the yeast to that well. Set machine to the dough cycle. Prepare the citrus filling. In a small bowl, add orange zest, lemon zest, and sugar. Stir together. Divide zest sugar mixture in half. Set aside. When dough cycle is complete, remove dough from machine. Place dough on medium sized nonstick cookie sheet. Punch dough down. Divide dough in half. Turn half of the dough out onto another medium cookie sheet. Press one dough portion into a rectangle on the cookie sheet. Spread with 2 Tbsp softened butter, then sprinkle half of the Citrus filling over the butter. Cut the rectangle into 6 strips. Stack the 6 strips on top of each other, then cut this stack into 6 pieces. Repeat procedure with remaining half of the dough. Oil 2 (9- x 5-inch) loaf pans (or you can use two oiled 8 x 8 inch glass pans instead, or one loaf pan and one 8 x 8 pan). Place stacked rectangles, cut sides up, into 1 prepared pan. Then do the same in the other pan. Prepare the glaze. Spoon the glaze topping over the loaves and spread it over the dough to completely cover. Cover the pans loosely with plastic wrap; let rise in a warm place (80° to 85°) for 1 hour or until doubled in size. Preheat oven to 350°. Bake 30 minutes or until golden brown, covering with aluminum foil after 25 minutes to prevent excessive browning, if necessary. Cool in pans for 10 minutes. Remove from pans. Pull apart slices. Serve warm, slathered with butter! To rewarm leftovers, cut a portion of the loaf and wrap it in foil. Bake in 350 degree oven for about 10 minutes.

You can also add a citrus glaze on top of the baked bread, mixing together 1 tablespoonful of lemon or orange juice with about 1/2 cup powdered sugar. I thought it might be too sweet to add another glaze, but if that is what you would like, give it a try!

Try this recipe another way...
+++By making a *Cinnamon Pull Apart Loaf!* Substitute the citrus filling for 3/4 cup cinnamon sugar and sprinkle the sugar over the layer of butter.

+++By making a *Parmesan Garlic Pull Apart Loaf!* Substitute the citrus filling with *Parmesan Garlic Butter*. To make the Parmesan garlic butter, mix together 4 Tbsps unsalted butter, 1/4 tsp meat tenderizer, 1/2 tsp garlic powder, 1/4 cup finely shredded Parmesan cheese. (Just remember to omit the glaze topping before baking.)

+++By making a *Buttery Pull Apart Loaf!* Omit the citrus filling and just spread on the butter. You can keep the glaze topping if you want a sweeter note to the loaf, or omit it for a more savory loaf.

Suggestion:
Try this bread's glaze on the **Challah Bread (January 1)** *or on the* **Hot Cross Buns (Good Friday)** *before baking. If using it on the Hot Cross Buns, omit the apricot glaze.*

Potatoes Au Gratin

I recently discovered the recipe for this A-list dish after Paul and I went out to celebrate his birthday this year. He ordered au gratin potatoes as his side. He had a bite, I had a bite, and we both thought they were absolutely delicious! I found the recipe when we came home and knew it was one I would be trying soon. Layers of potatoes, sliced paper thin. Cheese. Cream. Butter. Slow cooked in the oven for almost 2 hours until it's so tender, creamy, and cheesy, the ingredients unite together into a new culinary creation! This is one of those "labor of love" recipes which takes time and effort, but the ultimate result is definitely worth it. You can make it a day ahead of time, which is great, because it tastes even better the next day! What an amazing side dish to serve for an Easter dinner!

Ingredients:
- 2 Tbsps unsalted butter
- 1 - 2 cloves of garlic, minced
- 1 1/2 cups heavy cream (do not substitute!)
- 1 cup Colby jack cheese, shredded
- 1 cup brick, Muenster, or Colby jack cheese, shredded
- 1 cup Parmesan cheese, shredded
- 2 large or 3 medium russet potatoes, sliced paper thin
- Salt and pepper

Directions: In a small bowl, combine the melted butter, heavy cream, and minced garlic. Stir. Set aside. To a medium bowl, add the three cheeses, Mix together until combined. Set aside. Prepare a Corningware baking dish that has some depth for the many layers. Oil the bottom and sides well. Set aside. Preheat the oven to 350 degrees. Peel the potatoes. Using a mandoline slicer, slice paper thin slices of the potato. Be careful of your hands and fingers as you use the mandoline. (I have a spiralizer that stands up and has a hand crank. I chose the ribbon cut blade, which is held vertically in the cutter. I then just sliced the potatoes by hand on the vertical blade, without using the hand crank. It worked out beautifully! If you ever see a stand up spiralizer at a thrift store for a few dollars, pick one up! That's what I did! Most of them have never been unused. The same thing goes for bread machines!) When a third of the potatoes are sliced, place them in an even layer onto the prepared baking dish. Season with a little salt and pepper. Pour 1/2 cup of the cream mixture over the potatoes . Sprinkle 1 cup of the cheeses on top of the potatoes, in an even layer. Begin slicing another third of the potatoes. (By not slicing the potatoes all at once, this will prevent them from turning brown.) Place sliced potatoes over the cheese. Season. Pour another 1/2 cup of the cream mixture over the potatoes. Sprinkle 1 cup of the cheeses over the potatoes. Begin slicing the last third of the potatoes. Place slices over the cheese layer. Season. Pour the last 1/2 cup of the cream mixture over the potatoes. DO NOT add the last layer of cheese! We will save that last cup until the very end of the baking process. Cover the baking dish with the Corningware cover or with some foil. Bake for 1 hour and 20 minutes. Test the middle with a knife to see if the potatoes are tender. If not, bake for another 10 minutes. Remove from oven. Uncover and add the last cup of cheese to the top. Bake, uncovered, for another 15 - 18 minutes, until cheese topping is lightly browned. Remove from oven. Allow to cool for 5 minutes. Cut and serve. Refrigerate leftovers. Leftovers will last 3 - 4 days in the refrigerator.

Divine Mercy Sunday (Sunday after Easter)

"I am love and Mercy itself. There is no misery that could be a match for My Mercy, neither will mercy exhaust it, because as it is being granted -- it increases. The soul that trusts in My Mercy is most fortunate because I, Myself, take care of it."
-- Jesus, speaking to St. Faustina

Food for the Soul: Just like His amazing Love, His Divine Mercy increases. His precious gifts are in abundance for His people. All we need do is ask for them, and we shall receive.

Eternal Father, I offer You the Body and Blood, Soul and Divinity of Your dearly beloved Son, our Lord Jesus Christ, in atonement for our sins and of the whole world.

For the sake of His Sorrowful Passion, have mercy on us and on the whole world.

Holy God, Holy Mighty One, Holy Immortal One, have mercy on us and on the whole world.
-- Prayers of the Divine Mercy Chaplet

St. Faustina, pray for us.
Blessed Mother, graciously intercede for us.
Jesus our Redeemer, have mercy on us.
Jesus, I trust in You.
Holy Trinity, we adore You! Hear and answer our prayers.

Parmesan Crusted Caesar Chicken

*This has become one of our favorite chicken dinners!
It's inspired by a meal we frequently ordered at one of our local restaurants.
The marinade is the key to this juicy, tender, flavorful chicken,
but that crunchy, cheesy topping makes it a
winner, winner, chicken dinner, too!*

Ingredients:
- Chicken tenderloins, about 1 1/2 lbs

Marinade for Chicken Ingredients:
- 1/3 cup canola oil
- 1/3 cup + 2 Tbsps creamy Caesar dressing
- 2 Tbsps Worcestershire sauce
- 1 tsp apple cider vinegar
- 1 tsp lime juice
- 1 tsp garlic powder
- 1 tsp onion powder
- 1/2 tsp black pepper

Creamy Cheese Topping Ingredients:
- 1/2 cup Parmesan cheese, finely grated
- 1/2 cup brick, Muenster, or Colby jack cheese, grated
- 6 Tbsps creamy Caesar dressing

Crunchy Crumb Topping Ingredients:
- 4 Tbsps canola oil
- 1/2 cup panko breadcrumbs
- 1/4 cup Parmesan cheese, finely grated
- 1 tsp garlic powder
- 1 tsp ranch dressing mix

Directions: Mix together all of the marinade ingredients (canola oil, creamy Caesar dressing, Worcestershire sauce, apple cider vinegar, lime juice, garlic powder, onion powder, black pepper) in a medium sized bowl. Using a fork, poke holes into the chicken tenderloins, 3 - 4 times with each tenderloin. Turn them over and do the same on the other side.

Place the tenderloins in the marinade and mix until they are completely covered in the marinade. Pour the marinade and chicken into a gallon freezer bag. Remove as much air as possible from the bag, then seal. Refrigerate for two hours. (You can marinate up to 12 hours.) Right before you are ready to cook the chicken, combine the Creamy Cheese Topping ingredients (cheeses and creamy Caesar dressing) to a medium bowl. Set aside. Prepare the Crunchy Crumb Topping (panko breadcrumbs, Parmesan cheese, garlic powder, ranch dressing mix; mix in the oil right before you are going to use it) in a small bowl. Set aside.

In a large nonstick pan, heat 3 Tbsps of canola oil on medium heat. With a fork, remove the chicken tenderloins from the bag of marinade and place them in the pan. (Some of the marinade will still be coating the chicken. That is good!) Cook the chicken for about 3 minutes on each side, until cooked through. Don't worry about browning it. Be careful not to overcook. Set aside. (At this point, you could serve the chicken without the toppings, and it would still be delicious! But, the toppings do make this dish even better!) Preheat oven to 450 degrees on "Broil" setting. Line a 9 inch cake pan with foil and spray with nonstick cooking spray. Place the cooked tenderloins on the pan. Place the Creamy Cheese Mixture in the microwave for about 20 seconds. Stir. Return to the microwave for another 20 seconds. Stir. Do this until mixture is a melty goodness.

Top the tenderloins with the melted Creamy Cheese Mixture. Spread mixture over the tenderloins. Then top the cheese mixture with the Crunchy Crumb Topping. Place the pan in the oven and broil for 3-4 minutes, until lightly brown. Watch the topping carefully so it does not burn. Remove from oven and serve.

Feast of the Ascension
(Forty days after Easter, or the Sunday before Pentecost)

"At Easter, beloved brethren, it was the Lord's Resurrection which was the cause of our joy; our present rejoicing is on account of His Ascension into Heaven. With all due solemnity, we are commemorating that day on which our poor human nature was carried up, in Christ, above all the hosts of Heaven, above all the ranks of Angels, beyond the highest Heavenly powers, to the very throne of God the Father. It is upon this ordered structure of divine acts that we have been firmly established."

-- St. Leo the Great

Food for the Soul: As a member of the Body of Christ, we are united with Jesus in heaven. His divinity lies within us!
Seek it. Acknowledge it. Hallelujah!

St. Leo, pray for us.
Blessed Mother, graciously intercede for us.
Jesus, ascended into Heaven, have mercy on us.
Holy Trinity, we adore You! Hear and answer our prayers.

Feast of Pentecost
(Fifty days after Easter)

"O Holy Spirit, descend plentifully into my heart. Enlighten the dark corners of this neglected dwelling and scatter there Thy cheerful beams."

-- St. Augustine

Food for the Soul: Be plentiful within me, Holy Spirit. Bestow upon me Your gifts. Guide me in Your Plan for my life.

St. Augustine, pray for us.
Blessed Mother, graciously intercede for us.
Come, Holy Spirit, come! Set our hearts on fire!
Holy Trinity, we adore You! Hear and answer our prayers.

Post Pentecost Feast Days

Feast of the Holy Trinity
(One week after Pentecost)

"Eternal God, eternal Trinity, You are a mystery as deep as the sea; the more I search, the more I find, and the more I find, the more I search for You."
-- St. Catherine of Siena

Food for the Soul: Ask the Holy Trinity to draw you deeper into Their Presence.

Glory be to the Father, and to the Son, and to the Holy Spirit, as it was in the beginning, is now and ever shall be, world without end. Amen.

Praise the Holy Trinity, undivided unity;
Holy God, Mighty God, God Immortal, be adored!

St, Catherine of Siena, pray for us.
Blessed Mother, graciously intercede for us.
Holy Trinity, we adore You! Hear and answer our prayers.

Feast of the Body and Blood of Christ
(Two weeks after Pentecost)

"When you have received Him, stir up your heart to do Him homage, speak to Him about your spiritual life, gazing upon Him in your soul where He is present for your happiness; welcome Him as warmly as possible, and behave outwardly in such a way, that your actions may give proof to all of His Presence."
--St. Francis de Sales

Food for the Soul: Be sincerely present to Jesus in the Holy Eucharist. Allow Him to unite with you.

St. Francis de Sales, pray for us.
Blessed Mother, graciously intercede for us.
Body and Blood of Jesus, sanctify us.
Holy Trinity, we adore You! Hear and answer our prayers.

Feast of the Sacred Heart of Jesus
(Friday after the second Sunday after Pentecost)

*"I must strive to make the interior of my soul a
resting place for the Heart of Jesus."*
-- St. Faustina

*"As to persons living in the world, they shall find in this devotion, all the aids
necessary in their state of life: peace in their homes, consolation in their
work, the blessing of heaven upon all their enterprises, comfort in their
sorrows, a secure refuge during life, and especially at the hours of death.
It is plainly evident that there is no one in the world who will not receive all
kinds of heavenly blessings if they have a true love of Jesus Christ
manifested by a devotion to the Sacred Heart of Jesus"*
-- St. Margaret Mary Alacoque

Food for the Soul: Become devoted to the Sacred Heart of Jesus.
St. Faustina, pray for us.
St. Margaret Mary Alacoque, pray for us.
Sacred Heart of Jesus, sanctify us.
Blessed Mother, graciously intercede for us.
Holy Trinity, we adore You! Hear and answer our prayers.

Feast of the Immaculate Heart of Mary
(Saturday after the second Sunday after Pentecost)

*"He (Jesus) wants to establish in the world devotion to my Immaculate
Heart. I promise salvation to those who embrace it, and these souls
will be loved by God, like flowers placed by me to adorn His throne...
My Immaculate Heart will be your refuge and the way
that will lead you to God."*
--Words of Our Lady of Fatima to Sr. Lucia, Servant of God

Food for the Soul: Become devoted to the Immaculate Heart of Mary.
Our Lady of Fatima, graciously intercede for us.
Holy Trinity, we adore You! Hear and answer our prayers.

Sacramental Celebrations

Baptism

"Every baptized person should consider that it is in the womb of the Church where he is transformed from a child of Adam to a Child of God."
-- *St. Vincent Ferrer*

"Just as a man cannot live in the flesh unless he is born in the flesh, even so, a man cannot have the spiritual life of grace unless he is born again spiritually. This regeneration is effected by Baptism:
"Unless a man is born again of water and the Holy Spirit, he cannot enter into the kingdom of God." (John 3:5)
-- *St. Thomas Aquinas*

Food for the Soul: Pray for a spiritual transformation. Pray for a spiritual awakening.

St. Vincent, pray for us.
St. Thomas, pray for us.
Blessed Mother, graciously intercede for us.
Holy Trinity, we adore You! Hear and answer our prayers.

Reconciliation

"The devil may try to use the hurts of life, and sometimes our own mistakes, to make you feel it is impossible that Jesus really loves you, is really cleaving to you. This is a danger for all of us, and so sad, because it is completely the opposite of what Jesus is really wanting, waiting to tell you...
He loves you always, even when you don't feel worthy."
-- *St. Teresa of Calcutta*

"In my deepest wound, I saw Your Glory and it dazzled me."
-- *St. Augustine*

Food for the Soul: Let us ponder Christ's great Love, Healing, and Redemption.

St. Teresa of Calcutta, pray for us.
St. Augustine, pray for us.
Blessed Mother, graciously intercede for us.
Holy Trinity, we adore You! Hear and answer our prayers.

First Communion

"When you look at the crucifix, you understand how much Jesus loved you then. When you look at the Sacred Host, you understand how much Jesus loves you now."
-- St. Teresa of Calcutta

"If angels could be jealous of men, they would be so for one reason: Holy Communion."
-- St. Maximilian Kolbe

Food for the Soul: It is such an honor to receive Jesus, to be joined in union with Him. To fully embrace Him in love, amid all of His power and glory. Treasure this amazing moment the next time you receive Him.
St. Teresa of Calcutta, pray for us.
St. Maximilian Kolbe, pray for us.
Blessed Mother, graciously intercede for us.
Holy Trinity, we adore You! Hear and answer our prayers.

Confirmation

"Remember, then, that you received a spiritual seal, the spirit of wisdom and understanding, the spirit of knowledge and reverence, the spirit of holy fear. Keep safe what you received. God the Father sealed you, Christ the Lord strengthened you and sent the Spirit into your hearts as the pledge of what is to come."
-- St. Ambrose

"In Him, you also, when you had heard the word of truth, the gospel of your salvation, and had believed in Him, were marked with the seal of the promised Holy Spirit."
-- St. Paul

Food for the Soul: The gifts of the Holy Spirit are many! How generous is our God to share them with us!

St. Ambrose, pray for us.
St. Paul, pray for us.
Blessed Mother, graciously intercede for us.
Come, Holy Spirit, Come! Kindle in us the fire of Your Love!
Holy Trinity, we adore You! Hear and answer our prayers.

Matrimony

"I can do the things you cannot, you can do things I cannot; together we can do great things."
-- St. Teresa of Calcutta

"Marriage is a marvelous gift, which contains the power of God's own love."
-- St. John Paul II

Food for the Soul: The expression, "made for each other", is, no doubt, more than just an expression, when God is entered into the equation...
St. Teresa of Calcutta, pray for us.
St. John Paul II, pray for us.
Blessed Mother, graciously intercede for us.
Holy Trinity, we adore You! Hear and answer our prayers.

Holy Orders

"People who say that we priests are lonely are either lying or have got it all wrong. We are far less lonely than anyone else, for we can count on the constant company of the Lord, with Whom we should be conversing without interruption. We are in love with Love, with the Author of Love!"
-- St. Josemaría Escrivá

"The end for which God has instituted the priesthood has been to appoint, on earth, public persons to watch over the honor of His divine majesty, and to procure the salvation of souls."
-- St. Alphonsus Liguori

Food for the Soul: Conversing with God without interruption...
the secret to achieving intimacy with Him.
St. Josemaría Escrivá, pray for us.
St. Alphonsus Liguori, pray for us.
Blessed Mother, graciously intercede for us.
Holy Trinity, we adore You! Hear and answer our prayers.

Cream Cheese Butter Cookies
Tender, buttery cookies, ready to be shared at any special occasion!

Ingredients:
2 sticks unsalted butter, softened
3 oz cream cheese, softened
1 cup sugar
1 large egg yolk
1 tsp vanilla
2 1/2 cups flour, sifted
1/2 tsp salt

Directions: Preheat oven to 350 degrees. Prepare a cookie sheet, lined with parchment paper. In a medium bowl, cream together butter and cream cheese. Slowly add in sugar and mix well. Beat in the egg yolk and vanilla. Blend in the flour and salt. For these cookies, you can roll out the dough to 1/4 inch thick and use a cookie cutter, or... You can use a cookie press with any disc shape you choose, or... You can roll a teaspoonful of the dough into a ball and flatten with your fingers. Place cookies on the cookie sheet, 1 inch apart. Bake for 12 - 15 minutes. Remove from oven and cool completely. Sprinkle with powdered sugar, or decorate as you choose. Store in cookie tins.

Try this recipe another way...
+++By making ***Coconut Cherry Cream Cheese Cookies!*** Substitute the vanilla for coconut extract. Roll the teaspoonful of dough into a ball, then press some sweetened coconut flakes into the top of the ball, flattening the dough. Gently press a glazed red cherry half on the top.

White Chocolate Raspberry Bars

For me, making these bars could be very dangerous!
When they are around, I want to devour them all!

Ingredients:
- 1/2 cup unsalted butter
- 12 oz white chocolate chips
- 2 large eggs
- 1/2 cup sugar
- 1 cup flour
- 1/2 tsp salt
- 1 tsp almond extract
- 1/2 cup raspberry preserves
- 1/4 cup sliced almonds

Directions: Preheat oven to 325 degrees. Prepare an 8 inch glass pan, oil and flour pan. Set aside. In a small saucepan, melt butter. Remove saucepan from heat. Add 1 cup of the white chocolate chips. Let stand. Do not stir! Set aside. In a large bowl, beat eggs until frothy. Add sugar and beat into eggs until mixture is lemon-colored. Stir in white chocolate mixture. Add flour, salt, and almond extract. Mix until combined. Spread half of the mixture, about 1 cup, in prepared pan. Set remaining batter aside. Place pan in oven and bake for 15 - 20 minutes, or until golden brown. Stir remaining white chocolate chips into the remaining batter. Set aside. Lightly warm the raspberry preserves in the microwave so it is spreadable. Spread raspberry preserves over the warm, partially baked crust. Gently spoon teaspoonfuls of remaining batter over the preserves. Some preserves may show through the batter. Sprinkle with the sliced almonds. Bake for an additional 25 - 35 minutes, or until a toothpick inserted in center comes out clean. Remove from oven. Cool for 1 hour or until completely cooled. Cut into 16 bars. Store at room temperature.

Chicken Cacciatore

When I told Marge, our friend from the parish, that I was almost finished with my latest book, she was vey excited to hear the news! Then she said, "Chris, you have to include more Italian recipes!" So, I asked her if she would like to share one with me for this book. She was delighted to! Thank you for this family recipe, Marge!

Ingredients:
- 1 chicken, cut up, or chicken breasts
- 2 - 3 Tbsps flour
- Salt and pepper
- 2 Tbsps olive oil
- 1 large garlic clove, minced
- 1 large can of crushed tomatoes
- Mushrooms, chopped

Directions: Coat chicken with flour, salt, and pepper. Brown chicken in oil. Stir in garlic, cook, but do not brown. Add in tomatoes. Cover. Bring to a boil, then simmer for 45 minutes. Add mushrooms and simmer for 5 minutes more.

+++

**I pray this has been a year of
abundant blessings for you and yours!**

As you personally encounter God in your life, please consider freely sharing your story with me. You can share your God-encounters with me at christineramosauthor@gmail.com
With your story, please include your first name, along with the city and state in which you live. Thank you:)

I invite you to visit my website christineramosauthor.com for the latest "Good News" and information about future book launches. You can also share your prayer requests.
If you are located in the Chicagoland area and would like me to speak at your parish or school,
you can contact me at christineramosauthor@gmail.com

As I end this book, know that I will continue to pray for you and those you love, everyday.
Please keep Paul and I in your prayers, as well.

**Let us conclude this book, this prayer, this sacred year,
with the Sign of the Cross:
In the name of the Father, and of the Son, and of the Holy Spirit.
Amen!**

Recipe Index

Appetizers/Snacks
Caramel Apple Cream Cheese Dip, 45
Cheesy Pigs in a Blanket, 47
Chris' Caramel Corn, 43
Chrissy's Kettle Corn, 22
Cinnamon Sugar Popcorn, 22
Cinnamon Sugared Tortilla Crisps, 57
Confetti Veggie Wreath, 7
Confetti Veggie Pizza, 8
Cream Cheese Beef Dip, 46
Crescent Dog Wreath, 47
Ham and Pineapple Cream Cheese Dip, 130
Pigskins in a Blanket, 46
Pinwheel Roll-Ups, 45
Savory Cheese Flan Cups, 303
Sugar Crunch Pretzels, 79
Taffy Apple Salad, 142
Tortilla Chips and Salsa, 56
Tortilla Chips and Tropical Salsa, 57
Veggie and Cheese Flan Cups, 304

Beef
Chicago Style Italian Beef with Gravy, 72
Instant Pot Corned Beef, 69
Meatloaf Sandwich, 278
Porcupine Meatballs, 283
Ricotta Meatball Sandwiches with Red Gravy, 74
Saucy Meatloaf, 277
Saucy Turkey Meatloaf, 278
Sous Vide Corned Beef, 70
Sous Vide Filet Mignon with Seasoned Butter, 287
Swedish Meatballs, 181
Unstuffed Cabbage Rolls, 284
Unstuffed Sweet Peppers, 284

Biscuits/Scones
Apricot White Chocolate Scones, 49
Blueberry Raspberry Scones, 49
Cinnamon Roll Biscuits, 211
Citrus Roll Biscuits, 62
Dark Chocolate Cherry Sweetheart Scones, 49
Garlic Cheddar Scones, 50
Garlic Cheese Cream Biscuits, 15
Holiday Fruitcake Scones, 279
Maple Walnut Scones, 50
Old Glory Scones, 136
Pumpkin Spiced Biscuits, 200
Sweetheart Cherries and Cream Scones, 49
Tropical Fruit Nut Scones, 50
Whipped Cream Vanilla Biscuits, 14

Breads/Muffins
Aloha Bread, 143
Buttery Pull Apart Loaf, 314
Challah Bread, 6
Cherry Nut Bread, 81
Cinnamon Pull Apart Loaf, 314
Citrus Pull Apart Bread, 312
Colby Jack Cheese Bread, 88
Fry Bread, 237
Holiday Fruit Nut Challah, 6
Hot Cross Buns, 308
Garlic Butter Green Onion Naan, 306
Naan Bread, 305
Navajo Fry Bread Taco Shells, 238
Parmesan Garlic Pull Apart Loaf, 314
Pineapple Upside Down Cornbread Muffins, 54
Pumpkin Cinnamon Rolls, 210
Sope Shells, 285
Sugar Topped Blueberry Muffins, 243
Sugar Topped Cranberry Muffins, 243
Sugar Topped Raspberry Muffins, 243

Breakfast
Banana Nut Waffles, 94
Breakfast Burrito, 83
Carrot Cake Waffles, 185
Cinnamon Apple Waffles, 184
Cinnamon Apple Waffles ala Mode, 185
Crepes ala Chris, 183
Crepes with Scrambled Eggs, 183
Oatmeal with Apple Cinnamon Ice Cream, 37
Pumpkin Custard Pancakes or Waffles, 249
Ricotta Pancakes with Blueberry Topping, 64
Ultimate Banana Waffles, 93

Cakes
Amaretto Cake, 289
Black Forest Cherry Continental Cake, 258
Blueberry Lemon Pound Cake, 229
Brandy Cake, 289
Caramel Apple Cinnamon Continental Cake, 258
Carrot Pineapple Cake, 204
Cherry Berry Buckle, 148
Cherry Nut Cake, 80
Chocolate Pound Cake, 8
Cranberry Orange Pound Cake, 228
Flourless Chocolate Cake, 218
Green River Cake, 61
Heavenly Swedish Flop Cake, 168
Helen's Apricot Brandied Fruitcake, 280
Irish Cream Cake, 289
Lemon Blueberry Cake, 102

Cakes, continued
Orange Cranberry Cake, 103
Raspberry Continental Cake, 257
Rum Cake, 288
Rum ala Baba Cake, 289
Triple Threat Chocolate Cake, 31
Walnut Cinnamon Crunch Apple Cake, 189

Candy
Caramel Apples, 226
Fabulous Fudge, 225
Peanut Butter and Chocolate Bars, 161

Cheesecakes
Be My Valentine Mini Cherry Cheesecakes, 127
Caramel Apple Mini Cheesecakes, 127
Caramel Cheesecake Squares, 165
Caramel Cup Cheesecake Surprise, 117
Chocolate Caramel Cheesecake Squares 166
Chocolate Raspberry Cheesecake Squares, 166
Chocolate Overload Mini Cheesecakes, 127
Churro Crescent Cheesecake Bars, 166
Creamy Ricotta Cheesecake, 36
Fruity Mini Cheesecakes, 127
Mint Patty Cheesecake Surprise, 117
Peanut Butter Cup Cheesecake Surprise, 116
Santa Hat Mini Cheesecakes, 276
Sweet Heat Churro Crescent Cheesecake, 167

Coffeecakes
Almond Raspberry Cream Cheese Coffeecake, 85
Cheese Filled Paczki Coffeecake, 294
Chocolate Streusel Coffeecake, 116
Golden Streusel Coffeecake, 115
Polish Cheese Kowatz, 275
Polish Paczki Coffeecake, 293

Cookies
Brandy Butter Cookie, 208
Butter Pecan Butter Cookies, 92
Buttery Christmas Snowballs, 254
Buttery Starlight Cookies, 12
Candy Cane Chip Cookies, 261
Chippy Choco-Chip Cookies, 17
Chippy PB Chip Cookies, 17
Chippy Toffee Cookies, 17
Chippy Toffee Nut Cookies, 17
Chocolate Drizzled Raspberry Cookies, 120
Chocolate Peanut Butter Chip Cookies, 29
Cinnamon Apple Walnut Oatmeal Crisps, 256
Coconut Cherry Cream Cheese Cookies, 326
Cream Cheese Butter Cookies, 326
Delicate Butter Cookies, 214
Festive Cherry Walnut Chip Cookies, 262
Fruitcake Cookies, 281

Cookies, continued
Helen's Polish Kolacky, 268
Helen's Polish Walnut Crescents, 253
Maria's Sugar Cookies, 272
My Favorite Chocolate Chip Cookies, 172
Nutty Peanut Butter Chip Cookies, 29
Oatmeal Butterscotch Thin Crisps, 255
Peanut Butter Chip Cookies, 28
Peppermint Bark Chip Cookies, 262
Toffee Crunch Oatmeal Cookies, 18
Turtle Cookies, 119
Walnut Chocolate Chip Cookies, 173
WCCP Oatmeal Thin Crisps, 256

Dessert Bars
Almond Butterscotch Bars, 51
Almond Shortbread Bars, 51
Fried Wonton Cinnamon Crisps, 34
Chocolate Chip Walnut Bars, 52
Creamy Toffee Nut Shortbread, 260
Dreamy Strawberry Jello Pretzel Bars, 122
Peanut Butter and Jelly Bars, 29
Peanut Supreme Bars, 52
Piña Colada Cheese Squares, 154
White Chocolate Cranberry Pecan Bars, 52
White Chocolate Raspberry Bars, 327

Desserts
Apple Cinnamon Ice Cream, 39
Apple Pie Dumplings 38
Apricot Cream Cheese Wontons, 33
Baked Pumpkin Custard, 249
Chris-cent Donuts, 132
Coffee and Cream Dream, 193
Cool Whip Jello, 137
Easy Cream Filled Donuts, 196
Easy Frosted Donuts, 197
Easy Jelly Donuts, 197
Elephant Ears, 238
Fried Cream Cheese Wontons, 34
Perfect Polish Paczki, 291
Rosettes, 103
Stovetop Custard, 290

Glazes/Frostings
Buttery Lemon Glaze, 102
Buttery Lime Glaze, 133
Buttery Orange Glaze, 103
Cream Cheese Frosting, 204
Donut Frosting, 197
Peanut Butter Drizzle, 29

Gravy/Sauce/Butters
Alfredo Sauce, 11
Apricot Brandy Sauce, 34
Build-a-Burger Sauce, 100

Gravy/Sauce/Butters, continued
Honey Mustard Cream Gravy, 171
Creamy Onion Gravy, 25
Roasted Garlic Alfredo Sauce, 11
Savory Pecan Cream Sauce, 90
Seasoned Butter, 287

Pasta
Four Cheese Veggie Egg Noodle Lasagna, 300
Italian Sausage Egg Noodle Lasagna, 302

Pastry
Apple Strudel, 206
Banana Pudding Eclairs, 264
Banana Split Eclairs, 265
Chocolate Eclair Pastries, 263
Chocolate Filled Eclairs, 264
Eclair Christmas Wreath, 264
Strawberries and Cream Puffs, 10
Whipped Cream Puffs, 9

Pies/Tarts
Almond Pie, 91
Amish Fry Pies, 125
Caramallow Salted Peanut Cups, 223
Chocolate Coconut Cream Pie, 191
Coconut Cream Pie, 191
Cranberry Pecan Pie, 91
Nut Cup Tarts, 251
Pecan Pie, 91
Piña Colada Cream Pie, 155
Pumpkin Custard Pie, 248
Turtle Cups, 121
Walnut Pie, 91

Pizza
Chicken Alfredo Pizza, 221
Chicken Roasted Garlic Alfredo Pizza, 222
Southwest Side of Chicago Deep Dish Pizza, 42
Taco Pan Pizza, 213

Pork
Fried Bacon, 180
Fried Sous Vide Pork Chops, 24
Ham and Cheese Flan Cups, 303
Ham Salad Pie, 112
Instant Pot Baby Back Ribs, 141
Instant Pot Pork Tenderloin Medallions, 89
Sous Vide Pork Chops, 23

Potatoes
Chris-py Oven Roasted Baby Potatoes, 235
Easy Potato Pierogi, 273
Instant Pot Buttered Baby Potatoes, 71
Potato and Cheese Angel Dumplings, 177

Potatoes, continued
Potatoes Au Gratin, 315

Poultry
Chicken ala King ala Biscuits, 27
Chicken ala King Crepes, 184
Chicken Cacciatore, 328
Chicken Caesar Tenderloins, 14
Chicken, Cheese, and Bean Flautas, 108
Chicken Tamales, 107
Creamy Comfort Chicken Pot Pie, 26
Crispy Skinned Air Fryer Chicken, 128
Crispy Skinned Thanksgiving Turkey, 245
Fried Chicken Caesar Tenders, 13
Honey Walnut Chicken, 33
Instant Pot Apricot Chicken, 149
Instant Pot Honey Chicken, 162
Parmesan Crusted Caesar Chicken, 318
Sous Vide Boneless Turkey Breast, 244
Tropical Chicken Salad Pie, 111
Tropical Chicken Salad Sandwich, 112
Turkey Salad Pie, 112

Sandwiches
COBALT Sandwiches, 75
Monte Chris-to Sandwich, 231
Toasted Bolillo Sandwiches, 59

Sausage
Chicago Style Dogs on a Raft, 157
Instant Pot Brats, 205

Seafood
Cranberry Walnut Tuna Salad, 105
Cranberry Walnut Tuna Salad Pie, 112
Creamy Tuna ala Biscuits, 310
Crispy Shrimp Tacos with Pineapple Salsa, 297
Fish Fry Tacos, 295
Fried Lobster, 286
Honey Walnut Shrimp, 32
Perfectly Poached Lobster Tails, 287
Savory Tuna and Cheddar Flan Cups, 304
Tuna Pot Pie, 309
Velvety, Creamy Corn and Shrimp Chowder, 299

Sides
Autumn Sweet Potato Crisp, 247
Cornbread Cranberry Apple Stuffing, 24
Cheesy Creamed Peas, 97
Creamed Peas, 96
Cucumber, Radish, Apple Slaw, 97
Instant Pot Buttered Cabbage, 70
Instant Pot Onion Apple Kraut, 206
Tender, Butter Bathed Corn on the Cob, 139
Pickled Mini Cucumber and Onion Salad, 151

About the Author

Christine Ramos (nee, Stefaniak), was born in Oak Lawn, Illinois, at Christ Hospital, which is why her parents, Stanley and Helen, chose Christine for her name. She began the first five years of her life in the Back of the Yards neighborhood in Chicago with her older sisters Alice and Linda, but mostly grew up on the far southwest side of Chicago, attending St. Bede the Venerable Grade School. After graduating tenth out of 525 in her class from Bogan High School, she attended St. Xavier University and received her BA in Music Education in 1985, with a double major in voice and pipe organ. Christine has been an educator/director of music in Catholic schools and parishes for over 36 years. For the last six years, her most recent position has been as the Director of Religious Education at St. Patricia Parish in Hickory Hills.

Later in life, Christine married Paul, a widower and father of four, in May of 2016. They currently live on the far southwest side of Chicago with their furry "boyz", Samson, Louie, and Schubert, next door to the home where she had grown up. Paul and Christine are the proud grandparents of Andrew, Sofia, Maya, Lorenzo, Anthony, Maribel, Sean, Cameron, Christian, and Julian.

Acknowledgements

Thanks be to God the Father, Son, and Holy Spirit,
for Your divine inspiration. How awesome You are in my life! Each day I witness how You make Your presence known to me. I am continually amazed by Your loving, divine revelations. May this book, and all my books, bring all honor and glory to You! May You continue to walk closely with me, day by day, as I trust in You and in all the divine promises You have for my life! I love and honor You, Most Holy Trinity!

Thank you, Paul! *You are amazing! I praise God I have someone so strong, loving, and understanding to accompany me through my life. You keep me steady, you make me laugh, you inspire me, you cheer me on. Thank you for your amazing support, my love. I thank God that He has blessed us with each other. Here's to another year of faith, food, and celebrations together, in the Name of Jesus Christ, our Lord and Savior! I love you!*

Thank you, Mom! *This book is a loving tribute to you. You can be found everywhere in it! You inspired me so much in my life, in my faith and in my love for cooking and baking. I thank you for these beautiful gifts! I pray you will be able to have a copy of this book in heaven! If not, may it be written upon your heart. I love you!*

Thank you, Celia, Ellen, Linda, Marge, Michelle, Rafaela, Sandy, Susie, and Fr. Marc,
for your constant love, encouragement, and inspiration. I thank God that I am blessed to have each one of you in my life! I love you all!

Thank you, Mom and Dad, *for bringing me up in the ways of the Lord. You always pointed our family in His direction. I understood the Holy Trinity was accompanying me through my life because of you, and you encouraged me to accompany Them. What a precious gift you gave to me! I love you! May we be reunited, one day, with all those we love, in God's glorious Kingdom of Heaven!*